NEVADA DAYS

Also by Bernardo Atxaga in English translation

Obabakoak (1992)
The Lone Man (1996)
The Lone Woman (1999)
The Accordionist's Son (2007)
Seven Houses in France (2011)
The Fighter (2012)
The Adventures of Shola (2013)

BERNARDO ATXAGA

NEVADA DAYS

Translated from the Spanish by
Margaret Jull Costa

MACLEHOSE PRESS
QUERCUS · LONDON

First published in the Basque language as
Nevadako Egunak by Pamiela in 2013

First published in Great Britain in 2017 by

MacLehose Press
An imprint of Quercus Publishing Ltd
Carmelite House
50 Victoria Embankment
London EC4Y 0DZ

An Hachette UK company

1 3 5 7 9 10 8 6 4 2

Designed and typeset in 10/13½pt Galliard by Patty Rennie
Printed and bound in Denmark by Nørhaven

CONTENTS

SILENCE

Reno is always silent, even during the day. The casinos are airtight edifices, carpeted inside, and no noise spreads beyond the rooms where the slot machines and the gaming tables stand in serried ranks. You can't even hear the traffic on the busiest road, Virginia Street, or on the freeways that cross the city, the I-80 and Route 395, as if they, too, were carpeted or as if the cars and the trucks were moving very stealthily.

When night falls, the silence, or what you subjectively experience as silence, grows even deeper. The mere tinkle of a bell would put the city police on guard. If a firecracker were to go off in a house, they would race there in their patrol car, lights flashing.

The silence was the first thing we noticed on the day we arrived in Reno, on August 18, 2007, once the cab from the airport had driven off and left us alone in front of what was going to be our house, 145 College Drive. There was no-one in the street. The garbage cans looked as if they were made of stone.

We unpacked our cases and went out onto the verandah at the back of the house. In the darkness, we could make out shapes, nothing more: rocks, tall plants that resembled reeds, and cactuses. The garden was quite big. It sloped uphill and was flanked by trees and bushes.

Ángela pressed a red button next to the back door, and the spotlights on the wall lit up about 100 or so feet of the garden. At the top of the slope was a large house, and to the right, where the trees were thickest, a shack.

Izaskun and Sara ran towards the shack.

"There's something over there!" Izaskun exclaimed, grabbing her sister by the arm.

Near the cabin, I could make out two points, two small yellow holes, two shining eyes. They did not move or blink, inhuman in their fixity.

Before we left home, I had read a travel guide to Nevada, in which, among other dangers to bear in mind – in second place only to the sun – they listed rattlesnakes. However, according to the photographs and other information, they never left the desert. Those two small yellow eyes could not possibly belong to a reptile, I thought, but were more likely to belong to a cat. I couldn't be sure though.

There was a stick near the shack door. I picked it up and took a step forward. I was expecting some noise, some movement. Nothing. Only silence, the same silence we had noticed when we got out of the taxi.

My eyes were gradually getting used to the dark. I could make out a small head, and behind it, a striped tail.

"It's a raccoon," Ángela said.

Izaskun and Sara wanted to get closer, but, despite what Ángela had said, I told them not to. The guide to Nevada had not included raccoons among the possible dangers awaiting the visitor, but it had mentioned that some might have rabies.

THE HOUSE IN COLLEGE DRIVE

It could have been a mansion like the ones you find in wealthy areas in American cities, because it had steps and a porch, and there was a delicate harmony in the design of roof, windows, walls; the steps, however, were crumbling, and the porch was barely big enough for one rocking chair. Inside, the habitable space was, at most, 130 square feet. The house was a mansion, but in miniature.

There were two bedrooms, one of them a reasonable size, large enough for a double bed, but the other so small that two single mattresses only just fitted in. The bathroom was narrow, and the corridor even narrower. The rectangular kitchen was divided into two halves. There was a fridge, sink and cooker in the first half, and, in the second – which was lit by the window that gave on to the garden – a square table with four chairs. Since there was no living room, the sofa and the television had been placed in the hall.

The house was full of old newspapers, advertising flyers and unopened letters, and our first job, once we had unpacked, was to throw away anything that was clearly junk. We saved a few copies of the *Reno Gazette-Journal* and a letter from the Bank of America bearing a stamp saying *documents* and addressed to a certain Robert H. Earle.

SECOND NIGHT IN RENO

I got up at two o'clock in the morning and went into the kitchen for a glass of water. I found Sara in the hall, next to the sofa. Seen from behind, in her nightdress, she looked like a little doll. She was staring at the frosted glass eye of the front door.

Seen through that eye, the casino buildings were blurred shapes, in which the dominant colour was red.

I called softly to Sara. She didn't hear me. I picked her up in my arms and carried her to bed.

AUGUST 21, 2007
NIGHT

We went out for our first evening stroll and walked about a hundred yards down College Drive as far as the highest part of Virginia Street. From there we could see the whole city: a web of glassy white lights with the casinos all lit up in red, green and fuchsia. In the distance, the lights thinned out until they were a mere sprinkling. Beyond that lay the utter darkness of the desert.

We walked along Virginia Street as far as the point where the I-80 passes underneath the houses, and next to a Walgreens we saw a few beggars. On the other side of the road, parked at the Texaco gas station, two police cars lurked in the shadows, watching.

A helicopter flew by overhead, very low, signalling its position with a flashing red light. It passed over the highway and landed on the roof of St Mary's, the hospital we had unsuccessfully requested to be added to our health insurance, only to find that it was too expensive for our coverage plan.

We left the street and headed off towards the university campus.

3

It was dark. A single swan was swimming on Manzanita Lake, which skirted the building that housed the dining halls and the School of Mining. The swan glided effortlessly over the water, apparently carried by the breeze coming off the desert.

TELEVISION

They were showing a documentary about the Second World War on television, and I stayed up to watch it after Ángela and the girls had gone to bed.

The narrator spoke in suave, soothing tones, and the old soldiers, now in their eighties, were speaking sadly of the comrades who fell in Normandy. The soundtrack was Henry Mancini's "Soldier in the Rain" and another equally slow, sad tune that I couldn't identify.

I remembered what we had seen on our way through San Francisco airport: British and Spanish flags everywhere, posters talking about the "war on terrorism" or about "America's friends".

The documentary suddenly took on a new meaning. We were in a country at war. It had been four years since George Bush decided to invade Iraq, and the American army had lost thousands of men. The narrator's suave tones, the sad notes of "Soldier in the Rain", everything in the documentary that appealed to heart and guts was aimed at the present, not the past.

THE DREAM

I fell asleep in front of the television and found myself five and a half thousand miles away from Reno, in a hospital in San Sebastián. I was lying in a narrow bed, surrounded by metal bars, trying to attract the attention of the night carer my family had hired to watch over me. I needed to go to the toilet.

The carer took no notice. She was a young woman of about twenty-two. She was talking to someone on her mobile.

"Yes, I'm on the beach again," she said, patting the airbed she used to lie on to relax.

I knew that expression, and had heard it several times before. When she talked to her partner, she referred to the hospital room as the beach. It was her joke.

Afraid I might wet the bed, I tried to push down the bars keeping me penned in. When they wouldn't budge, I screamed at the carer to help me. She turned off her telephone and started scribbling on the pages of an illustrated magazine. I craned my neck over the bars and managed to read one of the things she had written: "I know that at times I may appear to be surrounded by an aura of sadness . . ."

I tried throwing my pillow at her, but only succeeded in getting tangled up with the I.V. line in my right arm.

"I want these bars removed! I'm not a monkey in a cage!"

I woke up and opened my eyes. The black-and-white images on the screen showed a burning tank.

The real things in the dream were all mixed up. There really was a night carer who referred to the hospital room as the beach and scribbled sentimental nonsense on the pages of magazines, and there was a bed with bars around it in that hospital. The one doing the protesting, though – "I want these bars removed! I'm not a monkey in a cage!" – wasn't me, but my father. Besides, the carer had nothing to do with it. I was the one refusing to remove the bars, so as not to disobey the nurses' instructions.

THAT NIGHT'S FILM

The military planes were getting closer and closer to the Empire State Building, aiming rounds of machine-gun fire at King Kong, who had climbed to the very top. We occasionally saw the half-naked girl the ape was holding in one hand, or the people in the street below, staring up at him; but what filled the screen most of the time were those attacking planes. First, a shot of the pilot; then, the machine-gun fire; lastly, the roar of the engine. Repetitive, wearisome images.

When he was living on the island, King Kong had already killed the dinosaur and the giant snake, as well as abducting whole legions of young women, so he was hardly a stranger to violence, but he understood nothing about life outside the jungle. He didn't know what the red stain on his neck was, the wounds inflicted by the invisible bullets from the machine guns, and he raged rather feebly at the planes. He finally caught one and brought it down, but he could do little else, for there was no let-up. The other planes continued hurling themselves at him, firing endlessly. *Ta-ta-ta-ta, ta-ta-ta-ta.*

King Kong lost his footing, and only the aerial on the Empire State Building saved him from falling. The end was near. Sara, our nine-year-old, began weeping silently, as if to herself, and would continue to do so for the rest of the film.

King Kong suddenly realised that his final moment had come and he made one last noble gesture. With his dying breath, he carefully leaned down and deposited the girl on the ground. Then he fell. The screen showed him lying in the street, and we heard a voice saying that he had been killed not by the planes, but by beauty. And the film ended. Sara's tears, however, did not, for she was weeping inconsolably now.

There was no way of reassuring her, and we began explaining:

"You have to understand. They did hurt him, it's true, but he hurt others too."

Still sobbing, Sara answered:

"Yes, but he didn't know what he was doing, and they did."

We couldn't argue with that, and so we took her off to bed in the hope that Queen Mab would bring her dreams that would make her forget King Kong's fate.

SUPPER AT TACOS

We went shopping in the mall at the junction of Northtowne Street and McCarran. As it was growing dark, around seven o'clock, we put our shopping in the boot of the car and went to have supper at a fast-food place, part of the Tacos chain. It was right there, on the other side of McCarran, on a hill.

You could see into the kitchen, which was only separated from the restaurant by a long counter, and the employees, all of them Latinos, were slaving away, preparing the food and putting it on metal trays like the ones you get in self-service places. The numerous customers would either collect their food in a bag from a window that opened onto the car park, so that they didn't even have to get out of their car, or at the counter itself. For people who preferred to eat in, there were about ten tables.

It wasn't an entirely run-of-the-mill place. It had a huge window that faced onto McCarran, framing the glittering, diamond-bright city as if it were a painting.

The girls chose the first table next to the door, just a few feet from a particular customer who had caught their eye. He was a young Latino, weighing about 280 pounds.

"Wouldn't you rather sit by the window?" I asked.

No, they wanted a table that gave them a good view of the young man. They were at once frightened and fascinated by his huge, round, shaven head, encrusted like a ball into a neck twice the size of any normal neck

The fat man kept glancing over at the kitchen. At one point, he got up and went to talk to one of the girls preparing the food orders. I assumed he must know her or that he was another employee on his break. He certainly wasn't a customer, because he wasn't eating anything. Apart from the girl in the kitchen, he only seemed interested in his telephone. He was constantly tapping at the keys, as if he were playing rather than actually making a call.

As soon as I sat down, I realised that my hands were dirty and so I walked over to the bathroom, just a short distance away. However, the toilet was occupied, and so I went back to our table.

"They're not really dirty," Izaskun said. "You've just got some of that Halloween make-up on them."

They called us to collect our trays, and before I did, I tried the toilet door again. Still occupied. A moment later, my hands were even dirtier than before, because the tray I picked up was sticky with grease.

"Why is this so dirty?" I asked one of the women serving.

Without a word, she gave me a clean tray and a handful of paper napkins.

There was a new customer in the restaurant now, standing by the door. He was dressed like a cowboy, in a fancy purple shirt with white piping. I guessed that he must have been the person occupying the toilet, which meant that I could now wash my hands. I was right. This time, the door opened.

There was toilet paper scattered all over the floor and a wet rag blocking the sink. I washed my hands thoroughly, doing my best not to touch anything. As I was leaving, I noticed that the wastepaper bin had fallen over, scattering bits of food, sweet wrappers and more toilet paper.

About ten people were now waiting at the counter. The last two were policemen. They had their caps tucked under their arms and looked rather humble, as though they were in a chapel rather than a fast-food outlet; however, the blue of their uniforms and the guns at their belts had the expected effect, and the other customers became strangely alert and silent.

The two policemen only stood in the queue long enough to observe the female employees, and ended up going over to the one who had been talking to the fat man. She pointed outside.

I thought perhaps a car was blocking the exit and asked Ángela if we had parked ours properly.

"You worry about everything," Izaskun said. "First it's your hands, and now it's the car."

The police left the restaurant as discreetly as they had entered and, for a moment, everything was very calm and quiet, as if Tacos really had become a chapel. Suddenly, the fat man sprang to his feet and ran over to talk to the woman at the counter. He moved lightly, quickly.

She was very offhand with him. Even though he was about eight inches taller than her and about 125 pounds heavier, she seemed to be the one looking down at him. At no point during their conversation did she stop filling plastic containers with food.

The place was empty now. There was no-one waiting at the counter, and only we and the fat man were sitting at the tables. He was still busy with his cellphone. Izaskun was reading a comic. Ángela and Sara were trying out the different-coloured make-up on a napkin. Seen through the window, the red, fuchsia and green casinos looked like cathedrals.

The door opened, and three policemen came in, the two from before and a third one, an older man. They went first to the toilet and then over to the counter and spoke to the offhand woman. In an attempt to understand the situation, I told the girls about the state of the toilet and about the dirty tray. Someone must have called the police to complain about the lack of hygiene. I remembered the cowboy in the purple shirt with white piping who I'd seen standing by the door.

The fat man got up again and went over to the three policemen and the young woman. They were talking in low voices; then the fat man and two of the policemen went outside. The third one, the older man, stayed chatting to the woman. She kept pointing angrily at the kitchen and raising her voice. She wasn't easily cowed.

Izaskun could see what was going on outside through the glass door.

"One of the policeman has put a little bag of white powder on the bonnet of the car," she said. "It looks like sugar or flour, but it's probably drugs."

We left the restaurant to go home and there was the fat man, sitting on the kerb, surrounded by policemen, with his hands behind his back in handcuffs. In that position, it was easy to see the tattoo that began on the back of his neck. A snake.

There were about ten police cars in the car park, and we had to drive around them to get out onto McCarran. Sara asked if the fat man would go to prison, and we all agreed that he would.

"For a month?" she asked.

I thought it would probably be for years, so I answered only vaguely.

"I don't think there was much stuff in that little bag, so I should think they'll let him out straight away," Izaskun said.

Just as had happened on the previous night with King Kong, the girls felt sorry for the arrested man.

Lying awake in our bedroom in College Drive, I remembered the cowboy in the purple shirt with the white piping. He was probably a policeman. He had rifled the bathroom at Tacos looking for drugs, while his uniformed colleagues had surrounded the place. They must have followed the fat man there. Or somehow tracked him via his phone.

I couldn't quite follow the plot, but it didn't matter. Thrillers were not as thrilling as they used to be. The main point now was the girls' reaction: What connection was there between justice and compassion? How far should society go in order to protect itself? What should the city do with King Kong?

The questions went round and round in my head. They were like ghosts in the room. I fell asleep feeling hopeless. Not even Queen Mab, the mistress of dreams, could have come up with an answer.

THE PAINFUL EYE AND THE VIGILANT EYE

We were caught by a gust of wind as we were setting off for Mount Rose School, and Izaskun immediately felt a sharp pain in her eye. We could see at once that her cornea had been damaged.

"There must have been some grit in the wind," she said.

We called our insurance company's contact number in America and raced off to the clinic assigned to us. It was at 1441 McCarran, about six miles away.

We had to wait half an hour in the waiting room because of a misunderstanding between the insurance company and the clinic. Then another half an hour, because the doctor had to cover the injured cornea with an orange liquid that was slow to take effect.

"It's a superficial wound and will heal on its own," the doctor said at last, cleaning her eye.

We dropped the girls off at school at about eleven o'clock in the morning, and five minutes later, we were back at the house, where we found an answerphone message from the police or some sort of security office informing us that Izaskun and Sara had not arrived at school at the appointed time.

The frosted glass eye in our front door might be able to trap the image of the casinos in the town centre, but the other eye, the Vigilant Eye, was sharper still and could even see inside the houses.

AUGUST 27, 2007
MARY LORE

Mary Lore Bidart was the director of the Center for Basque Studies (C.B.S.). She was about forty years old and had very pale blue eyes.

"If you want us to do all the paperwork later, that's fine by me," she said.

I was sitting immediately opposite her, but didn't say a word. I was finding it hard to think.

"I'm still jet-lagged. My head feels like it's full of lead," I explained.

It took me almost fifteen minutes to fill in the forms that the University of Nevada required of visiting writers. Shortly afterwards, Ángela arrived and picked up the card that would allow her to use the library and access the archives.

Before leaving the office, we gave Mary Lore the letter addressed to Robert H. Earle from the Bank of America, the one we had saved during our clearing-up session at College Drive.

"So they're still writing to him at that address," Mary Lore said when she saw it. "He used the house as his study until he retired, but that was at least three years ago."

This explained the size of the house in College Drive. It was intended as a study, not as a family house.

Mary Lore gave us more information. The house was a gift to the university from Robert H. Earle or "Bob" as he was known, and the C.B.S. was using it to store books and to accommodate writers spending time in Reno.

"Bob lives in the big house at the top of your garden. Pay him a visit. He'd like that."

"We'll go and see him as soon as we've recovered from our jet lag."

We left Mary Lore and started going down the stairs connecting the university offices with the library. Ángela said that I looked ill.

"I've got a headache, but it's not the jet lag, it's Nabokov," I said. "While Mary Lore was speaking, I was remembering that other Mary Lore, the nurse in *Lolita*. Don't you remember? Nabokov has Humbert Humbert insult her, calling her "rumpy" and "a plump whore". Then, again for no reason, he takes a sideswipe at Mary Lore's father, some old joke about Basque shepherds having it off with sheep. It's a vile passage."

"No, it's the jet lag," Ángela said. "I wasn't thinking about Nabokov's Mary Lore, but I've got a terrible headache as well."

DENNIS

Mary Lore made all the arrangements with the university and found us an office. It was in the library, behind the shelves reserved for dictionaries and other reference books. It was small and windowless and fairly sparsely furnished, with two desks, two computers, a filing cabinet, and a phone attached to the wall. Still, it was a privilege to have a place to work in, and, during a brief "ceremony", we were given the keys and our computer passwords.

One of the university's I.T. people came to see us in our office. At first, I thought he was a young man, because he was very slim and sported a kind of Beatles haircut, but he must have been at least thirty or thirty-five. He introduced himself to us as Dennis.

"Everything O.K.? Computers working?" he asked.

He sat down in front of one of the computers, tapped a few keys, then went to the other computer and did exactly the same. It took him all of thirty seconds.

"Right, you're in the system now," he said, getting up and going over to the door.

He left the office, but immediately came back. Five seconds, maximum.

"I've been talking to Bob about security at your house. When can the exterminators come in?"

We realised that "Bob" was our neighbour Robert H. Earle, but we didn't know what Dennis meant by the "exterminators".

He was standing up, arms folded, one hand cradling his chin. He took a while to tell us what was on his mind.

"The cellar is full of books, and there are a lot of trees and bushes around. There might be spiders," he said at last. "Normally, that's not a problem, but it's best not to have them under your bed."

He pursed his lips before telling us the name of the spider in question: the black widow.

"You wouldn't mind staying home for one day, would you?" Ángela said. "That way the exterminators can come whenever they like." She wanted to be in the C.B.S. archives first thing in the morning, whereas I had no timetable to keep to. We were in Reno because of my work as a writer, not for me to give classes or do research.

"They can come tomorrow, if you like. The sooner we get rid of any black widows the better," I said.

"Great!" Dennis said, giving me the thumbs-up.

We saw him walking briskly away through the library, taking short, quick steps. He was clearly a popular man. Several students, sitting at their computers, looked up and said hello.

THE SPIDER

In the images I found on the Internet the spider was black and shiny, as if it were made of a mixture of metal and plastic. It had a red mark like a diabolo on its belly. Its legs were long and strong and hairless, almost polished. Its body was no larger than a hazelnut.

According to the article accompanying the image, the poison of the black widow was a neurotoxin, and its bite, which might seem innocuous at first, caused severe pain, like the pain of a heart attack or appendicitis, only simultaneously. It also caused tremors, faintness, dizziness, nausea and, worst of all, a sudden rise in blood pressure. The article emphasised, however, that the bite was rarely fatal, and was only really a danger to children and the elderly.

PHONE CALL TO MY MOTHER

"I'm phoning you from the office they've given us at the university," I told my mother. I had to speak standing up because the phone was fixed quite high on the wall. "I can't phone you when I get home because that would be too late. How are you?"

"It's late enough as it is," she said. "I've already had my supper."

"We're going to have our lunch shortly. We usually go to one of the dining halls in the university, which is quite nice really, with a view over a lake with swans on it. Normally . . ."

"What did you say? You're going to have lunch? You mean supper, don't you?"

"No, we're going to have lunch. We're in Nevada, remember, in the United States. It's twenty past twelve in the afternoon here."

"Twenty past twelve! That's amazing! Here it's twenty past nine at night. That's why I've already had my supper. Normally, I have my supper at eight and by nine, I'm in bed."

"Don't you watch any television? There are some good programmes on."

"I don't like television. I prefer to go to bed. I'm in bed by nine most nights. I don't necessarily go to sleep, but at least I'm lying down."

THE EXTERMINATORS

"Here we are! The exterminators!" one of the two men said as soon as I opened the front door.

If they had said it in unison, I would have thought they had come to advertise a variety show, or that they were two comics from the television. They seemed excessively cheerful, spoke very loudly and sang. They were wearing blue jumpsuits and red baseball caps, and carrying plastic cases and fumigation guns with long tubes attached.

Talking all the time – I couldn't understand a word they were saying – they went to their respective posts. The younger man, who seemed to be a trainee, went to the girls' bedroom, and the boss, a big fellow of about sixty, went down with me to the cellar. He looked everywhere: in the corner where the washing machine and the boiler were, in the carpeted room that served as a junk room and play area for the girls, and, above all, in the garage, where the books published by the C.B.S. were stored on metal shelves. He moved from one place to another, his hands in his pockets, whistling and singing to himself. Every now and then, he would sigh and exclaim: "Terrible place!"

He put the plastic case down on the floor and began taking out various containers. One was full of a yellow liquid; another contained a black powder like soot; the third a kind of green slime.

The big man stopped his sing-song commentary for a moment and gave me his verdict. He repeated, in rather less prolix form, what Dennis had already told us. Our cellar was the perfect habitat for black widow spiders. And not just spiders either, but for a large number of creatures that the Bible deems beyond the pale: snakes, scorpions and so on. He would have to use some particularly aggressive substances.

"Do you have a cat in the house?" he asked.

I felt like saying that the only animal around was the raccoon in the garden, but the word "raccoon" escaped me and so I simply shook my head.

"Just as well!" he boomed, then added with a laugh: "For the cat, I mean!"

He indicated to me that I should leave the cellar and then he put on a kind of surgeon's mask.

I waited in the kitchen. I couldn't see the raccoon in the garden, but I could see the blue jays, who were sitting in the trees, cackling. About thirty or so feet away, at the top of the hill, the sun was glinting on the windows of the house belonging to our neighbour, Robert "Bob" Earle.

The trainee exterminator was moving around outside. He directed his fumigation gun at one corner of the porch and squeezed the trigger, then repeated this operation on the stone steps and, as far as I could see, outside the garage too. He, too, was humming to himself, although not any particular tune.

The big man did not emerge from the cellar for a quarter of an hour. He went straight to the truck he had parked outside the house and put his fumigation guns and his plastic case in the back.

"So, did you see anything?" I asked when he returned to the house.

"There was a spider on the bookshelves. Don't worry, though, I killed it," he said. At least I think that's what he said.

"A spider?" I asked, surprised.

He nodded, but without looking at me. He was leaning over the table, filling in an invoice. When he had finished, he smiled and showed me how much I owed him. One hundred and forty dollars.

"One hundred and forty dollars?"

He said something else I didn't understand, but at least there was no doubt about the figure. One hundred and forty dollars.

It seemed to me that the engine of his truck started up very cheerfully, almost burst into song, in as good a mood as its owners, the exterminators. It reached the junction of College Drive and Sierra, turned on its left blinker and disappeared.

THE BOTTLE IMP

There was a stall at the entrance to the library where they made coffee to go, so that you could take it with you into your class or to your desk. They served it in plastic cups with a lid on so that it wouldn't go cold. I met Dennis while I was queuing up, and he asked me about the exterminators.

"Apparently, they found a spider in the garage," I told him. "But they didn't show me the body."

The more time passed, the more convinced I was that there had been no spider in College Drive.

"I doubt he was lying," Dennis said, reading my thoughts. "There are a lot of them about this year."

Our cups of coffee were ready, and the student in charge of the stall set them down before us after first fitting them with a cardboard ring so that we wouldn't burn our fingers.

Dennis adopted the same pose as he had the day he came to connect us up to the university computer network – arms folded, one hand cradling his chin.

I paid for the coffees and handed him his cup.

"Have you got five minutes?" he asked.

"Of course."

We walked through the library to his office. It was as small as ours, but his had windows with a partial view of Reno and of the desert mountains beyond. I counted seven computers on his desk and on the floor.

The thing he wanted to show me was on top of a metal filing cabinet: a glass jar with a round metal lid, and inside it was a spider like the one I'd seen on the Internet, a black widow.

"I caught it yesterday," Dennis said.

He picked up the bottle and held it in the air so that I could see it from below. There was the spider's belly and the red mark in the form of a diabolo, or, to use Dennis's word, an hourglass.

The spider moved its long legs.

"Watch this," Dennis said.

He shook the bottle. The black widow raced up and down the glass walls.

"Incredible energy, eh?"

Dennis returned the bottle to its place on top of the filing cabinet.

"I'd better go and do some work," I said. I wanted to get back to my office and drink my coffee.

Dennis told me that his plan was to test the spider's powers of endurance, to see how long it could live without food and with a limited supply of oxygen.

"If it's still alive in two weeks, I'll let it go."

Two weeks seemed a long time to me, but I said nothing.

HELICOPTERS

I was woken by the noise of engines and immediately identified the metallic buzz, the rhythmic beating of a helicopter blade. It wasn't just one helicopter transporting a patient to St Mary's hospital. There were a lot of them, and they seemed to be flying very low. The windows in the house vibrated.

I ran out into the garden. The sky was full of red lights, and the noise seemed to affect everything, the house, the trees, the air. One of the helicopters passed immediately overhead, and I could see the lettering on it and the colours. It was one of those big-bellied ones they use for carrying troops.

Silence returned to the garden. Next to the shack, the raccoon was looking at me with its two yellow eyes, as if nothing had happened.

A DOSE OF MORPHINE
(A MEMORY)

A week after being admitted to hospital, my father was given an overdose of morphine. When I went to see him, he mistook me for a man who had worked with him in the forests of the Pyrenees sixty years before.

"Where are the oxen?" he demanded. His eyes were watery.

"What oxen?" I said.

"What do you mean 'what oxen'? The ones we need to transport the timber! We have to load it onto the train tomorrow!"

I placed one hand on his arm. He brushed me off.

"Just get those oxen, will you! The timber's too heavy to haul with a rope!"

His shouts could be heard in the corridor. I pushed the buzzer next to his bed to summon help.

A young nurse appeared.

"Are you the owner of the oxen?" my father asked.

"Is he off his head?" said the nurse.

"Mind what you say! Show some respect!" That would have been my older brother's response, but I wasn't quick enough and said nothing. However, she could see that I was annoyed and she blushed.

"I've been in the timber business for three years, and nothing like this has ever happened to me before," my father said.

The matron came into the room then. She spoke to my father, calling him by his name and asking him all kinds of absurd questions before attaching a pouch containing a tranquilliser to the tube in his arm.

"Would you come with me for a moment. There's something I'd like to say," she said, indicating the door.

A patient was walking slowly down the corridor, holding a bag containing urine. Two women were supporting him, one on either side. The matron let them pass before speaking.

"The young woman who looks after your father at night is not to be trusted," she said at last. "She puts up the bars around the bed and then goes off to the snack machines. She spends all her time reading magazines or talking on her mobile."

"Well, she shouldn't do that. We're paying her a fortune."

"That's nothing to do with us," she said. "What's worrying us is that your father keeps trying to get out of bed. The other night, we found him with one leg over the top of the bars. If he has a fall, it could be very serious."

I had been about to protest at the sheer nerve of the younger nurse, but what I had just heard made me forget all about that.

"He always has been very strong," I said.

I went back into the room. My father's eyes were less watery now.

"What do you want?" he said in a nasal voice. A second later, he was asleep.

SEPTEMBER 12
WHAT TO DO IN DANGEROUS SITUATIONS

Izaskun and Sara came home from school talking about what they had been taught to do in the event of some potentially dangerous situation.

"If the siren sounds eight times, that means there's a fire," they explained. "In that case, we all have to line up and walk in an orderly fashion to a particular part of the playground. Each class is allocated a different area."

We thought that was it, but it wasn't.

"If bears appear in the playground, we have to turn out the lights and crawl under our desks. And it's the same if a gunman starts firing at us. You have to turn out the lights and hide under the desk."

The automatic door to the Eldorado Casino opened just as we were passing, and the first thing I saw was a gigantic screen showing Elvis Presley. He was wearing a tight white sequinned jumpsuit and singing one of his hits, "In the Ghetto". The people at the fruit machines took no notice, their eyes fixed on those other screens.

A young woman was standing at the corner of Virginia Street and 2nd, peering upwards, craning her neck like a bird. She was wearing dark glasses and carrying a white stick in her right hand. She was blind.

"Can you help me, please?" she called out when she felt us close by.

She asked us where the Greyhound bus station was, and we only knew where it was because it was close to the public dispensary where we had gone for the vaccinations required by the school, and so we explained that she had to go down 2nd, then count six streets along. The bus station was on the left. She walked briskly off, tapping the ground with her stick.

We continued along Virginia Street, listening to the cling-clang of the metal signs on the street lamps being blown about by the wind. The street suddenly became very brightly lit, as if we had just emerged from a tunnel. We walked another hundred feet or so and found ourselves beside the Truckee river. The waters boiled and churned like a mountain stream, swirling round the rocks.

We had been told that some young people in Reno used to amuse themselves racing from one bridge to another on the inner tubes of old truck tyres; that day, we saw only ten or twelve hippy types sitting on the bank. One of them was rather unenthusiastically playing with a black dog.

We crossed the bridge and reached a monument, the war memorial. Engraved on the marble panels were the names of all the Nevadan soldiers who had died in America's various wars – the First World War, the Second World War, Korea, Vietnam, Iraq, Afghanistan. On the panels dedicated to the fallen in Iraq and Afghanistan, the names occupied half of the surface or slightly less.

I copied the last five names into my notebook:

Raul Bravo Jr. Marines. Died March 3, 2007. Iraq
Anthony J. Schober. Army. Died May 2, 2007. Iraq
Alejandro Varela. Army. Died May 18, 2007. Iraq
Joshua R. Rodgers. Army. Died May 30, 2007. Afghanistan
Joshua S. Modgling. Army. Died June 19, 2007. Iraq

A twenty-something girl in glasses went over to the monument and stood there, slightly hunched, head bowed, for two minutes or so. Then she straightened up, shot a disapproving glance at Izaskun and Sara, who were running around among the panels, and told us off, saying that we should show some respect for the dead. We called the girls over and left.

We caught the free downtown bus that took us back up Virginia Street to College Drive. Ahead of us, during the whole journey, stood a huge cross lit up in pink neon, looming out of the darkness. It was on a hill the other side of McCarran. We had never even noticed it during the day.

THE VISIT

There was a knock on the door of our office in the library. A man of about sixty, with blue eyes and white hair, stood there.

"Hi, I'm Bob Earle, your neighbour," he said, shaking my hand.

I felt guilty about not having visited him as I had promised Mary Lore I would.

"I've been meaning to come up to your house to say hello, but just haven't got round to it. I'm sorry," I said.

"Nonsense. I'm the one who should have come and introduced myself the day you arrived, and brought you a couple of pizzas too. Trouble is, I thought Mary Lore was going to bring them, and Mary Lore thought I was going to. What a welcome to Nevada! Straight to bed with only what you were given to eat on the plane!"

He held out his card.

"I'm afraid I don't have a card," I said and started writing down our number on a piece of paper.

"Oh, don't worry, I know the number. The College Drive house was my study when I used to teach at the School of Mining."

"Of course. Mary Lore told me. Ángela's working in the archives at the moment. I'll introduce you to her later. And to the girls."

"Everything alright at the house? According to Dennis, the insect problem has been resolved. I hope they didn't bankrupt you."

Earle was wearing jeans and a sky-blue shirt. He was a strong, good-looking man and, perhaps because of that, because of the confidence he felt in his own physical strength, he seemed warm and direct, with none of the awkwardness of the very shy.

"Very nearly!" I said. "They charged us a hundred and forty dollars!"

Earle's smile concentrated itself in his eyes.

"I reckon Dennis has a share in the business. He sends those robbers in as soon as he finds out someone new has arrived in town."

Then he changed the subject.

"Would you like to go for a drive in the desert? I'd be more than happy to show you around," he said.

The invitation caught me by surprise, but I accepted immediately.

"Great. How about tomorrow morning, Tuesday?"

I again said yes.

"Good. I'll pick you up in College Drive at eight o'clock," he said. "Bring something to eat and something to cover your head, a cap or a hat."

A silence fell.

"I wouldn't be at all surprised if it isn't sunny in the desert tomorrow," he said with just a hint of a smile, then strode off to the C.B.S. office.

A DRIVE IN THE DESERT

Earle was looking from side to side, screwing up his eyes, and I couldn't imagine what it was he was looking for. We had left the roads behind us by then – the 80, the 50, the 361 and the 844 – and were deep in the desert, and all I could see was a barren plain and the occasional hill covered in sagebrush, the plant that appears on the Nevada flag. Now and then, we saw the tyre tracks of another vehicle, but, generally speaking, there was nothing but earth and rocks and more earth and rocks.

Suddenly, far off in the distance, I spotted a trapezium-shaped mountain, and the sense I had of being in a totally empty space only intensified. The mountain somehow lent depth to the landscape.

"When I was a boy, I used to come here to catch rattlesnakes," Earle said. "Then I would sell them to zoos or pet shops. It paid pretty well."

He tended to pause between speaking, but after three hours in his company, I no longer felt embarrassed by these silences. After a while, he went on:

"I'd pin them down with a forked stick, then put them in a canvas sack, the kind that lets in the air. Easy. I loved it."

I imagined the rattlesnakes squirming around in the sack, trying to pierce the fabric and bite the hand of the hunter.

"If you keep the sack away from your body, there's no problem," Earle said when I told him what I was thinking. "And even if it does bite you, it's not really that bad. A rattlesnake bite is rarely fatal."

I had read in the *Reno Gazette-Journal* that a young man had spent four months in hospital after being bitten by a snake, and had only survived because he was helicoptered out of the desert. I didn't say anything though.

Several orange-coloured mountains appeared behind the one shaped like a trapezium. That's where Fallon must be, Fallon being the nearest town according to the map, about sixty miles away. A two- or three-hour drive in that terrain.

We started to climb a hill. The road was stony and flanked by trees that looked like rather scrubby pines. Earle told me they were pinyon pines.

"They're ugly trees and nobody much likes them nowadays," he said. "But for thousands of years, the Indians used the pine nuts to make flour."

Earle was gripping the wheel hard. It wasn't easy to control the Chevrolet Avalanche as it lurched over the rougher stretches of road. It took us a quarter of an hour to climb the slope.

The hill was flat on top and there was a canyon running through it, nearly a thousand feet long. We got out of the car and stood looking down into the depths of the canyon to see what was there: clumps of grass, a few alder trees, and some intensely red rocks protruding from the walls. Not a sign, as Earle pointed out, of the Citabria single-engine plane piloted by Steve Fossett, who had disappeared about two weeks before while flying over that same desert.

"Seems like God gave up on him," Earle said. "He doesn't give up on the birds, mind; he provides them with pine nuts to eat, but he wasn't so generous with Fossett."

Steve Fossett – the "Adventurer's adventurer" or the "American hero", depending on which newspaper you read – was famous throughout the United States for his exploits in the field of extreme sports. He held more than a hundred world records, including being the first man to fly solo non-stop around the world in a balloon. His disappearance was one of the most talked-about events in Nevada and all over the country.

A lizard poked its head out of a crack in a rock, then instantly vanished. Earle made another remark about Fossett.

"I'm not really surprised God gave up on him. He asked too much of him."

We went back to the car and set off again.

"What shall we do if we meet Fossett's ghost?" I asked.

"We'll ask him to tell us exactly where he crashed."

"That will save the search parties a lot of work."

"Not to mention money. I hate to think how much gas they've used on rescue planes and helicopters."

We drove downhill, parallel to the canyon, and my feeling now was that we were leaving one sea behind us and entering another still vaster sea. For miles and miles around, as far as the eye could see, there were only a few isolated mountains, mostly trapezoid in shape and black and ochre in colour. I looked for the orange mountains I had seen earlier, and, when I couldn't find them, thought that perhaps they were only that colour because the sun had been shining directly on them, and that they, too, were ochre and black. I was wrong. There they were, to our left, the orange mountains. We weren't driving in a straight line, but were gradually veering to the right.

We reached an area where the earth was wet and the colour of plaster, and we left the tracks of our tyres imprinted in it. In the distance, we saw what looked like a pinkish object, a mother-of-pearl box.

Earle pointed.

"It's a roulotte, you know, a caravan. Hunters come here looking for antelope."

I looked hard at the roulotte. There were no hunters. No antelopes either. The only moving thing was our car.

We drove another five or six miles across completely flat terrain, then started to go down another slope. The mountains we could see ahead of us now looked like mounds of earth emerging from the sea, the islands of an archipelago. I remembered the time I spent in Villamediana, a village in the Spanish province of Palencia, and reading somewhere that Castile was like a sea of earth. I told Earle this.

"Here, it's something more than a metaphor," he said. "Each of these mountains is a unique system with its own flora and fauna. The reptiles and the insects you find on one don't exist on another. And that's exactly what happens on islands in the sea."

We could make out a road, a straight line, which was a slightly paler colour than that of the earth. When we reached it, Earle began to accelerate as if we were driving onto an approach road to a freeway. The car threw up clouds of dust behind us.

"What's going on over there?" he asked, accelerating still more.

About five hundred yards further ahead, next to a rocky outcrop, I saw a FedEx delivery van. The two front doors stood open and the van was parked at a strange angle, neither perpendicular to the road nor facing the rock nor parallel with it.

We stopped about fifty feet from the van. Earle took a rifle out of the boot and released the safety catch. He told me to stay in the car.

He went over to the rocky outcrop and started walking round it, rifle at the ready. A minute later, he reappeared on the other side and approached the van. Suddenly, he stopped. Then he lowered his rifle and signalled to me that there was nothing to worry about.

He returned to the car and took a forked aluminium pole out of the boot.

"Come with me."

The windscreen on the driver's side of the FedEx van was shattered. Earle told me to look through the other side.

On the driver's seat I noticed what appeared to be a pile of brown cloth. It was a rattlesnake. It had its head up, looking first at me and then – its coiled body shuddering as it moved – at the other door, where Earle was standing with the metal pole. There was a sound like maracas. The snake was flicking its tongue frantically in and out.

Earle failed to pin the snake down properly and as he was picking it up, he managed to drop it onto the roof of the van. Then it slithered towards me, fixing me with its two black eyes . . . No, that only happened in my head. Earle playfully scolded the snake, saying that the driver's seat was only for drivers, not mouse-hunters. The snake hung limply from the forked pole, like a belt.

Earle went round the back of the rock, and I followed.

"I had to remove it from the seat," he said. "People don't take care and just open the doors of vans without even looking."

He released the snake, and it vanished among the clumps of sagebrush.

We returned to the Chevrolet Avalanche, and Earle called the police on the radio he'd had installed. They answered instantly.

"Fallon Police Department," the voice said. It sounded as if it were speaking from underneath the earth, not from Fallon.

Earle provided his personal details and our position on his G.P.S. The subterranean voice took only a few seconds to tell us that we were near a ghost town called Berlin. Then it asked for the van's licence-plate number.

"Wait a moment," Earle said. He started the engine and drove forward a few feet before dictating the relevant letters and numbers.

"Anything else we need to know?" the subterranean voice asked.

"The windscreen on the driver's side was broken, and the interior was a complete mess. Looks like a robbery," Earle said.

"Sure."

The subterranean voice sounded grubbier now, as if mingled with sand and grit, and I couldn't quite understand what it said. It referred several times to that abandoned town called Berlin and to Fallon prison. The conversation seemed very relaxed, and before it ended, Earle gave a loud guffaw.

"They found gold and silver in this desert, and they gave the mine the name of the man who found it, a man called Berlin," Earle explained when we set off again. "But it was never as big as the mines at Tonopah or Virginia City. By the beginning of the twentieth century, it was a ghost town."

Berlin, the ghost town, appeared to us just half an hour after leaving the FedEx van: a dozen or so wooden shacks and a larger building, also made of wood, with a single-eaved roof, the slope of which matched the slope of the mountain. Several paths led off from there, two still quite clearly marked. The first crossed a plain thickly covered with sagebrush, and that path, according to Earle, led to Fallon; the second, perpendicular to the first, went up a hill through a small gorge into an area of bushes and trees.

I told Earle a true story Ángela had told me. Two young men got off a train somewhere in Nevada and set off on foot to Berlin, about sixty miles away, with only a bottle of water. They had never seen or even imagined a desert like this.

"They arrived half-dead and nearly blind," I said. "One of them never recovered and died shortly after starting work at the mine."

"I don't think we'll meet *his* ghost either," Earle said.

After spending all morning with him, I was beginning to get used to his sense of humour. He meant that Berlin was so empty that it didn't even have any ghosts.

We stopped outside the larger building, the centre of mining activity in the age of gold and silver. All the mining machinery and tackle was still there, and so were all the birds in the area, taking advantage of the shade cast by the roof. Most were flying from beam to beam or perching on the cables; some came and went constantly, in and out of the large windows that faced onto the hill.

Earle smiled.

"The powers-that-be in Nevada keep the building maintained so as to attract tourists. And they have actually succeeded in attracting a few. In fact, we'll probably see them soon."

We set off in the direction of the gorge and the trees and shrubs. About a couple of hundred yards further on, we saw two white vehicles. They were parked by the side of the road; near them, about ten or so men were standing in a line, working. Their overalls were white too.

As we approached, the conversation about the FedEx van between Earle and the subterranean voice began to make sense. I knew now who those people in the white overalls were: prisoners.

"What do you think of Berlin's tourists?" asked Earle, slowing down.

I recalled something I'd seen many years ago when I was driving to New Orleans and was kept hanging about for half an hour in a traffic jam, while about twenty men wearing orange overalls and shackles were working with spades and hoes to clean the hard shoulder of the freeway. Two policemen were watching them, rifles cocked.

The Berlin prisoners weren't shackled together, and they stood to one side to let us pass. Most were Latinos. The youngest must have been about twenty-five and the oldest about sixty. The young men looked really strong and healthy, the older men looked scrawny.

Earle accelerated once we had passed them, and we started to drive up a hill that led to the gorge.

"I didn't see any guards," I said.

"The desert is their guard," Earle said. "And what better guard could you have?"

He remained thoughtful for a while.

"There were a couple of guys I really didn't like the look of," he went on. "The two non-Latinos. Did you notice? Their eyes lit up when they saw us. Especially the guy with the little beard."

I glanced in the rear-view mirror. All I could see were white dots against a background of stones.

"A big, strong guy?" I asked.

"A real brute. He's probably in jail for having strangled someone."

We were in the gorge now, and the trees and shrubs transformed the landscape with their intense green. Earle braked for a moment and, turning to the right, headed downhill. A little stream interrupted the path, and we were across it in an instant, before, slowly, we began to climb again.

We travelled about two hundred yards and arrived in a small square, which was in marked contrast to the desert and the landscape around Berlin. It was partly surrounded by a concrete wall, and there was a wooden shack with a notice saying TOILETS and another structure with a roof that seemed to reach right down to the ground with no supporting walls.

"Time to see the lizard!" Earle cried. "And it's pretty big, as you're about to find out."

And there was indeed a giant lizard painted on the wall in the little square. A plaque told us it was an ichthyosaur, a marine reptile that had lived about two hundred million years ago and reached a length of over sixty feet. The actual fossil was in the building with the low roof.

In the painting, the ichthyosaur bore a striking resemblance to Flipper.

The building was closed, and we could only see the fossil through some small windows at ground level in the side wall. It was uncomfortable crouching there, with the sun burning your back.

At first, the ichthyosaur that had swum in the sea two hundred million years ago looked like the dried-up bed of a stream. In the part corresponding to its head, there was a slight bulge and at the other end there was what looked like a real tail.

"Great place, isn't it?" Earle said.

He meant the building, which was a lot taller than I'd thought when I saw it from outside, and inside was a large empty space, uninterrupted by any columns. The only source of light was provided by the rectangular windows in the roof, which lit up the whole area.

It was very hot, more than thirty degrees, and I felt as if my shirt was burning. The shrill whirring of insects buzzed in my ears. I stood up.

"We need to find some shade," Earle said.

We sat down next to a tree trunk, on a rock, and ate our sandwiches and our tangerines in silence, while we gazed at the Flipper painted on the wall. The painting was not at all appropriate. That cartoonish style had the effect of infantilising a dolphin, even an ichthyosaur, which was fine on screen, but not in the desert.

I was picking up the orange peel, when I heard a voice. It rang in my head. The prisoner with the small beard was whispering to one of his companions, and I could hear it as if in a dream:

"I've had enough of breaking stones out here in the desert, and there's no way I'm going back to jail. Did you see the car those two guys were in, the ones who've gone to see the fossil? It was a Chevrolet Avalanche. If we stole it, we could be in Fallon in no time. I have a buddy there who could hide us until the police get tired of looking for us."

Absurd as it may seem, I could hear the voice as clearly as I could smell the tangerine peel.

"They might have a gun in the car," the man with the little beard said. "We would have to move fast once we'd stopped the car."

His companion said something I couldn't hear. The "radio" inside my head was not tuned in to him.

"If we take anyone with us, it should be Gonsalves," the man with the beard said. "He knows quite a lot of people in Las Vegas, and that could be useful once we get out of Fallon."

A small bird rather like a thrush hopped over to us; Earle said it was a sage thrasher, and emptied a few crumbs from his sandwich bag onto a rock.

"I should have brought a handgun with me too, not just the rifle," he said. So *he* had heard the prisoner whispering in his ear too.

"Do you know how to drive?" he asked. He was serious.

The Chevrolet Avalanche was almost twice as big as our Ford Sedan, but I said I'd be happy to drive.

"I'm worried about that prisoner with the little beard. I'm sure that when he saw us, he immediately thought of a plan. He may have taken me for an old man, an easy target."

I got into the driver's seat.

"What do I have to do to cross the stream down below?" I asked.

"Close your eyes and step on the gas."

Earle smiled, and I felt reassured.

I found it hard to get the pressure right on the accelerator, because it was very sensitive and the slightest touch sent the car lurching forward. When we crossed the stream – way too fast – I managed to flatten all the bushes on either side.

The stones and rocks on the road – loose stones and rocks sticking up out of the ground – slowed our progress, making us bounce and sway about; but we soon recovered our balance. A hundred yards further on, the road became smooth again.

The prisoners working near the two white vehicles no longer looked like white dots, as they had when I saw them in the rear-view mirror, but real people with heads, arms and legs. Earle grabbed the rifle and placed it between his knees, barrel downwards.

The prisoners were not all working together. First, there was one, then behind him another; then a group of five or six, then about twenty yards further on, three more men, backs bent.

The first of the prisoners, the one nearest to us, was the man with the small beard. He stepped into the middle of the road and signalled to us to stop, as if he were a traffic policeman. He was holding a spade in his right hand.

"Shall I stop?" I asked.

Earle nodded, then lowered the window about an inch.

The prisoner with the beard came over.

"Could you give me a couple of cigarettes, one for me and one for my friend here?"

He spoke very politely, pointing with his free hand at the other non-Latino prisoner.

"You're not supposed to do this. You know that, don't you?" Earle said.

The man with the beard did not move a muscle. He was considering his response.

"Prisoners have no right to stop a vehicle. You know that, don't you?" Earle said again.

The man's eyes were dull, as are the eyes of anyone who has spent years in prison. For a few seconds, he stood there, still thinking. Then he looked down.

"Yes, sir," he said, stepping back.

I put my foot down too hard on the accelerator, and the Chevrolet Avalanche leapt forward. The bearded prisoner's companion jumped out of the way. Those who were working a few yards further on stepped back too, even though there was plenty of room for us to pass. Earle closed the window and put the rifle on the back seat.

When we reached Berlin, I stopped the vehicle outside the mining building and we changed seats.

"After that test, I have no doubts about your skills as a driver," Earle said, giving me that half-smile of his, "but I think I would prefer to take the wheel, if you don't mind. It makes me feel young again."

We set off. The plain stretched out ahead of us as far as the horizon. The sky was completely blue.

We drove ten, twenty, thirty miles. On some stretches, the green of the sagebrush disappeared and the terrain looked as black as if it had been scorched by fire, or else white or off-white; elsewhere, the earth became sand and formed dunes like those in "Lawrence of Arabia". I suddenly felt very sleepy and closed my eyes.

When I opened them again, I saw a chain of mountains ahead of us. They seemed as flimsy as light clouds and not made of rock at all.

"Carry on sleeping, if you like. There's not much to look at in the desert," Earle said.

Then suddenly there was. Two black blades crossed the space between us and the Fallon mountains at supersonic speed.

I sat up in my seat.

"Military aeroplanes," Earle said. "F-16 fighters probably."

The air base at Fallon is home to more than three thousand people, military and civilians, and the surrounding area is the U.S. Navy's biggest air warfare training centre. They perform daily practice bombing raids. The 1963 atomic test took place there too.

"At least the navy was considerate enough to make it an underground explosion," Earle said.

He turned on the radio and pressed some buttons. All that emerged from the speakers, though, was a metallic whistle.

"Last time I drove past here, I could hear the pilots' conversations, but today nothing doing," he said. "I'm going to tune in to the air base radio station instead and see what music they're playing."

The names of singer and song appeared on the small screen on the radio. Elvis Presley, "Love Me Tender".

We were coming into Fallon. The first sign was a horse ranch, then some very green alfalfa fields, with the irrigation sprinklers going full blast. Fifteen minutes later, and we were in an urban area, at a round-about adorned with an old fighter plane, painted in the colours of the American flag.

I noticed the new song being announced on the radio screen. Johnny Cash, Willie Nelson. "Ghost Riders in the Sky".

"Time doesn't pass in Fallon. They were playing that song last time too," Earle said.

We stopped outside a respectable-looking bar and went inside. The bartender – who had a helicopter tattooed on his arm – made a joke when I ordered a Budweiser. I didn't quite understand and merely smiled.

The walls were covered with framed photographs, mostly of planes, but the one in the corner near the door showed three young marines. They were in dress uniform, gold buttons on their navy-blue jackets. All three had died in Afghanistan, killed in action.

The door opened and in came two marines. They walked past, ignoring us completely, not even bothering to say hello, and sat at the back of the bar. We paid for our beers and left.

We took Highway 50 heading for Reno, and Earle continued telling me about Fallon. It was always sunny there, clear blue skies every day. There were a lot of deserted, empty places in America, but none of them had the right climate for pilots being trained to drop bombs on specific ground targets.

"In planes like those ones over there," he said, pointing to one side of the road.

"Those ones over there" were black flies against a mineral-blue sky.

The sun was already going down, and to the west, above the horizon, the sky was tinged with red. The black flies grew to the size of birds; gradually, the birds became metallic objects and the metallic objects became helicopters. They crossed the road in front of us. Three of them, then ten seconds later, another three. The second group flew very low, making the sand on either side of the road swirl about.

"Our Berlin tourists stood no chance of escaping anyway," Earle said.

He hadn't forgotten them. Neither had I.

On the radio, Nancy Sinatra was singing. "Bang Bang, My Baby Shot Me Down".

Even though I didn't have any cigarettes, I thought I would have wound down the window on the Chevrolet Avalanche to speak to the prisoner with the beard, and would have said a few friendly words to him, saying – guiltily aware that my words were purely rhetorical – how sorry I was, how I pitied him and his companions, wasting their lives in that way, clearing rocks from a road that was barely usable. A memory accompanied that thought. Around 1980, I was in a café in Gold Street in New York, and the waiter took me for a fellow Latino and said to me in Spanish: "How come they're so rich and we're so poor? How can God allow that?" His eyes filled with tears. He was so depressed that he didn't even mind showing his feelings to a complete stranger. It was a small café, but very luxurious. He was wearing an extremely elegant uniform: maroon jacket and bow tie, white shirt. He himself was handsome, with dark, curly hair. I asked how much he earned. "These people pay nothing," he answered. "Their hearts are made of stone. They are jackals." His words did not shatter any of the shop windows in that street of gold; they did not even reach the ceiling of the café. They affected me though. After that day, I could never go to America without seeing, in every other suffering face, the face of that exploited waiter. And now in the face of that prisoner. "Could you give me a couple of cigarettes, one for me and one for my friend here?" I would have said: "I'm sorry, but I don't have any." "Never mind. Thanks anyway." "Why are you in prison?" "I was accused of strangling a girl, but it's a lie. I'm innocent."

I felt confused. Thoughts and memories kept getting mixed up in my head.

On the radio's small screen another song came up. Dolly Parton. "I Will Always Love You".

Earle was driving along with his eyes narrowed. Perhaps he was looking for antelopes, as he had been at the beginning of the trip or, more likely, he was finding it hard to see the road. The sun was about to vanish, the shadows were becoming ever more numerous. The sagebrush on either side of the road was not green any more, but black.

Earle's response to the prisoner was, doubtless, the right one, and perhaps the fairer one too. He couldn't have spoken to the prisoner in a friendly manner, not even a prisoner who was easy to intimidate and keep at bay, as was the case then. A nine-year-old child, our daughter Sara, could feel sorry for King Kong or for a drug trafficker arrested in Tacos, but a grown-up? I wasn't sure what the answer was. The tear-filled eyes of the waiter in New York's street of gold stood in the way.

The Rolling Stones. "Angie".

Night was falling. In the sky, it was hard to tell blue from black.

Earle slowed the car almost to a halt. Before us we saw what remained of a gas station. The pumps were all blackened, the trash cans a twisted mass of plastic. A fire.

"It used to be a brothel," Earle said, turning off the radio. "The women who worked the pumps didn't wear many clothes. And inside, they didn't wear any at all."

Another half-smile.

An hour later, we reached the junction of Highways 50 and 80. Suddenly, we were driving among trucks. From the other direction too it was mostly trucks, many of them with extra lights on the cabin, like the cars on carousels. We were driving home, and I felt as if I had been away for a whole month. Time was different in the desert.

"Nevada!" Earle exclaimed. He sounded almost elegiac. I could nearly smell the scent of sagebrush that word gave off.

"This is a state that flourished thanks to four things," he said. "Divorce, gambling, prostitution and mining for gold and silver."

And the highway, I thought, looking at the trucks. But I said nothing.

"Most of the mines were mined out years ago," Earle went on. "There are still a few in Virginia City and in Tonopah, but not many. And divorce isn't what it was in the days of Vanderbilt, because people can get divorced anywhere now. Fortunately, the other two mines are still active, and I shouldn't think they'll ever be exhausted."

"Although that depends on the Indians," I said. I had read in the *Reno Gazette-Journal* that the casinos owned by the Chumash and the Mission Indians in California were giving Reno and Las Vegas a lot of competition.

"Well, we all have to live," he said with a smile.

We came round a long bend and, suddenly, the lights of Reno appeared, as if they had just been turned on.

THE SHEPHERD AND THE DESERT

Ángela brought back from the C.B.S. archives a copy of *National Geographic*, containing an interview that the writer Robert Laxalt had made with his father Dominique. His father was talking about his experiences in the desert during his years as a shepherd.

"If a man was unlucky enough to be sent there when he first came, it was a terrible shock.

"I remember how it was for me. I wasn't much more than sixteen years old, you know. And they sent me into the desert with a dog and three thousand sheep.

"I can remember waking up in the morning, and, as far as I could see in any direction, there were only sagebrushes and rocks and runted little junipers. Though the Basques are used to being alone, these deserts were something else. In the first months, how many times I cried in my camp bed at night – remembering my home, remembering the beautiful green Basque Country.

"In the summer, the desert burned your lungs, and every day you had a scare with rattlesnakes and scorpions. In the winter, the blizzards tore at you and soaked you so that you were wet and freezing day and night.

"Those first few months, you thought you would go insane. Then, suddenly, your mind turned the corner and you were used to it, and you didn't care if you ever saw people again."

MESSAGE TO MY FRIEND L.
RENO, SEPTEMBER 18, 2007

Two days ago, my neighbour, Bob Earle, drove me into the desert in his Chevrolet Avalanche. We drove through Churchill County and visited a ghost town called Berlin.

Initially, I kept looking for a kind of "Lawrence of Arabia" landscape, because that was the image I'd expected after seeing that film forty or so years ago. But the Nevada desert, the part I saw anyway, is different. It isn't a sandy desert. Parts of it are covered in trees and shrubs; other parts are a succession of trapezoid mountains and piles of rocks in an area that extends for hundreds of square miles.

Seeing those trapezoid mountains in the distance, I got quite confused. I lost all sense of time and space. If someone had told me that I was travelling in the *Discovery* space shuttle rather than in Earle's Chevrolet Avalanche, that we were crossing outer space and not the Nevada desert, I would have believed them. Just as I would have believed that we were back in the days when pterodactyls were still flying about and ichthyosaurs were swimming in the sea, and not in the year 2007. Looking at those mountains – far, far, far away, so far away that the most distant ones looked like mere maquettes – I was keenly aware of the world's utter indifference to us. This wasn't just an idea either, but something more physical, more emotional, which troubled me and made me feel like crying. I understood then that the mountains were in a different place entirely. They weren't just distant from me in the way a bird in Sicily is distant from a tree in Nevada, but, as I said, in a different place entirely. In another dimension? That's what I would say if I were just chatting to a friend. But the word "dimension" doesn't include the important element of indifference. Those trapezoid mountains have been in the desert for millions of years. They are nothing to do with us, they are nothing to do with life, and it's hard to imagine why they are there, or why we even occupy the same physical space.

As you see, I've gone all Byronic and highfalutin. I will come back down to earth now.

Bob Earle is very used to being in the desert, and he broke the spell I was under by making jokes about the whereabouts of Steve Fossett, who was into extreme sports and spent his life beating world records in endurance and speed. He disappeared some weeks ago.

Leaving the desert had its moments too. In Berlin, we saw a group of prisoners clearing the road, and a fossil ichthyosaurus.

BUYING BOOKS IN BORDERS

The bookshop was light and spacious and a really pleasant place to be. We used to visit it often, normally on a Friday. Izaskun and Sara would spend several hours lying on the carpet in the children's section, reading picture books, while Ángela and I, sitting in the café, would leaf through the books and magazines we had picked from the shelves.

The first books we took to our table in the café on Friday, September 19 were written by various members of the Laxalt family: a special edition of *Sweet Promised Land* by Robert Laxalt, *The Deep Blue Memory* by Monique Laxalt Urza – which we had only read before in the Basque translation – and a book of poems by Bruce Laxalt, which we didn't even know existed. Then, from the table of new books, we chose *Dempsey in Nevada* by Guy Clifton, and a catalogue of photographs taken on the set of John Huston's "The Misfits", which included a long interview with Arthur Miller.

We intended to buy the Laxalt books, and so spent our time looking at the other two. Individually, the photographs in the catalogue were really good – Huston and Marilyn at a gaming table in Reno, a wild horse galloping through the desert, Clark Gable smiling, Clark Gable looking tired, Montgomery Clift looking thoughtful – but perhaps because the photographs were the work of different photographers, seeing them all together jarred somehow. And the interview with

Arthur Miller was uncomfortable to read. The print was faint and the typeface ugly and the spacing too big.

"I wouldn't buy it," Ángela said. And I agreed.

The Guy Clifton book included photographs too: Dempsey and Willard fighting in the ring, the fight between Dempsey and Carpentier in front of thousands of people, Dempsey with his mother, Dempsey with a hippopotamus at a circus that visited Reno in 1931 . . . To our surprise, Paulino Uzcudun appeared in one of the photographs. The caption said: "Actor and wrestler Bull Montana, Paolino Uzcudun and Dempsey pose at Uzcudun's camp at Steamboat Springs, 1931."

There were more photographs of Uzcudun, several with Max Baer; there was also a panoramic shot of the Dempsey Arena in Reno on the day of the fight. According to the book, there were more than 15,000 spectators.

My father was born a few miles from Uzcudun's house and had a lot of things to say about him, none of them good. I found him an interesting character.

"I'd love to find that training camp, Steamboat Springs," I said to Ángela.

A man who looked like a tramp was sitting nearby, and he suddenly snatched up the Guy Clifton book and started studying the back cover, then read out loud: "My God, that's when men were men!" It was part of the publicity puff Angelo Dundee had written.

"Totally agree!" the tramp exclaimed, handing the book back.

THE SPIDER IS STILL ALIVE

I met Dennis in the university library while I was looking for a copy of Nabokov's *Lolita*. I asked him about the black widow spider he had imprisoned in a bottle.

"It's exactly as it was on the first day," he said, and his face lit up like a child's face.

"Really?"

"Would you like to see it?"

I looked doubtful.

"What's the book you're looking for?" he asked.

"*Lolita*."

"And the author's name?"

"Nabokov."

"Na-bo-kov," he repeated, as he searched the shelves, quickly running his fingers over the spines of the books. A few seconds later, he had two different editions of *Lolita* in his hands, in Spanish and English. I took the Spanish and he took the English.

We went over to the library counter to have the books stamped, and went from there to his office.

The spider was sitting motionless in the bottle. It really did seem perfectly healthy: its back had the same metallic sheen as when I saw it the first time, unblemished and undulled.

Dennis tapped the bottle, and the spider moved its legs. Then he shook the bottle, and the spider raced from the bottom to the top and from the top to the bottom. Just as it had the first time.

"It's been in there quite a few days, hasn't it?" I said.

"Nineteen."

"That's incredible."

"Fascinating," Dennis said.

EXCURSION TO PYRAMID LAKE

Pyramid Lake, a Paiute Indian reservation, is 35 miles north-east of Reno, in a remote desert area south of Washoe County. It is 15 miles long and 11 miles wide. In 1993, the population was 1,603. *Guidebook to Nevada*

I was sitting on the lake shore, and Sara and Izaskun were pointing at the white pelicans flying towards us from the pyramid-shaped rock, but my mind wouldn't fix on that place – Pyramid Lake, Washoe County, Nevada – or on that moment – Sunday, September 23, 2007, a cold, blue day – and was instead recalling what had happened to two boys I knew when I was a child; it focused in on them like eyes homing in on a particular object.

They were twin brothers, Carmelo and José Manuel. Their father worked in Madrid, and so they lived there and only came to the village, to Asteasu, for the summer, and then they would hang out with us boys, who were the same age as them. We would go down to the river or up into the hills, or we would cycle to some nearby cinema.

One of those summers, towards the end of August, José Manuel went back to Madrid to prepare to re-sit an exam he had failed. Shortly afterwards, I realised that his brother, Carmelo, was missing and I assumed that he had left too. But he was still in the village, confined to the house because he was ill.

"He's got a bad headache," a cousin of his said.

That same night, I heard my mother talking to a neighbour in our kitchen.

"They say he's in a really bad way," the neighbour said.

I thought she meant Carmelo, but they were talking about José Manuel. Apparently, there had just been a telephone call from Madrid to warn the family.

The woman's voice dropped to a whisper.

"They're afraid he might have meningitis."

Her tone of voice seemed in keeping with the grave state the patient was in, and I adopted the same tone to give them my news: that afternoon, José Manuel's twin brother, Carmelo, had come down with a bad headache and was lying in the dark in his room, unable to get out of bed.

I had invented the business about the dark room, driven to exaggerate by my excitement.

My mother and the neighbour listened to me intently.

"That's all we need – for them both to get ill," my mother said.

After supper, my two brothers and I used to sit in the living room, reading comic books about Red Ryder and Hopalong Cassidy. I mentioned that José Manuel was ill, adding information gleaned from my mother's conversation with the neighbour. Meningitis gave you a fever of forty degrees. And the back of your neck went as hard as a stone. But, despite the seriousness of the illness, we shouldn't worry, because the hospitals in Madrid were very good.

My two brothers moved their heads up and down. Easy enough.

I did the same. The backs of our necks were not as hard as a stone. We were fine.

We carried on reading, but I couldn't concentrate. I couldn't rid myself of an idea that was going round and round in my head.

"It's really strange," I said to my brothers. "Carmelo started to get a really bad headache here in Asteasu at precisely the same time José Manuel fell ill in Madrid. Or the other way round. José Manuel fell ill in Madrid, and Carmelo got a really bad headache here. Both at the same time."

I was hungry for mystery, and I started to adorn the facts with invented details. No-one knew the exact moment when the twins had fallen ill.

"It's as if they were telepathic," I explained, not entirely sure what the word "telepathic" meant.

My two brothers continued reading their comics and showed not the slightest interest.

The following morning, I met Carmelo in the baker's. He didn't seem ill, but he was quieter than usual. When the shop assistant asked about his brother, he simply shrugged. When he left, he didn't even say goodbye.

"It all depends on how advanced the illness is," a young woman waiting to be served said. It seemed that no-one was talking about anything else in the village.

The two women and a third who came into the shop shortly afterwards went over the various cases of meningitis that had happened locally, and I was surprised to find it was so common, but the biggest surprise came when I heard the name of a cousin of mine. I couldn't remember her ever being ill. Besides, my cousin was still alive.

That day, we went down to a pool in the river, and the older boys tried to show us a new way of diving in. At first, Carmelo didn't want to join us, but then he cheered up and stayed in the water until it was getting dark. I never took my eyes off him. I wanted to see if he showed any sign of having a headache, but I saw nothing. He just seemed more silent than usual, as he had in the baker's, and he kept away from the rest of us when we started noisily splashing about in the water and fighting.

I couldn't accept that show of normality and, over supper, I again brought up the subject of telepathy between twins.

"He felt a really bad headache at the precise moment when his brother fell ill in Madrid."

"Oh, not that again!" protested my older brother.

"Twins *are* always quite special," my father said.

Once supper was over, we all went into the living room to read comics. Shortly afterwards, the telephone rang, and my mother was talking to someone for a few minutes. Then she pushed open the door to the living room.

"So José Manuel has died, eh?" she said, just like that, adding that final "eh?"

"And how's Carmelo?" I asked. But my mother was no longer there.

PYRAMID LAKE (2)

The only sound by the lakeside was the lapping of water on rocks, and it was hard to comprehend the origins of a legend according to which, if you listened carefully, you could hear, on the shores of Pyramid Lake, the crying of the children who had drowned in its waters. Perhaps its origins lay in the nature of the human mind, which is incapable of keeping control of its memories or of tying up bad memories in a canvas sack, as Earle used to do with those rattlesnakes. And out of bad memories ghosts were born, and out of ghosts, legends . . . The lake, its ghosts and its legends certainly had an influence on me. It had been thirty or possibly forty years since I had thought of the twins Carmelo and José Manuel, and suddenly I had seen them again as clearly as when we were all children together.

I had to drag myself back to reality. I was at Pyramid Lake, Nevada. It was September 23, 2007.

A large fish stuck its ugly head out of the water, and I tried to call my daughters over to see it, but they were standing some way off, next to a couple of Paiute Indians, who were sitting on fold-up chairs, fishing. Ángela was even further away, taking photographs of some white pelicans.

The two Paiutes were big, strong fellows. The older one wore his hair in a braid. When I went over to them, he was saying to my daughters:

"I feel proud that my people have been able to take care of this place. It's always been a beautiful place, and it still is."

The second Paiute added:

"This is a sacred land. The mountains, the desert, the lake, they're all sacred."

They both spoke without looking round, as if they were addressing the lake itself. I wondered if they really believed what they were saying or if they were merely repeating, once again, the script they reserved for foreigners.

I sensed that Izaskun and Sara were about to ask something.

"We'd better go," I said. "If you ask too many questions, you'll frighten away the fish."

They obviously considered this to be a good enough reason, and the three of us walked over to our car, where Ángela was waiting for us.

From the road, the lake looked dark blue; the pyramid-shaped rock off-white; the desert grey. On the shore in the distance, we could see dark pillars, the sort you might see when a really violent rainstorm is approaching, but these were pillars of sand or dust, whipped up by the wind.

In the guidebook to Nevada I had read that Las Vegas was an anomaly. The same could be said of Pyramid Lake: nearly 200 square miles of lake in a place where it never rains. An anomaly that gave life to the two towns on the reservation, Nixon and Sutcliffe. We drove towards the second of those towns, which was nearer the road back to Reno.

Sutcliffe looked like a housing development, with individual houses just slightly larger than the sort of cabins you might find on a camp-site, and it had clearly been dreamed up in the office of some town planner. All the houses were the same, so were the streets, so were the cars, both the new – every one of which was a pickup – and the old, the ones destined for the junkyard, with no wheels and with the guts of their engines exposed to the air. At one end, near the lake, in the middle of a grove of trees – which gave the place the appearance of an oasis – was the only non-identical building, the service area of Crosby Lodge: gas station, motel, shop and bar.

We parked in the shade and went into the bar. The thermometer fixed on the door frame read eighty-one degrees.

The place was quite busy. A man wearing the uniform of a trucking company was playing pool with a Paiute Indian. Watching the game were another ten men, most of them wearing fishing hats. Sitting at a table were three young Latinos who looked like construction workers. On the other side of the circular wooden bar was a girl with very blonde hair. She came over to us and waited while we decided what to have.

"Ah, Basque!" she exclaimed when she heard us talking.

She explained that she was from Idaho and had worked in Boise. She had recognised the sound of our language.

The main wall of the bar was covered with photographs of fishermen, and there was a plaque informing us that the large fish with the ugly head they were all proudly holding was a cui-ui. Having recently leafed through that book about "The Misfits" in Borders, I was surprised to find not a single image from the film shoot. There was one, I seemed to remember, that would have been perfect: Marilyn Monroe and Clark Gable lying next to each other on the shores of Pyramid Lake. I asked the waitress, but she had never heard of the film. Nor was she interested in Marilyn Monroe.

"I'm more into politics," she said.

She took a leaflet from a box under the counter.

"We're going to see what's in the shop," Izaskun said, and they both rushed off.

"He'll be the next President of the United States," the waitress said, showing us the leaflet.

We had heard about a black politician who was contesting the

Democratic leadership race with Hillary Clinton, but this was the first time we had seen a photograph of Barack Obama.

"Go along and listen to him," she said.

According to the leaflet, Barack Obama would be speaking in Reno on October 14. The meeting would take place in the hotel-cum-casino Grand Sierra Resort.

"We'll try," Ángela said.

It took the girls just five minutes to review the souvenirs in the shop. Izaskun wanted to buy a silver bracelet, and Sara wanted a plastic version of the Nevada state flag, about the size of a newspaper; it was cobalt blue with a single white star. They also wanted to buy Ángela some turquoise earrings and me a dream- (or, rather, nightmare-) catcher adorned with a small eagle's feather. We gave them some money and they went back to the shop.

Sara had her little Nikon camera with her and, before we set off back to Reno, she took some photographs of an old telephone box that had caught her eye. It stood by the entrance to the bar and bore a sign on which the name of the company was written in large letters: NEVADA BELL.

About five miles from Sutcliffe, the road climbed up to the official lookout point. The wind was blowing so hard that Ángela and I had to fight our way over to the information board. We finally managed to read what it said: the waters of Pyramid Lake came from Lake Tahoe, and the river that brought them, the Truckee, ended there. For the Paiute, Tahoe was "the higher lake" and Pyramid "the lower lake".

I stood for a while staring down at the lake below. It looked like a piece of smooth turquoise. Too beautiful. Too still. On some American night, it would doubtless come back to haunt me, unless it was caught by the dream-catcher Izaskun and Sara had given me.

FROM SUTCLIFFE TO RENO

Outside the Paiute reservation, the desert was less harsh and the road long and straight. As we drove along, gliding over the grey asphalt, our Ford Sedan seemed like a small solitary animal, a black mole. Suddenly, an eagle appeared. It dived down and picked up the mole – our car – in its beak.

I jumped and raised my head.

"You fell asleep."

Ángela's voice merged with the hum of the engine. The sun was shining directly in my eyes.

"Very few people have understood the desert as well as Daniel Sada," I said to Ángela, as if I had been thinking about him all the time. "I remember hearing him say that, compared with the desert, any other landscape looks like a stage set. He was quite right."

Ángela indicated the back seats. Izaskun and Sara were both asleep.

I thought of Arthur Miller and went on talking, but more quietly.

"Do you remember what he says about Nevada in his memoirs? He didn't much enjoy being here. He wanted a divorce so that he could marry Marilyn Monroe, and that meant spending three whole months in Nevada."

Ángela had given me a copy of Miller's autobiography a few months earlier. She nodded.

"He found this whole area around Lake Pyramid particularly inhospitable," I went on. "He said it was like a piece of the moon. But I prefer Daniel Sada's description: 'Compared with the desert, any other landscape resembles a stage set.' He was spot on."

I would have liked to expand on this, but my eyes were closing again. The hum of the engine was growing denser and denser. It seemed to come from the sun itself.

I saw Arthur Miller. He was talking to Marilyn Monroe from the telephone box in the Crosby Bar, and the breeze blowing in through the cracks made his trousers flap chap-chap-chap. "I love you, I love you," he was saying, and the chap-chap-chap gave a rhythm to his declaration of love: "I love you chap-chap-chap, I love you chap-chap-chap." I wanted to catch Marilyn Monroe's voice, but all I could hear was a little doll's voice saying: "Oh, Pa! Oh, Pa!" I listened harder, and the sheer effort woke me up again.

"Relax. Go back to sleep. I'll tell you when the landscape changes," Ángela said. Sometimes she shared Bob Earle's sense of humour.

Over where the sun was setting, I could see whirlpools of dust swaying tirelessly, as if they were taking part in a dance. I saw Marilyn Monroe outside a cinema in New York. She was wearing a satiny white dress that fell in soft folds to her knees. In the dark street, it looked even whiter. "It's a shame the monster had to die like that. It's sad!" she sighed. "What did you expect? That he would marry the girl?" retorted the man with her. "The monster isn't evil," insisted Marilyn. "If he felt loved, he wouldn't act like that." Then there was the roar of a subway train, and the breeze suddenly whooshed up through a ventilation grille and lifted her skirt, revealing her thighs. "It's refreshing that breeze, isn't it?" the man said. The images then vanished from my head, but not the noise: chap-chap-chap, chap-chap-chap. I glanced round at the back seats. Sara was awake and had stuck the plastic Nevada flag out of the window. That was where the flapping noise was coming from.

On a hundred-yard stretch of road I saw four snakes squashed by cars. I started wondering if eagles ate snakes that had been dead for a while, and in my head there was another whirlpool, the memory of my father. He would have been about forty then. I was about seven. There was a dead snake lying in the grass. My father looked at it and said:

"The eagle sees the snake from far away. He swoops down, grabs it in his talons and flies up again as fast as he can. Then he drops the snake. The snake suffocates during the fall, and the eagle follows behind and snatches it up again just a second before it hits the ground. Then he carries it back to his nest or to a hole in some rock and eats it."

My father pointed at the snake lying in the grass.

"Can you see the marks left by the eagle's talons?"

He was right.

"For some reason, the eagle didn't manage to pick it up again. Perhaps a dog appeared and he got frightened, who knows. Anyway, he lost his lunch."

48

The memory vanished from my head like another pillar of dust.

We passed several ranches surrounded by trees. Shortly afterwards, at an airfield protected by metal fences, I counted five light aircraft that resembled insects – grasshoppers or mosquitoes. I thought we were reaching the edge of the desert, and that we would soon come across another inhabited area, but in the miles that followed, the landscape reverted to its usual self – more wide, flat expanses, more squashed snakes on the road, more sun.

The road dipped down, and on the hillside above us, in a corral, we saw more than a hundred horses. A lot of them were at the drinking trough, but most were standing alone, scattered about in the corral.

"I think they're wild horses," Ángela said in response to a question from the girls. She stopped the car on the hard shoulder so as to get a better look.

Most of the horses stood as still as statues and were utterly silent. It was strange: more than a hundred horses in a corral and not a sound from them.

Ángela started up the engine again, and we continued on down the highway. From the back seats, the girls continued to ask questions. What were the horses doing there? Were they really wild horses? They were thinking of the mustangs, the fiery-eyed horses they had seen in comics and films, galloping across the desert in a cloud of dust.

"They're waiting for someone to adopt them," Ángela said. "I read something in the newspaper the other day about how some horses can't cope on their own and need help."

This was partly true and partly false. The scriptwriter of "The Misfits" had not invented the fact that wild horses were killed and used for dog food, but now it was the Paiutes and other native Indians who, being exempt from federal laws regarding protected species, hunted and sold the horses. Animal rights organisations had to buy them from the Indians, take them away from the reservation and then release them into the wild again in some protected area.

We were leaving behind us the houses in Sun Valley now and coming into the outskirts of Sparks. In another fifteen minutes we would reach Reno and our house in College Drive.

I was assailed by more memories. I saw myself in the village where I was born. The pig they were killing in the butcher's back yard kept screaming, and I could hear it as clearly as if it were there in my bedroom. This was followed by another incident, which took place in the slaughterhouse. The slaughterman slit the throat of a cow, and the little boy standing next to me, seeing the cow's legs twitching even after it had fallen to the ground, asked: "Did they electrocute it?"

Neither that cow nor all the thousands of other cows who had met the same fate were anything like the drawing on the Laughing Cow cheese triangles; the screaming pig was nothing like Babe, the Sheep-Pig; the mustangs in the comics or in the films were nothing like the horses we had seen in the corral on the hill. However shiny or cute the wrapping, the contents were still terrible. As Daniel Sada might have said, reality was the desert, and representations of reality the stage set.

DEATH OF A HORSE
(A MEMORY)

The electrocuted horse lay in the alleyway all day, and the children keeping watch over it, waiting for something to happen, felt duly rewarded when two Civil Guards and a group of other people arrived and began an inspection.

"You see," one of the men said, addressing the crowd and holding in one hand the electric cable hanging from a post, "this is what killed the horse. Because it wasn't properly attached, it fell on him and killed him."

I knew the man. He was the horse's owner as well as the owner of the village's only restaurant. People called him Franquito because, during the Civil War, he had been a great admirer of General Franco.

"He looks like a Percheron. How much did he weigh?" asked another of the men, dressed in suit and tie. Someone next to me said he was the judge.

"I was only about three yards from the horse. If I'd been any closer, the cable would have killed me too," Franquito said.

"Excuse me, sir," one of the guards said, addressing the judge. "Draught horses tend to weigh anything from 1,700 to over 2,000 pounds, and he was one of the bigger ones."

"I've never seen a horse that big before," the judge said.

"I just want something to be done about it," Franquito said, raising his voice. "That cable could have killed me. They should slap a big fine on the owner of the electricity substation. He lives right here, on the square. His name's Jacinto."

"Calm down, please," the magistrate said. "We'll do whatever needs to be done."

Then he went over to another member of the group, a young man wearing glasses.

"Write a report, will you?"

I ran to my house. Jacinto, the man Franquito had mentioned, was my father. The substation belonged to him, and so did the cables. The horse was lying dead in the street. What would happen? I wanted to ask my mother.

I went into the house, but no-one was there, not my mother or my brothers. I escaped to the pelota court and stayed there watching a game until it was dark.

Over supper, my father repeated the story he always told us when there was some problem at the substation. His father, my grandfather, had gone to the provincial capital to study technical drawing and get a good job in some government office, but his efforts proved fruitless, because every post was assigned beforehand depending on who you knew. He was so disillusioned that he decided to leave it all behind him, and when he came back, he built a substation in the valley, in a place that wasn't even accessible by road.

This was doubtless a mistake. A wrong decision. But it wasn't my grandfather who paid for the mistake, it was my father. At the age of ten, when the other children were coming out of school and going to play pelota or run around in the square, he would have to go to the substation to check all the machinery. He was often left alone too, because his mother, my grandmother, worked for a dressmaker in the next town and only came back to the village at weekends, and because

51

my grandfather used to spend his afternoons and evenings in the local bar.

"When will you be back, Pa?" my father would ask him.

"Before they ring the angelus bell."

But he used to take longer than that, and my father would get frightened there in the dark valley, and would walk again and again up to a bend in the path just to see if his father was coming. Fear seethed inside him like eels in water.

Normally, my father's crises lasted only as long as it took to recall the history of the substation, but the day after the horse died, when my brothers and I went into the kitchen to have breakfast, the first thing we heard were these bitter words, a continuation of what he had said the night before:

"I wish I'd burned the place down the day I inherited it!"

He was smartly dressed, in a jacket and blue shirt.

"Your father has to go to San Sebastián," my mother said.

"To see the judge?" I asked, remembering the man I'd seen standing next to the horse, the one in the suit and tie. My mother spun round, amazed that I should know what was going on.

Three hours later, we were leaning out of the kitchen window and looking across at the place where they were going to bury the horse. There were a lot of children hanging around the grave, among them my two brothers.

"They might impose a really big fine," my mother said.

"How much?"

"I don't know, but possibly fifty thousand pesetas. That's what *he's* saying anyway."

Franquito was directing the burial and gesticulating angrily. He was the 'he' my mother was referring to.

"Look at the horse's swollen belly!" I cried.

A team of labourers began dragging the horse towards its grave.

"Franquito has no shame!" my mother said. "He was an informer during the war. That's how he ended up owning the restaurant. The real owner had to escape because Franquito reported him."

My mother left the window to go and prepare lunch.

"Your father will be having a hard time of it in court," she said and launched into a litany of complaints. It wasn't his fault, but they wouldn't give him a chance to defend himself. It had been an accident, completely unforeseeable, but the judge was sure to take Franquito's part, because they were on the same side, the side that had won the war. That's why he had been summoned to court so quickly. They wanted to punish him.

"That's it. They've buried the horse," I said from my position at the window.

"Good!" my mother exclaimed.

My father found the judge sitting in a leather armchair, resting his chin on his clasped hands. On the wall behind him hung a portrait of General Franco.

"I summoned you here urgently because I need to know something before I proceed with the case."

He made no attempt to be friendly. Still in the same pose, he went on:

"What is your relationship with a man called Iruain? He lived in the village and had the same name as you."

"He was my father. That's what people called him: Iruain."

The judge stirred in his armchair and placed his hands on the table. He studied my father's face.

"Do exactly as I am about to tell you to do," he said at last. "Go back to the village and give the owner of the horse a thousand pesetas, so that he can buy another one. That way, we're all square."

The judge got to his feet, and my father did the same. They shook hands.

"So there won't be a fine, then?" my father asked.

"Do exactly as I told you and everything will be alright. As I said, that way, we're all square."

My father would have liked to know the reason behind that decision and ask the judge how he had known his father, Iruain, but he didn't dare. The judge's attitude did not invite him to ask any further questions either, for he remained strangely aloof throughout the interview.

The years passed, and the substation was bought by a large energy company. The question that had gone unanswered in court was often brought up at family celebrations: Why had the judge not imposed a fine? What was the relationship between that man and our grandfather, Iruain?

If life were like literature and facts could be manipulated, if we could set up a stage in the desert, this book would say that the son of Iruain, my father, died in peace, reconciled with, or at least with a better opinion of, *his* father because he had discovered the judge's motives. But that isn't what happened. The answer came much later, too late, at the beginning of summer 2007. That was when I found out, purely by chance, that the judge was the illegitimate son of a woman who had come to work in the village, only to spend weeks looking for somewhere to live, because no-one wanted to rent a room to a single mother. Iruain, our grandfather, was the exception. He let the first floor of his house in the square to the woman and her son. That is why the judge had favoured my father; that is why he had said twice: "That way, we're all square."

OCTOBER 2

THE FIRST SNOW

I was sitting on the verandah at the back of the house in College Drive reading the *Reno Gazette-Journal*, when I felt something cold touch my hand. It had started to snow. Two hours later, the sky was blue again and the peaks of the mountains that separate Nevada from California were touched with white.

"I think the raccoon has gone," Ángela said later on.

We went out to look. The creature's bright yellow eyes had disappeared from the garden.

"Perhaps the snow was a signal for him to leave," I said.

"He's probably gone south," Ángela said. But she didn't really believe it.

TELEPHONE CALL TO MY MOTHER

"We're all fine," I told my mother. "But from now on, things might not be so easy here. Winter has arrived. It snowed yesterday afternoon."

"Well, it's been drizzling here all week. I'm fed up with it," she said.

"Where are you phoning from?"

"From my office at the university. Like I said, if I don't phone you from here, it will be too late for me to call you once I get home."

"Well, you don't want to let it get too late. You need your sleep. I'm just about to go to bed myself. This weather's really getting me down."

"I've arranged to meet Ángela for lunch. We almost always have something called a 'Combo'. The dining room is really spacious, and we usually get a table by the window so that we have a view of the lake. There's a swan that swims up and down. I think I mentioned that the other day . . ."

"Lunch, did you say? You mean supper, don't you?"

"No, we're going to have lunch, not supper. We're in the United States, remember, in America. I told you the other day. It's midday here, well, a quarter to twelve."

"No, no, it's a quarter to nine! That's why I've already had my supper. I'll be going to bed soon."

"You'll watch a bit of television first, though, won't you?"

"I don't like television. Besides, I'm fed up with this weather. It's been drizzling all week and shows no sign of stopping."

IN HOSPITAL WITH MY FATHER
(A MEMORY)

My father spoke Spanish reasonably well, but he always retained a strong Basque accent and tended to resort to Basque proverbs and set phrases to express himself.

Two doctors came into his hospital room while he was asleep. Without waking him, they felt first one leg, then the other, and invited me to do the same. His left leg was warm, but his right was as cold as marble.

55

They showed me the result of the M.R.I. scan they had done the day before. At first sight, it looked like a satellite picture of Amazonia: a thick line – the Amazon river itself – with a few thinner lines coming off it – the tributaries – and finally a mass of tiny threads – the tributaries of the tributaries. But it wasn't a map of far-off Amazonia, it was an image of the veins in my father's right thigh.

The doctors directed my attention to the thick line. It was the femoral vein, which was damaged and even blocked. One of the doctors pointed to the blockage with his pencil and indicated a few smaller veins, which ran only a short distance, before returning to the femoral vein. They explained that because the main route was closed, the blood was trying to find a way through by making all the other veins it met en route work harder. However, in my father's case this wasn't enough. They needed to insert a stent in order to open up the blockage to the femoral artery.

They needed our permission to carry out the operation. One of the doctors said cheerily to my father, who had just woken up:

"And what do you think, Jacinto?"

"Me? I say that when two or three shepherds are gathered together it can mean only one thing: a dead sheep."

OCTOBER 12, 2007
DIFFERENT MESSAGES

It was snowing heavily when I arrived at the university, but that didn't seem to worry the red-haired man in the car park distributing booklets. He came over to me, beaming, and thrust one into my hand. He had several teeth missing.

The title of the booklet was: *Have You Ever Faced Death?*

Shortly afterwards, while I was waiting in the café at the entrance to the library, two young men gave me a full-colour leaflet bearing a photograph of Barack Obama.

The first booklet was not exactly reassuring. It opened by saying: "Most of us imagine we will die at home, in our sleep, but very few of us will die like that." It then continued its ascetic message, taking examples from recent history: "When General McArthur took up the reins during the Korean War, the first thing he did was to remove all the awnings that were put on trucks during cold weather, leaving the soldiers exposed to the elements and at the mercy of enemy fire. Well, that is how we live our lives."

The statements grew weirder and weirder. In the fourth paragraph, the writer declared that a belief in immortality was common to human beings and dogs, but not to cats.

I abandoned the booklet and began reading the Barack Obama leaflet instead. It was advertising his forthcoming appearance at the hotel-cum-casino Grand Sierra Resort. "Turn the page on Iraq," it said in big letters. There was also a photograph of the candidate standing beneath a placard bearing the word "Change". A slender man in a dark suit and white shirt, but no tie, was pictured waving to his followers in a way that was neither entirely serious nor entirely upbeat.

OCTOBER 14

BARACK OBAMA'S SPEECH. "TURN THE PAGE ON IRAQ"

The queue of five or six hundred people who had come to hear Barack Obama filled the elegant, carpeted ground floor of Grand Sierra Resort from end to end. The dim lighting – casinos are always dimly lit – emphasised the gaudy, strident colours of the slot machines. The players moved the levers or pressed the buttons without once looking up, clinging to the machines like limpets, and they seemed annoyed by the presence of all these intruders.

It was a striking scene. Those who were concerned about the Big Game – the war, working conditions, the arms trade, the health system – were calmly chatting among themselves or reading the leaflet distributed by the organisers. Those devoted to the Small Game, on the other hand, seemed riddled with anxiety, as if they were dealing with a matter of life and death.

"Turn the page on Iraq," the leaflet said. Beneath the heading was a statement Barack Obama had made in the past: "I don't oppose all wars. What I am opposed to is a dumb war. A war based not on reason but on passion, not on principle but on politics."

On the second page of the leaflet was a space for him to set out his general intentions: "I'm not running for President to conform to Washington's conventional thinking – I'm running to challenge it."

Next came a four-point plan to end the war, and this was followed by various contact telephone numbers and a repetition of the main slogan: "End the war. Join the movement."

The loudspeakers of the Grand Sierra Resort were blasting out hits from the sixties. "The House of the Rising Sun" by the Animals; "Dedicated to the One I Love" by the Mamas and Papas; "Fly Me to the Moon" by Frank Sinatra. After a thirty-minute wait, we all started filing into the room where the event was to be held. One of the young men on the door looked approvingly at the long queue. "More people than we expected, eh?" he said to his colleagues. It was a quarter to eleven in the morning.

Barack Obama made his entrance discreetly, taking advantage of a brief interval in the constant comings and goings of organisers and technicians, and few of us would have noticed his arrival had his supporters on stage not stood up to applaud him. He shook hands with four or five people there and went straight over to the microphone. The loudspeakers blared out the introductory words: "Barack Obama, future candidate for the Democratic Party, future President of the United States."

A huge satin flag occupied the back of the stage, and it gleamed, softly and warmly, in keeping with the friendly atmosphere in the room. The main spotlight trained on Barack Obama was equally soft, as were the colours he was wearing: light brown suit, white shirt, maroon tie. A complete contrast to the colours on the slot machines or, generally speaking, to the colours of American popular culture. The aesthetics of the event and of the whole campaign seemed to follow the guidelines established by Jun'ichirō Tanizaki in his book *In Praise of Shadows*, and were, in that respect, rather Japanese.

Barack Obama began by echoing a lot of the slogans that appeared in the leaflet. In the moderate speech that followed there was just

58

one barb: he had been against the war from the beginning. Hillary Rodham Clinton, on the other hand, along with other Democratic politicians, had not hesitated to fall in line with the stance adopted by President George Bush. The matters in hand, however, had to do with the present, not with the past. It was a question of who had and who didn't have the necessary qualities to confront the grave problems facing us in the future.

When it was time for questions from the floor, thirty or forty hands shot up. By then, Barack Obama was in shirtsleeves and walking slowly back and forth on the stage.

An Afro-American man sitting in front of us asked if he felt particularly pressured because he was black. Barack Obama said no. Who cared if he was green or red or white or yellow or black? The United States had more important things to deal with.

He listened with particular attention to the person who asked the next question, an old lady from the Pyramid Lake reservation. The living conditions of the Paiute Indians were dreadful, she said. Some Paiutes were so poor that, "without the help of kind neighbours", they would die of hunger or of easily treatable illnesses. Barack Obama replied sympathetically, and promised to do what he could to change the national health system.

The old lady from Pyramid Lake was followed by a veteran of the Korean and Vietnam wars. His situation and that of all veterans was, he said, truly pitiful. The country paid lip service to their contribution to the nation, and Veterans Day was widely celebrated, but the reality was quite different. You should see the terrible state the veterans' hospitals were in. Barack Obama repeated what he had said before. He would try to change the national health system, and the hospitals for those who had risked their lives defending their country would be included in that plan. When Obama finished speaking, the veteran thanked him effusively and gave him a military salute.

There were more questions, and in answering one of them, Barack Obama told a story. When he was campaigning to be a senator for Illinois, a woman asked him to come and speak in her town, and he agreed. When the day arrived, and he realised that the town in question,

59

Greenwood, was a long way away, he was tempted not to go; he had too much work, he was tired out. When he did somewhat reluctantly travel to Greenwood, he was met by only four people, the woman who had invited him and three of her friends. He thought it might be better to cut the visit short. However, the woman asked him to give her just half an hour. She would go from house to house and bring everyone from the town to meet him. And she did. Half an hour later, the room was packed with people, and the meeting was a wild success. And all thanks to the willpower and enthusiasm of one woman.

As he reached the end of this story, Barack Obama began a kind of crescendo: "One voice can change a village! A town can change a valley! A valley can change a county! A county can change a state! And a state can change a nation, and if it can change a nation, it can change the world!"

For the first time since the event began, Barack Obama was using the rhetoric of all such political meetings.

"Only an American candidate could make such a statement without seeming ridiculous," Ángela said. "Because what happens here really will influence the whole world."

When we left, the slot-machine addicts were still there, brows furrowed, faces taut with anxiety. The people who had attended the meeting, on the other hand, looked much happier than they had when they went in.

In the car park, we found our Ford Sedan surrounded by a small group of people. We soon understood why: one of the teachers at the C.B.S. had chosen to change our license plate to read "Obaba", which could have been mistaken for "Obama".

TEXTBOOK BROKERS

On the corner of Virginia Street and 9th, I noticed a small shop I hadn't seen before. It was called Textbook Brokers. Inside, as far as I could make out, a fifty-something man was apparently sorting through a pile of books. He had a long ponytail that came halfway down his back. When I went in, I saw that I was the only customer.

It wasn't books the man with the ponytail was sorting through, but vinyl records, and the sound of him riffling through L.P. covers was all that could be heard in the shop. Everything else was still and quiet. The books on the shelves and the postcards in the drawers were still, and so were the black-and-white photographs on the walls: desert landscapes, Indian teepees, horses, the streets of Reno as they were in the early twentieth century. They seemed to have been there for many years and would stay there for many more until someone's eyes or hands alighted on them.

The ray of light coming in through the window was filled with dust motes. These were not entirely still, like the other objects in the shop, but they were moving very sedately. They rose and fell, turned and rose again. Like a slow-motion dance.

The man with the ponytail went over to one end of the counter and put on a record. In a way, I was disappointed. Music is perhaps an attempt to improve on silence, but it often fails. Besides, the silence in Textbook Brokers was so delicious.

The record began to play. I immediately felt good. The song was "Summertime": "Summertime, and the livin' is easy, fish are jumpin' and the cotton is high, oh yo' daddy's rich and yo' ma is good lookin', so hush, little baby, don't you cry . . ." The song was even sweeter than the silence. And this was a version I had never heard before.

I had been in Nevada for about two months, but like some-one going into a house simply to deliver a message and leaving the front door open on the assumption that he won't be staying, I didn't feel I really belonged. This changed when I heard that music. Just as Dominique Laxalt had said of Basque shepherds and the desert, my mind turned a corner, I became an inhabitant; I closed the door. "Summertime, and the livin' is easy, fish are jumpin' . . ." It wasn't summertime, and there were no fish in the campus lake. There weren't even any swans to be seen. But that music, that song lent Nevada a pleasant lightness and suddenly it didn't seem so very difficult to live there.

The man with the ponytail handed me the record cover, which showed the members of a family, each holding his particular instrument: guitar, double bass, banjo and violin. The name of the record was "Elementary Doctor Watson!".

"Doctor Watson?"

"Traditional American music," the man said.

The vinyl records weren't for sale. I bought several old postcards and a second-hand guide that contained maps of various areas of Nevada and the whole of the West. It cost me fourteen dollars for the lot.

SEXUAL ASSAULT

We were subscribers to the *Reno Gazette-Journal*, and a copy was delivered to us every day at half past four in the morning. The delivery guy arrived in a white Toyota and tiptoed to the door so as not to disturb the silence. The vehicle must have been specially adapted, because the engine purred, and the noise the doors made when they closed was no louder than the sound of the newspaper landing on the porch.

On October 22, I was awake when the white Toyota came to call, because the dream-catcher that Izaskun and Sara had bought me at Pyramid Lake wasn't working and I was still sleeping badly. At a quarter to five, I was already sitting at the kitchen table with a cup of coffee and the newspaper. The garden was deserted, as it had been for the last few weeks. No sign of the raccoon.

On the page reporting local news was an article headlined "Sexual assault". The attempted rape of a university student in somewhere called the Whalen Parking Complex. I turned on my computer and studied a map of the city. The car park was on campus, less than two hundred yards from our house.

Three hours later, Ángela and I went to the university and were astonished at how normal everything seemed. There were no policemen in sight, no huddled groups of students, no cuttings from the newspaper on the noticeboard in the library. When we went up to the C.B.S., no-one said anything, not even Mary Lore. At the coffee stall, I met a French teacher who had the office next to ours, and I mentioned what I had read. She was surprised. No-one had said a word about it.

At the entrance to the library, there was always a big pile of copies of the *New York Times*, which, thanks to a benefactor, teachers and students could pick up to find out what was happening in the fifth or sixth circle of reality – the government crisis in Russia, the war in Iraq or in Afghanistan, U2's latest tour – or to read comments on these events by the seventh circle. On the other hand, they didn't read the *Reno Gazette-Journal*, they didn't buy it. For economic reasons, of course – the monetary unit on most campuses is the cent – but also, above all, because of a kind of tropism. Someone preoccupied with what is happening in the fifth or sixth circle finds it hard to lower his gaze and notice what is going on around him in the first circle.

There was no message from the campus police on my computer. They probably didn't have much to say. Their headquarters was in a building facing the Whalen Parking Complex, where the attempted rape had taken place.

FAREWELL TO STEVE FOSSETT

Two months after Steve Fossett's disappearance in the desert, and when there was still no sign of him, the news programmes on radio and television issued a bulletin announcing that all search operations were to be halted. No more planes or helicopters would scour the desert, no more search parties would tramp the mountains.

The bulletin only confirmed what most people thought, namely, that the chances of finding the "American hero" alive were zero. Richard Branson, owner of Virgin, said his farewell in *Time* magazine:

"I first met Steve Fossett on a freezing January evening at the Busch stadium in St. Louis, Mo., in 1997. He was about to attempt a solo circumnavigation of the world by balloon, and although we were rivals, I decided to see him off in the spirit of sportsmanship that still inhabits the world of record-breaking. As I neared his balloon, a television crew approached, and I found myself being filmed chatting with a man I thought was on his team. I said one had to be a bit mad to test oneself in this way. The quiet American in front of me looked at me sympathetically and said: 'I'm Steve Fossett.'"

Richard Branson added that their friendship had begun right then, and that the number of world records Steve Fossett had accumulated over a period of twenty-two years – one hundred and sixteen in total, more than anyone else in history – was truly admirable. His circumnavigation in the carbon-composite jet, the Virgin Atlantic *GlobalFlyer*, flying at altitudes of fifty thousand feet for three and a half days, alone and without rest, had been one of his most amazing achievements, and, given what it taught us about saving fuel, possibly one of the most beneficial too.

At the end of the article, along with some sad words of farewell – "It's hard having to say goodbye to a true American hero" – Richard Branson described Steve Fossett's final project: to beat the land speed record by driving his *Sonic Arrow* at more than 800 miles an hour. Indeed, on the day of his final flight, he may well have been looking for alternative sites for this attempt.

I looked on the Internet to learn more about Steve Fossett's final project, and found a forum discussing precisely that. Most of the participants rejected the official version out of hand and refused to believe that he had disappeared or that he was dead. In their view, the accident was merely a publicity stunt. The problem was that, despite all his amazing world records, Steve Fossett was far from being a star in the United States, mostly because he was middle-aged and slightly chubby. And because he wasn't handsome and sexy like Richard Branson, he needed something extra, a mystery that would ensure him plenty of publicity on the eve of his attempt to beat the world land speed record. In short, there was no need to worry. Fossett wasn't dead, he was merely hiding. He would reappear at any moment beside his *Sonic Arrow*, wearing his trademark astronaut outfit and giving a V-for-victory sign.

Almost everyone taking part in the forum was merely hypothesising and, generally speaking, did not seem quite right in the head. One of them, though, signing himself 'Snowflake', offered what seemed to be some more reliable facts. The best proof that Steve Fossett was dead, he said, was what had happened to the project since. The vehicle was up for sale. The people selling it were asking three million dollars for the project *and* the vehicle, which was way below the nearly four million dollars that the project had cost so far.

Snowflake concluded by giving still more concrete information: "Official photographs of the vehicle will be taken in the last week of October at the salt lake bed where they had been planning to do the test run, and will be published in the second week of November, giving full details of the machine."

I called Bob Earle from my office and told him what I had just read. Ever since our trip into the desert, Steve Fossett had become one of our regular topics of conversation.

"It's nearly the end of October already," he said, when I told him what Snowflake had said.

"There was no mention of the name of the salt lake bed where Fossett was thinking of carrying out the test," I said.

"Give me ten minutes. I'll call you right back."

Less than eight minutes later, the telephone rang.

"The vehicle will be in the Black Rock Desert this weekend. They're going to take photographs of the *Sonic Arrow*," he told me. "This is reliable information. A friend at the town hall told me, and he only deals in twenty-four-carat gold."

We decided to go. It would be quite a long drive, but it wasn't every day you had the chance to see a vehicle that could travel at more than 800 miles an hour.

"I think Izaskun and Sara might like to come too," Earle said.

"We'll all go, then, the whole family. And what about Dennis? Do you think he'd be interested?"

"I'll ask him. He'll find it hard to be apart from his spider, but I think he'll come."

"Is the spider still alive?"

"Well, I'm certainly not going to go sticking my finger in that bottle."

We agreed that we would set off on Sunday. He would pick us up in College Drive at eight in the morning.

Black Rock was in a remote part of the desert, quite some way beyond Pyramid Lake, and, as Earle said, you'd have to be an insomniac not to drop off at the wheel on the journey. However, the atmosphere in the car was very lively, and even I managed not to succumb to sleep. There were six of us: Earle and Ángela in front, with me in the middle row; and in the back seat, playing with a laptop, Sara, Izaskun and Dennis.

"We're nearly there," Earle said.

Whitish depressions, small dried-up salt lakes, began to appear on one side of the road. They looked like ulcers.

We drove another eight or so miles, and the ulcers grew larger. On the other side of the road was what looked like a wall of rocks.

Conversation in the Chevrolet Avalanche revolved around Steve Fossett. It was paradoxical that a man capable of surviving all those dangers and breaking 116 world records should die like that, in a little plane.

"He was flying a Citabria," Dennis said. "I wouldn't call that 'a little plane'."

"What seems odd to me is that the search should have taken so long," I said. "The longest you can survive in the desert is three days, isn't it?"

Earle looked at me in the rear-view mirror.

"And another question," he said. "Who's paying for it all?"

On the Internet, Dennis had found photographs of various racing cars that had set land speed records in the past, and he was showing them to Izaskun and Sara: "This one is the *Bluebird*. And this is the *Spirit of America*. And this is the last one to beat the record, *Thrust* . . ."

I remembered the *Bluebird* as soon as I heard its name. It was there in my memory as clearly as when I first saw it fifty years ago in the magazine my mother used to read at the time, *Reader's Digest*. It was similar to the cars that used to compete in Monaco, but about six feet longer.

The threads of my thoughts easily found other issues of *Reader's*

Digest, and I remembered a story that had appeared in one of them. It took place on an ocean liner travelling from the United States to Europe and described an altercation that took place between an Indian entertainer on board ship and one of the passengers. The passenger mocked the Indian, saying that he had obviously removed all the venom from the snake he used in his performances, thus rendering it completely harmless. The Indian entertainer insisted he was wrong. The story ended tragically. The writer was Somerset Maugham.

The road began to skirt round a white plain. In the distance, blocking the view ahead, was the top of a mountain.

"Black Rock," Earle said, pointing.

A roadside bar appeared. It was a rectangular box about fifty feet long with very small windows and an adobe roof, and even more run-down than the Crosby Bar at Pyramid Lake. Two Harley-Davidsons were parked to one side under a carport.

"It's not very elegant, but it will probably have the basics," Earle said.

Dennis was handing round pairs of dark glasses for when we eventually reached the white plain.

"I'm going to the bathroom," Earle said. "I'll be right back."

I followed him as far as the bar, which was so dark that I had to wait for my eyes to adjust to the contrast between the fierce light outside and the darkness inside. My ears, though, needed no period of adjustment to recognise the song coming out of the loudspeakers. It was "Rockin' in the Free World" by Neil Young.

The two Harley-Davidson riders and the barman were drinking beer at one end of the bar. The walls were almost completely bare apart from a six-foot-by-one photograph on the wall facing the entrance: a racing car. I copied down the information in my notebook: "Black Rock Desert, 15 October, 1997, Andy Green, ThrustSSC, 763.035 m.p.h." It was a monster of a car. A black needle with two protuberances, two huge turbo engines.

763.035 m.p.h. That was the record Steve Fossett had wanted to break with his *Sonic Arrow*. I imagined the pilot after the accident, lying in some remote place in the mountains or the desert and

repeating with his dying breath: 763.035 m.p.h., 763.035 m.p.h.
. . . I imagined, too, a couple of climbers crouching beside him, both
wondering: "What does he mean? What mystery lies behind that
number?" I brushed the thought away like a fly.

Earle returned from the bathroom and we ordered two beers. The
barman held up the bottles that he and the motorcyclists were drinking. It was a brand I had never seen before: Sierra Nevada.

"Is that O.K. with you?" Earle asked me.

"Fine."

"We're here because of something we read the other day," Earle
said to the barman when he came back with the beers. "Can I just run
it past you?"

The man beckoned him over to where the two motorcyclists were
standing.

The loudspeakers were now blasting out Neil Young's "Love and
War". But which was better, the quiet Crosby Bar or here? It was hard
to say.

There was another sign next to the photograph. "The first vehicle
to break the sound barrier." I thought back to my physics classes at
Colegio La Salle. What was the speed of sound? I couldn't remember.
The threads of my thoughts couldn't reach that far back.

Earle went over to the door, telling the barman we would be back
in an hour.

"I'll be here," the man said. The two motorcyclists raised their
hands in farewell.

Outside, the sun filled everything, brazenly occupying the space
between earth and sky. Dennis, Ángela, Izaskun and Sara were all
wearing their dark glasses as well as caps advertising some I.T. company. Earle and I were in agreement: we would wear the dark glasses,
but not the caps. There was no need, since we would not be getting
out of the car on the drive through the Black Rock Desert.

"I think we're going to be in luck," Earle said as we set off. "According to the barman, a huge truck arrived at the salt lake yesterday. I may
be wrong, but I reckon the *Sonic Arrow* was inside that truck."

"Where's the entrance?" Ángela asked.

"There is no official entrance," Dennis said from the back seat. "It's not like a national park."

We followed the road for another mile or so, then, turning to the right, drove another mile off-road. We were on the shore of the salt lake.

"Let's go driving!" Earle said, putting his foot down on the accelerator.

We were travelling at sixty miles an hour over that white surface, and everything around was ablaze with light. I tried to make out something through the window, but all I could see was whiteness, the sun bouncing off the salt bed, a kind of blinding white mist.

According to Dennis, it was the custom in the desert for the driver to let go of the steering wheel or to allow a child to drive. He suggested to Earle that he let Izaskun and Sara drive for a minute, but Earle didn't hear him. He was hunched over the wheel, looking to right and left. There was nothing to be seen, only whiteness upon whiteness. Then, for an instant, the mountain that gave its name to the place, Black Rock, appeared in the distance.

I took off my dark glasses and immediately had to close my eyes. If, in a normal desert, you could only survive without water for three days, what hope would we have in the Black Rock Desert? The threads of my thoughts started making troubling associations. I felt nervous.

"No, this isn't right!" Earle yelled. He seemed annoyed. "There's no way they would have brought the car this far! All they want is a few photographs!"

He slewed the car round 180 degrees without braking. The car tilted slightly to one side.

"Slow down, Earle," I said. "We don't want the car to overturn."

"O.K.," he said, braking slightly.

Ahead of us lay a blue lake. Izaskun and Sara both started yelling with excitement.

"There's no water in that lake," Dennis said. "It's a mirage."

Earle was looking all around him, this time with Ángela's help. We were once again travelling at sixty miles an hour.

"There's something over there," Izaskun said from the back seat. She spoke unemphatically, as if what she said was of no importance.

"Where?" we all asked at once.

She pointed. On the white plain was an equally white shape, except that it was more geometric, more solid. As we approached, I thought – not very intelligently – that it was a rectangular panel, part of some kind of solar energy plant. It wasn't. It was a trailer truck. Some men were moving around nearby. They were wearing overalls and red caps.

"They've probably already put it back in the trailer!" Earle said. He was feeling very tense, as was Ángela. Dennis, Izaskun and Sara sat up in their seats.

I did not share their excitement. The threads of my thoughts wanted to disconnect from it all. I was tired of chasing after the *Sonic Arrow*. I wanted to leave the Black Rock Desert.

And yet, when we saw it, the car was amazing. It was parked in a corner formed by the trailer and a pickup truck, and seemed to be watching us, as if it were not a machine, but a bird or an insect come from some unknown planet. It was white, with a green-and-yellow stripe along each flank, and two short wings at the back sticking out at right angles.

"It looks like a fighter plane," Earle said.

"Or a missile," Dennis said.

When Earle opened the door of the Chevrolet, one of the men working next to the *Sonic Arrow* walked towards us, waving his arms about above his head, telling us to go away. A colleague of his emerged from the cabin of the trailer truck and made some even more explicit gestures. We couldn't stop there, we had to leave.

"I got a photograph of it," Dennis said quietly.

Izaskun and Sara began rummaging around inside their backpacks. They were looking for the camera.

"Did you take a picture?" I asked when we set off again. They made me turn round to look at the little screen on the camera. There was their treasured shot: the image of the *Sonic Arrow* along with one of the men in overalls and a red cap.

"It's astonishing that something so slender can reach 800 miles an hour," Ángela said.

We were once again on the shore of the salt lake bed. We made our way slowly back to the road, heading for the bar, all of us silent, deep in thought. We had the photographs, but we wanted to store the image of that car away in our memories: white, with a green-and-yellow stripe along each flank; a bird from another planet, an insect about to take flight.

"Let's go eat," Earle said, stopping outside the bar. There were now five Harley-Davidsons parked under the carport.

The motorcyclists were eating lunch in one corner of the bar. At the counter, two women, also in leathers, were chatting to the barman and smoking. From the loudspeakers came a song I didn't recognise.

The photograph of the *ThrustSSC* on the wall looked bigger than before, and the car itself uglier.

"The British will be happy," Dennis said. "The record they achieved in the *ThrustSSC* will remained unbroken until another Steve Fossett comes along."

The barman offered us hamburger or pizza. We all ordered hamburgers, including Izaskun and Sara. To drink, Earle and I ordered the same beer as before, Sierra Nevada. The others preferred Pepsi.

Sara put her camera on the table.

"I took two photographs of the racing car," she said.

Dennis laughed:

"I took five!"

He showed us the pictures on his camera screen. The "racing car", Steve Fossett's *Sonic Arrow*, the bird, the insect, suddenly looked rather pathetic, as if it felt sad to be stuck there waiting for a truck to take it away from the Black Rock Desert when it was perfectly capable of travelling at 800 miles an hour.

Earle spoke about the regulations surrounding special vehicles like that. We had better be careful. Dennis and Sara should think twice before posting the photographs on the Internet. It could be illegal.

The threads of my thoughts again took me back to the age of the *Reader's Digest*, and I saw my mother, one summer day, sitting on the balcony of our house in Asteasu, reading. I remembered another story, also by Somerset Maugham. As in the story about the snake, the characters were travelling on an ocean liner, but in this case the subject of the dispute was a pearl necklace. One of the protagonists, an expert on precious stones, was put to the test during a gala supper given by the captain: he had to analyse the necklaces, diadems, bracelets and rings worn by the ladies sharing his table and verify which were authentic and which not. The expert wasn't keen on having to play the entertainer, but, on the captain's insistence, he finally agreed. It immediately became clear that he knew a lot about the subject. "That's not a diamond, it's quartz," he said after merely glancing at the pendant one woman was wearing. "He's right," confessed her husband, and there was applause from the travellers following this improvised performance. Then it was the turn of a ring. "An excellent sapphire, probably from India," the man said – more applause.

They showed him other items of jewellery, and he was always right.

Then came the turn of a pearl necklace worn by a particularly beautiful woman. The expert saw a look of anxiety in the woman's eyes and thought that perhaps the pearls were imitation and she didn't want to be shown up in front of the other passengers. He was wrong. The pearls were of excellent quality, probably Australian. He smiled at the woman, but she only looked even more anxious. "The pearls are genuine," he said. His words provoked a guffaw from the woman's husband. "I'm afraid you've failed, my friend. The pearls are fake!" he cried. He was rather like the fatuous fellow who had made fun of the Indian entertainer with the snake. The expert had to think quickly. There was real panic now in the woman's eyes. He suddenly remembered something he had overheard during supper. She had spent several months alone in New York while her husband was away in Europe on business. "Let me have another look," he said. A moment later, he gave his verdict. "No, I was mistaken. The pearls are false." The other people present clapped him on the back. Not to worry, what did one mistake matter when he had been so right about the others?

When the other supper guests retired to their cabins, the expert went up on deck to take the air and smoke a cigarette. There he found a fellow passenger with whom he had struck up a friendship. "The pearls were real, weren't they?" he said. The expert answered enigmatically: "If I had such a pretty wife, I certainly wouldn't leave her alone in New York." And that is how the story ended.

Again I saw my mother reading the *Reader's Digest* on the balcony of our house in Asteasu. After a moment, she put down the magazine and started hanging out the washing.

Earle was at the counter paying for the food. I suggested we go halves, but he refused.

"In Black Rock, lunch is on me, and you can buy me lunch when I come and visit you in the Basque Country. You're getting the bad end of the bargain, I'm afraid."

Before we left, I asked the barman about the music he was playing.

"The Grateful Dead," he said, giving me a thumbs-up.

On the way back, we took different positions in the car: Earle and Dennis in the front, Ángela and me in the middle, Izaskun and Sara at the back. After a mile or so, we stopped at a small viewing point and took one last look at Black Rock. The sun was no longer shining directly on the salt surface, and we could clearly see the trailer that would take the *Sonic Arrow* back to its hangar.

"Thirty years ago, I was tempted to buy into Craig Breedlove's attempt to beat the world land speed record," Earle said. "But my wife at the time thought I was mad wanting to invest thousands of dollars in the project and managed to dissuade me."

I wasn't surprised by this statement. Mary Lore had told me that Earle was seriously wealthy, part of a family who owned half a dozen roadside casinos.

Dennis turned to us and winked.

"That's a shame! Now, if you'd bought into the *Sonic Arrow* project, those guys in the red caps would have shown us around for sure."

Earle turned on the engine.

"If it's any consolation, Dennis, I can always drive a little faster than usual."

In the back seat, Izaskun and Sara clapped their hands.

We set off. Forty miles an hour, fifty, sixty, seventy. Earle was in a hurry to get back to Reno.

THE WOMAN WHO READ *READER'S DIGEST*
A REFLECTION ON PEOPLE FROM POOR PLACES

People who spent their lives in poor places died unknown to the world or, even sadder, unknown to themselves. How could they know themselves, when there was no midwife, no school to help them find out what it was they carried within them, in their blood, in their D.N.A.; what lay latent in their mind, their temperament, waiting for something to bring it to the surface. They lived their lives, of course, but it was a life lived all on one level, reduced to the basics, to the elemental. Then, when they died, they were forgotten. "My father's name was Juan," someone would say. "No, my mother didn't work in a canning factory, she was a dressmaker," another said. But such recollections, plus a few photographs, a silk handkerchief, a particular perfume or the way they lit a cigarette, were not enough to create a lasting image, an emblem. They were mere detritus for the memory, or, rather, a succession of dust motes. "You are dust and to dust you shall return," Genesis says. A very exact description of what happens to most people born in poor places.

Of course, a miracle might occur as it did for the shepherd Ambrogiotto, who, according to Giorgio Vasari in his *Lives of the Most Excellent Painters, Sculptors, and Architects*, became Giotto, the finest painter of his day, purely by chance, when Cimabue happened to pass through his village and saw the sheep Ambrogiotto had drawn on the rocks. However, given that miracles are very thin on the ground, there were no such transformations or advances in poor places, not at least in the country areas of the Basque Country in the days when the woman who read *Reader's Digest* was young, at the beginning of the twentieth century. The only way out was the Church. The convents. The seminaries.

The children's crusade . . . For much of the twentieth century, children left villages and farms in droves, heading for a convent or a seminary, forming long queues at train stations. After all, it was an attractive option, given that education and bed and board were free, but an inhuman one too. The Catholic Church did not accept that those children had bodies, or only as a secondary factor subordinated to the myth they called the soul. Their thousands of rules and regulations came down to one thing: No sex!

The price was high for everyone, but especially for girls. They were impoverished twice over. Most of the boys went on to become priests and would be put in charge of the biggest, most powerful edifice in whatever village they were sent to; the girls, however, would end up in a cell in an enclosed convent or in a hospital. It's impossible to imagine, as one can with certain priests, that any of them would have broken their vow of celibacy.

On the drive back from the Black Rock Desert to Reno, I kept thinking of all those poor people. Now and again, the image of my mother would resurface, either reading the *Reader's Digest* or hanging out the washing. She had been the beneficiary of a miracle. Despite being born into an extremely poor family, she managed to avoid the potato fields and the convent and was given a chance to study. However, when the Civil War broke out in 1936, she had to leave university and go back to her village. She was nineteen at the time.

HALLOWEEN. MONSTERS

We were in a neighbourhood in north Reno, with Mary Lore and her family: the children were getting more and more excited, banging on doors and being given sweets, while the parents were getting chilled to the bone. It was a freezing cold night.

Sweets, laughter, children: but Halloween was nothing like Christmas. You just had to look up at the sky, at the red light of a police helicopter hovering above us, and there they were, floating in the air: the rumours. "Five years ago, a boy was kidnapped and has not been seen since"; "Three years ago, three girls were raped in Sparks"; "Two years ago, a student taking part in an orgy died from the alcohol and drugs he had consumed." Plastic spiders on long plastic threads, but real monsters too.

We were on our way home with the bag of sweets that Izaskun and Sara had collected, when Mary Lore met a niece of hers, who played hockey for the university team. I didn't quite understand what they were saying, but they were talking about how some men brandishing guns had gatecrashed the Halloween ball being held by the university sports department.

We found out the end of the story later from Mary Lore. One of the gatecrashers had killed three people.

By the end of the day, the *Reno Gazette-Journal* had posted on their website the photographs and names of the people involved. The man who fired the shots was Samisoni Taukitoku, a nineteen-year-old Samoan; his accomplice was another Samoan of the same age, Saili Manu. The victims: Nathan Viljoen, twenty-three, ex-student; Derek Kyle Jensen, the same age, student; and Charles Coogan Kelly, twenty-one, a world-class snowboarder, who was just about to turn professional.

ANOTHER MONSTER: LEVIATHAN

This information was followed by a note about a man called William Castillo. According to the judge, he ought to pay with his life for the life he took from Isabelle Berndt in 1995. An eye for an eye, a tooth for a tooth.

A group of about twenty or twenty-five people were calling for clemency from the Leviathan – the Nevada State Government – holding up a placard at the prison gates: "We are here for Peace and against the death penalty". A blurred photograph, taken at night, showed the group's spokesperson, a Latino Catholic priest.

WARNING FROM THE LEVIATHAN THREE DAYS AFTER HALLOWEEN
MEMORY OF A RURAL HALLOWEEN

A friend of my father's came to visit him in hospital. He was a bald, burly fellow, but even at the age of seventy, he still had the face of a child. Determined to keep the conversation light, he told us what had happened to a logger from his village. He was, he said, a man who believed in witches, lost souls and other such superstitions. One day, in the local bar, a few young men started winding him up.

"Sure, you used to be a big, strong guy, but now you're old and will have to get using to staying sat in your chair."

"Shut your mouth! I'm still stronger than the whole lot of you," retorted the logger.

The young men continued to taunt him, until, finally, the furious logger decided to resolve the matter with a fight.

"O.K., why doesn't one of you come outside with me, and we can sort this out once and for all?"

"We don't want a fight," the young men said, "but we'll make a bet. If you win, we give you twenty pesetas, if you lose, you give *us* ten bottles of wine."

They explained the bet to the logger. He had to run from the bar to the cemetery and back in less than half an hour. In the dark.

"And another thing. You have to run round the inside of the cemetery."

"Why inside?" the logger asked.

"Well, apparently, you're afraid of graveyards, or so we've been told. And we wanted to make the bet that little bit harder."

The logger was not amused by this condition, but he thought he could easily win those twenty pesetas, even if he walked the distance, and so he accepted. It was already dark, and he set off at once, followed by the young man charged with making sure that he fulfilled all the conditions.

The others stayed in the bar, laughing. They knew that waiting for the logger at the cemetery were at least ten other young men all wearing white sheets smeared with earth. As soon as they saw him walking among the graves, they would start howling and moaning. That was the joke. They thought the logger would then flee in terror.

"Let's just hope he doesn't have a heart attack," the owner of the bar said.

Even someone who didn't believe in ghosts or phantoms would get the fright of his life if he saw corpses in shrouds wandering around a cemetery at night, so just imagine the reaction of someone who *did* believe in those things?

Time passed. The half-hour was nearly up. The young men were growing increasingly nervous. No-one came, not even the colleague who had gone with him as a judge. Then the logger burst in through the door.

"Where is he? Where is he?" he yelled, completely beside himself.

The young men didn't know who he meant.

"Where is who?" they asked.

"What do you mean 'who'? The gravedigger, of course!"

"The gravedigger?"

The young men had no idea what was going on.

"They've all come out of their graves!" bawled the logger, waving his arms about. "I went into the cemetery and almost went mad with the noise they were making. All the dead have left their graves!"

The young men said nothing. Then, finally, they asked:

"So what did you do?"

"What could I do? I knocked them to the ground. I tackled as many of them as I could, but some escaped. They're probably still there."

When old people laugh, their laughter tends to be very superficial. You can't say of them what the Jacques Brel song says, "*le rire est dans le cœur*", "laughter is in the heart". But when he heard the logger's story, my father roared with laughter.

"When did this happen?" I asked the friend.

"A few years before the war," he said, staring up at the ceiling while he tried to remember the date. "I think it was the year Uzcudun became European champion."

"1926 then," my father said.

"There's nothing wrong with his brain, is there?" the friend said to me cheerily.

"It's certainly in better shape than my legs," my father said.

He was a polite enough man, from the city; he sold pharmaceutical products. He told us he had a blocked vein in his neck, and that they had decided to operate on him because he ran the risk of having a stroke. He was terribly rude to women, though. He spoke as peremptorily to the nurses as if they were his maids, and when his wife visited him, he looked visibly annoyed.

"I told you not to come," he would say, then go back to his crossword, his favourite pastime.

A few days after the visit from my father's friend, he asked us:

"That brute you were talking about the other day, who was he? Was he Uzcudun the boxer?"

On his neck, beneath his left ear, he had a dressing the size of the palm of his hand.

The question was addressed to my father, who had known Uzcudun from the village fiestas of his youth, but he said nothing. He may not even have been awake.

"No, it wasn't Uzcudun," I said. "That business in the cemetery happened in another village, not in Régil."

"Ah, that's right, Uzcudun was from Régil. A real King Kong. During the war he used Republican prisoners as sparring partners."

He made as if to spit, then went on talking about the war. He described how two of his uncles and an aunt had been shot dead.

"They got on a boat, hoping to get from Santander into France, but the captain had been bribed and, under cover of night, he changed course and landed in Pasajes instead. The following day, all three were shot."

In his opinion, San Sebastián was a city full of fascists, although a lot had quickly put on a democratic mask when the dictator died.

"The usual thing," he said.

I noticed that the dressing on his neck was becoming stained with red, then it began dripping blood, thick drops that spattered the floor. I pointed this out to him, and he pressed the button to summon the nurses.

They put another bandage round his neck and whisked him away.

I went over to my father. His eyes were open, but had a somewhat glazed look about them.

"When I was young, there were always fights at fiestas, but it was simply a matter of knocking your opponent down, not punching him," he said, talking slowly and clearly. "But Uzcudun would insult people, saying, "Your mother is a whore," and things like that. His rivals would get furious, of course, and put up their fists, and then he would give them a terrible drubbing. He was an animal. So was his father."

He smiled wanly.

"But he eventually got a taste of his own medicine. In one of his first fights in America, his opponent broke all his teeth. From then on, he wore gold dentures."

STEAMBOAT SPRINGS

After seeing the photographs of Paulino Uzcudun in Guy Clifton's book *Dempsey in Nevada*, and knowing they had been taken in the Steamboat Springs training camp, I tried several times to locate the place. I looked on the computer and there was a black dot next to that name on the road between Reno and Carson City, but when I drove there, I found nothing. Just a small church, an ordinary building that would have gone unnoticed but for the pitched-roof porch and the metal cross.

Everything seemed to indicate that this was the place I was looking for, and Ángela agreed. After all, as still further proof, there was the hot spring that gave the place its name. It was, besides, a rather beautiful place, a shady garden cooled by a small stream. It wasn't hard to imagine a boxer training there, but it had been more than eighty years since Paulino Uzcudun fought Max Baer, and perhaps there was no trace of the camp left. They must have pulled it down to build the little church. That, at least, was what we thought.

At the beginning of November, we started taking Izaskun and Sara to a ranch where they could learn how to ride, mainly to fill their time, because they had been without friends for three months, wondering where "American children" went to outside school. When we found a ranch a few miles from Steamboat Springs, we used to drive through there every week, going and coming back. I would see the column of steam and the small church and again wonder about Paulino Uzcudun's training camp.

One day, we were driving back from the ranch, when Ángela spotted a car parked next to the church and drove over to join it. She passed the car – I saw a man with a white beard at the wheel – and stopped a few yards further on, immediately opposite the column of steam. It suddenly seemed to me a very neglected place. An old engine had been dumped at the edge of the spring, as if someone had wanted to get rid of it by throwing it in. A little further on, next to some bushes, the ground was littered with broken beer bottles.

The man with the white beard went over to the door of the church and invited us in, arms outstretched and palms uppermost. He had the somewhat old-fashioned look of a priest in civvies, but his neatness was in stark contrast with the otherwise neglected air of the place. He made this welcoming gesture rather half-heartedly, knowing we wouldn't take him up on it.

I apologised, then explained the reason for our visit. We were looking for the training camp used by a boxer called Paulino Uzcudun. That was all.

"Well, you've found it," he said.

I wasn't expecting such a straightforward response, and I stood there, not quite sure what to say, rather moved to have found what I was looking for. I pointed to the small church. That's what had confused me. It didn't seem appropriate for a boxing camp.

"We built it ourselves when we took over the place," he said.

"It's very nice," I said.

Sara called to us from the car. She was bored with waiting.

The man with the white beard looked at us sadly. I asked if we could take a few photographs. We wouldn't be long. He again held out his arms, palms uppermost, as if to say: "It's all yours." He then took out his keys, opened the door and went into the church.

On the drive back to Reno, I remarked to Ángela how very

different the inhabitants of one house could be. If the stories I had heard throughout my life were true, Paulino Uzcudun and the new owner of Steamboat Springs could not have been less alike.

THE FIGHTER

THE STORY OF PAULINO UZCUDUN'S FATHER

It was a velvety summer's night, and the trees in the wood were lit by the gentle light of the big, round moon. However, the all-pervading calm failed to touch the man's heart. He was walking along the path, oblivious to everything around him, and with just one thought in his head: there had been no fighting at the fiesta held in Mugats. He could understand no-one wanting to start a fight initially, but it infuriated him that hours had passed without one of those lads taking a swing at him, and there were at least a hundred of them, all a good thirty years younger than him and stoked up on drink. He couldn't bear it. How could they be so cowardly, so lily-livered! Giving them a shove or insulting them had no effect whatsoever. Instead of confronting him, they would slip away among the couples on the dance floor, like lizards on a wall, joking with the girls to hide their fear. And it was a long walk too, a whole hour from his house to Mugats, and longer still on the way back, because most of it was uphill. What a waste of time. Besides, it wasn't just that they didn't want to take him on; they didn't start any fights among themselves either, for fear he might get involved and begin dealing out punches.

Leaving the woods behind him, he reached the edge of a stream. Grass and roots hampered the flow of water, so that it slipped silently, slowly along, adding to the dense calm of the night. Despite this, his mood remained unaltered. He was wondering what would have happened if the lads at Mugats had started fighting; if he would have hurled himself on them as he had when he was twenty or twenty-five, him against five, six or more opponents, and if he would have beaten them all, smashed in their faces and himself ended up with nothing but a bruise on his back from being punched in the kidneys by one of those opportunists who always attack from behind.

This thought only made him grumpier still. More than twenty years had passed since those big fights, and he was no longer the same man. He noticed this when he was working with the axe. He could still fell five trees one after the other, but would have to sit down afterwards. His older brother had warned him that once he passed forty-five, any slight over-exertion, even an ejaculation, would affect him and leave him feeling weak. But then his older brother was already sixty, which was quite a different matter.

There was a fountain next to the stream, protected by a little wall on which stood a statue of the Virgin, surrounded by flowers. He drank some water from the metal bowl provided, then set off again. From there the path rose steeply.

How many young men could he take on and still be confident of winning? The question lingered in his mind, and the answer wasn't easy. He had grown more cautious, more calculating. If there had been a fight among the lads in Mugats that night, he wouldn't have taken them all on, unless provoked.

Behind his doubts lurked the final and most insidious of questions: had his decline already begun? There was the nub of the matter, the anxiety underlying all the others.

The hill was so steep that the oxen used in the mines had great difficulty coming down it with heavily laden carts. He suddenly decided to test his strength and walk up the hill as quickly as possible, as if it were a race. He started running and his body responded. He could feel his strong thighs and knees, the air smoothly filling his lungs. The lads in Mugats would have had difficulty overtaking him. And even if they could, they would not have dared. That would have been a snub to the best fighter in the province of Guipúzcoa.

The mine-workers were afraid of him too. He had challenged them before, sometimes in Mugats, but usually on their own territory, in the big hut near the mine that served as their dining room. He would go over to them and, without saying a word, grab hold of one end of the table, leaving plates and bottles of wine in danger of sliding off. But no-one got angry; on the contrary, they would invite him to join them.

83

He burst out laughing. One of the mine-workers was an evil-looking fellow called Ayerra, a nasty man who would whip out a knife at the slightest provocation. One afternoon, Uzcudun had deeply offended Ayerra simply by ruffling his hair, and Ayerra had lunged at him.

The memory of what followed made him laugh even louder. As soon as Ayerra was within reach, he had grabbed his wrist and twisted it so that the knife fell to the ground. Then, putting his arms around his waist, he had picked Ayerra up, carried him out of the hut and thrown him some twelve or fifteen feet as if he were a sack of potatoes. "What do you expect, you stupid fool?" he said and slapped him across the face so hard that he split his lip.

He stopped laughing and carried on up the hill, more slowly now. The images from that memory continued to parade through his mind. The foreman had whispered to him: "You'd better watch out for Ayerra. He'll stick his knife in you one day when you're not looking. He'll never forgive you for what you just did to him." Uzcudun went and sat down on the ground next to Ayerra and put his arm around his neck. "Ayerra, we've got to be friends, otherwise, you know what will happen." He tightened his grip. "You do know, don't you? You know what will happen if you start following me around, hoping to take me by surprise?" Ayerra let out a moan. His face turned scarlet. "I'll break your neck." Ayerra tried to say something, but couldn't get a word out. Uzcudun loosened his grip. "I promise you one thing, Ayerra, for your own good. I won't tell my sons that you drew a knife on me. If they ever find out what happened, they'll be after you like a shot," he said.

He had nine children, five of them boys, the oldest thirty-two and the youngest twenty. They would not hesitate to defend a member of their family. "But they're friends of mine," gasped Ayerra, rubbing his neck with his hands. "You're friends with my sons, are you?" Uzcudun had said. "Ah, now I understand. You were just joking when you threatened me with your knife . . ." And he laughed and slapped him on the back. Ayerra did not respond.

Halfway up the hill, the terrain flattened out. The mine-owners had widened the path to create a level area for loading up the minerals onto the carts. To the left was a rough stone cross bearing a metal plaque in memory of a murder that took place there. In 1898, the landlady of the inn at Mugats had fled into the hills after seeing her son kill his father, but the son had caught up with her on that very spot and killed her as well.

He could not recall the details of the crime, but he was sure that the son had murdered his mother by smashing her head in with a rock and had killed his father with a knife, as Ayerra had wanted to do to him.

He snorted like a horse and stood looking at the cross. The murderer must have been a complete imbecile! All he could think of doing after killing his parents was to go off to the Copacabana nightclub in San Sebastián and make a spectacle of himself there, buying champagne for all the girls and singing to his captive audience. If he hadn't made such a scene, the police might not have suspected anything. However, when they heard about it, they immediately arrested him: "You were just making sure that people would know you were in San Sebastián and not at home," they said. He soon confessed and was garrotted the following year in the square in Azpeitia.

Uzcudun's eyes, nimbler than his thoughts, had lost interest in the metal plaque on the stone cross. Someone was standing a few feet away, leaning against a wooden fence, his arms outspread. Although only a shadow, he was clearly defined by the light of the moon: the image of a crucified man. The vague idea flitted through his mind, as if in a dream, that it could be that same Mugats murderer, condemned to stay like that for all eternity; however, he immediately rejected this idea and took a few steps towards the figure.

"What do you want?" he asked, and the question rang out in the silence of the night. There was no reply.

The figure seemed not to move. For a moment, Uzcudun thought it was a tree trunk that the loggers had left there as a joke, with its two branches resembling arms, but when he moved still closer, he rejected that idea too. The figure was the size of a man, a big, strong man like him, and his arms were real arms, not branches.

"Ah, I know who you are!" he cried, going closer still.

The previous year, he had gone with his five sons to watch a bout of catch wrestling in San Sebastián, and the wrestler they had all liked best was one who called himself the Masked Man. Suddenly the scene made sense. The figure before him also wore a mask, a piece of black cloth covering his whole head. He had adopted the same pose as the wrestlers had when standing in the corner of the ring. Yes, he was hanging on to the fence just as the wrestler had hung on to the ropes. There was no doubt about it: the shadow was imitating the Masked Man.

He advanced another step, and the figure straightened up.

"What do you want?" he asked again.

It was obvious. The faceless man wanted to fight. He suddenly let go of the fence and gave Uzcudun a shove. Uzcudun weighed more than 240 pounds, and yet even so he had to take a step back to steady himself. The man wasn't going to be an easy opponent to beat. He wouldn't be able to lift him in the air and throw him down like a sack, as he had with Ayerra.

"Just a moment," he said and went over to the stone cross, where he urinated. Never fight on a full bladder. When he came back, his trousers were tightly fastened at the waist and his shirtsleeves rolled up.

Side by side, they walked over to the loading area. Before they got there, Uzcudun stuck out his leg and tripped the masked man up. The man stumbled, but did not fall.

"Who are you?" Uzcudun asked.

Again he received no reply, and so he aimed a punch at his opponent's head. His faceless adversary dodged the blow with a slight movement from the waist.

"You move well, Mr Wild Cat!" Uzcudun said and laughed.

The man might dodge him the first time, the second and possibly the third, but Uzcudun would eventually manage to tear the hood from his head. Then a lot of things could be cleared up. Who was this man trying to beat him, and why had he not challenged him at the party in Mugats, in front of everyone else, as was the custom? Catch wrestling was always done before an audience too, that way everyone knew who the champion was. The man with no face jabbed him in the ribs with his left fist.

"Steady, wild cat!" Uzcudun said, butting him like a ram.

Utter silence reigned, apart, perhaps, from the rustling of leaves, the frogs in the stream and the night insects, but otherwise, nothing, as if the big, round moon had absorbed all the noises and cancelled them out.

The silence did not last. A dog started barking furiously, and, a moment later, another dog barked just once, striking a deeper note. They could hear people shouting.

Five or six other dogs joined in from the hills round about, near the mine. A confused clamour of barking briefly disturbed the silence; then the dogs grew bored and fell silent, first the one in Mugats, and then the others. The final bark came from far off and immediately died away.

The fight lasted almost as long as one of those catch-wrestling matches, and when it ended, Uzcudun watched his opponent stride off up the hill.

"Don't leave without telling me who you are," he shouted after him from where he was sitting on the ground.

He had not succeeded in removing the man's hood; he didn't know who he was, that man who had beaten him so soundly, and who, for the first time since Uzcudun was fifteen, had left him sprawled on the ground.

Whenever he went to Mugats or into some bar, there would always be someone who shouted out: "Here comes the strongest man in Guipúzcoa!" And he would answer "Hungry!" or "Thirsty!" and a bottle of wine or a plate of stew would appear on the table. If the other customers were playing cards, they would make room for him and invite him to join them. From now on, though, he would have to behave with more humility. There *was* a better fighter than him in Guipúzcoa. The man who could strip him of his reputation had finally been born.

He staggered over to the stone cross and sat down on the base. He was very tired and felt lightheaded and dizzy from the blows he had received. His thoughts, though, were perfectly clear. If someone in a bar greeted him with the words: "Here comes the strongest man in Guipúzcoa!" and he accepted the greeting, then the worst could happen: someone – the masked man – might call out: "That's not true. *I'm* the strongest man in Guipúzcoa!" And then he would have to fight him in front of everyone, knowing that he would lose, because the stranger was better than him, of that there was no doubt.

He felt a wave of heat rising up his neck to his face. He felt ashamed to have lost like that. How easily the masked man had landed punches on him! How nimbly he had walked up the hill when the fight was clearly over! He moved just like a wild cat, both walking and fighting. That's why Uzcudun had been unable to remove his hood, despite trying again and again.

He bent forward, rested his head on his folded arms and closed his eyes. He again thought about what had happened. After spending all evening and part of the night in Mugats, the stranger had chosen to fight alone. Uzcudun could not understand why.

When he woke in the morning, he could feel precisely the points on his body that had received the hardest blows. His top lip hurt, as did his nose, but the ribs on his right-hand side hurt most of all. The skin on his right knee felt tight. He rolled up his trouser leg and saw that the skin was broken and covered with a bloody scab. He took a few steps and was relieved to find that he could still walk. He was also hungry, which was a sign that he was alright inside. He touched his lip, then probed the inside of his mouth with one finger. His lip was swollen, but all his teeth were intact.

The dogs round about were barking gaily, the sun was filling everything with light. He set off uphill, just as the stranger had after the fight. He remembered how quickly the man had climbed the hill, with not a hint of tiredness. Yes, a wild cat, he muttered. Yesterday's sombre thoughts returned. He was not as strong as he once had been. The best days of his life were over. He would no longer enter any bar in Guipúzcoa like a champion.

The last stretch of the hill was a real effort, because the pain in his knee meant that he couldn't bend it properly. Once at the top, he thought of going to the mine to eat something in the hut along with the miners. However, although his stomach was aching with hunger, he walked straight past and headed down the hill to his house.

In a shady corner of the path there was a fountain and a drinking trough. When he took off his shirt and bent over to wash himself, he saw a snake swimming through the water. He made to grab it, but missed. When he missed again, he left the snake in peace and began scrubbing himself clean. His ribs no longer hurt quite as much, but his lip did, a lot. He would have to eat on the other side of his mouth.

He took off his trousers and rested one foot on the edge of the drinking trough so that he could wash the bloody scab on his right knee in the water flowing from the pipe. Then he got dressed again and continued on his way. He was already very close to his house.

When he went into the kitchen, he found nearly all the family waiting for him, his wife, his five sons and two of his daughters. His other two daughters worked as servants in San Sebastián.

"Where have you been?" his wife asked. She was standing up, as were all his children.

Uzcudun saw five axes on the table.

"Haven't you been to work yet?" he asked.

"I told them to wait until you got back," answered his wife. She was tall and very thin.

"Fry some eggs for everyone," he said. Then he spoke to his sons: "Take your axes off the table and sit down. And you," he spoke this time to his daughters, "outside."

"What happened, Pa?" his oldest son asked.

"Can't you see? He's been in a fight," his mother said. She had put the frying pan on the stove and had the basket of eggs beside her.

"First, let's eat," he said, sitting down at the table.

"How are you going to eat with your lip all swollen like that, Pa? Who did it? He must have punched you right in the mouth!" said the youngest and boldest of his sons.

"Be quiet, and fetch a loaf from the chest!" ordered his mother. "And the rest of you, set the table!"

They were big lads, with muscular arms and shoulders from working in the woods felling trees, but they obeyed their mother like meek little boys. The table was soon ready: plates, knives, forks, wine, glasses and a large loaf of bread. His wife set the dish of eggs down in front of her husband. He helped himself to three, dipped a piece of bread in one of the yolks and raised it to his mouth.

"You're not as bad as I thought, Pa," his youngest son said. "I thought you wouldn't even be able to open your mouth. I would have bet on it."

"Be quiet and pour him some wine," his mother said from the stove. She had finished frying the eggs and had started on the bacon.

The narrow kitchen windows barely let in the morning light. Once the meal was over, the five boys picked up the plates, forks, knives and bread, leaving only the wine and the glasses. When they returned to the table, their mother sat down with them. They were all waiting. He leaned back in his chair and turned to look at the fire.

"Tell us what happened, Pa. Something bad?" his eldest son asked.

"Couldn't be much worse. Today, I stopped being number one," he said.

His youngest son protested, laughing:

"What are you saying? If I'm not mistaken you've just eaten seven eggs and three rashers of bacon. And you drank more wine than anyone else too. How can you say you're no longer number one?"

"He's right there," his eldest son said, and the other three nodded their agreement.

He got up from the table and, pacing up and down, started telling them what had happened. He had gone to spend the evening in Mugats, but no-one had wanted to fight. Afterwards, when he was walking back in the dark, a man had appeared. A man with his face covered by a black hood.

"Do you remember the masked man we saw at the wrestling match? Well, he was just like that."

His sons and his wife were listening attentively.

He gave them a detailed description of the fight. The stranger was as agile as a wild cat and very quick with his left hand. He had kept delivering low jabs with his left fist, then flung a right at his face, fortunately with less success, because he didn't keep his arm close enough in to his body. That was why he hadn't come off worse really, because most of the time the other man had missed.

"That left fist of his, though, was really something. I lost count of the number of times he got me in the ribs. He knocked the breath out of me. If his right had been as good as his left, I wouldn't have made it home."

"But you gave as good as you got, didn't you, Pa?" his oldest son asked.

Uzcudun stood with his hands on his hips and looked up at the ceiling. He was not far off six foot five.

"For a long time, the strongest man in Guipúzcoa has lived in this house," he said. "But that's all over now. From now on, that wild cat will be the champion."

The youngest son had stood up, his arms flung wide.

"Don't be sad, Pa! The strongest man in Guipúzcoa still lives in this house!"

"What do you mean?"

"I'm the wild cat, Pa. I was the one who beat you last night!"

Everyone else had now sprung to their feet too.

"Is that true?" he said.

"Yes, Pa," his son said, going over to the cupboard and taking out a black scarf. "Here's my mask!"

Uzcudun also flung his arms wide.

"Let me give you a hug, my boy!"

They exchanged a long embrace.

"So the strongest man in Guipúzcoa *does* still live in this house!" another of his sons cried.

"That's all fine and good, but now you've got to take up your axes and go off to the woods," their mother said, silencing the hubbub filling the kitchen. "It's time to do some work."

"Not the wild cat, though," Uzcudun said. "He can stay with me. I need to teach him to improve his right hand. If he can do that, then one day, with that strong left hand of his, he'll be world champion."

THE BOXER MEETS THE PRESS

In June 1931, Paulino Uzcudun gave a press conference at the Steamboat Springs training camp, where he was preparing for his fight with Max Baer. It was attended by journalists from the most important newspapers and magazines in the American West: *Ring Magazine*, *Sporting News*, *Nevada State Journal*, *Reno Evening Gazette*, *Los Angeles Daily*, *Sacramento Bee*, *Sacramento Union* and *Las Vegas Evening Review-Journal*. Sitting next to Paulino Uzcudun was the ex-boxer, Jack Dempsey, who would be refereeing the fight as well as promoting it, along with the owners of various local casinos.

The first question came from a reporter from the *Sacramento Union*, the only female journalist.

"How should we spell your name – 'Paolino' or 'Paulino'?"

When he first arrived in America, the press tended to Italianise Uzcudun's first name, calling him "Paolino".

"Primo Carnera is Italian. I am not," he said in fluent but heavily accented English.

The journalists from *Ring Magazine* and *Sporting News* asked him what he thought about his major fights, at the same time congratulating him on his knockout victory over Les Kennedy in Los Angeles three months before. Uzcudun talked about that fight in jovial tones, but frowned angrily when he spoke of his defeat by Primo Carnera. In his view, the only reason the Italian had won was because he had been able to take advantage of his greater height – Uzcudun was nearly six foot five – which meant Carnera had merely used him as a punchbag. The fight should have been declared a draw.

The talk turned to the matter of referees, and a discussion ensued among the journalists about certain controversial decisions made in recent years.

Dempsey waited for them to finish talking, then said:

"All I can say is that I couldn't think who to pick as the best referee for this fight. In the end, I was asked to take it on, and I accepted. I just hope that wasn't a wrong decision."

Dempsey laughed when he said this, and most of the journalists present laughed too. They knew he would go down in history as one of the greatest boxers of the twentieth century, and they were just glad to be there, sitting only a few feet away from him in that warm, friendly atmosphere. The only ones not to laugh were the journalist from the *Sacramento Union* and a young man sent by the *Reno Evening Gazette*.

"I get what you're saying, Jack," the young man from the *Reno Evening Gazette* said, "but what are people going to think? Forgive my frankness, but aren't you afraid they might think you don't trust the boxing associations in Nevada?"

"That's a fair enough question," Dempsey said. "Nevada is a place very dear to my heart, so I wouldn't want there to be any misunderstandings. The fact is that, before taking the decision, I got together with the representatives from the Reno race track and with the city's mayor, Mr Roberts. They were the ones who asked me to referee the match. Actually, the mayor didn't ask me, he ordered me."

The young man gave Dempsey the thumbs-up.

"That's a great answer, Jack. Thank you."

"Mr Roberts is clearly an intelligent man. If he manages the city's affairs as well as he manages boxing, Reno should do just fine," the journalist from *Ring Magazine* said.

The woman from the *Sacramento Union* was holding up her pencil again. Her question was once more directed at Uzcudun:

"In boxing circles, you're often referred to as 'the woodcutter' or 'the Basque woodchopper'. Were you really a woodchopper? Do you know how to handle an axe?"

Uzcudun smiled and revealed a mouthful of gold teeth.

"The men in my family in the Basque Country have always worked in the woods," he said. "My father worked in the woods; my four brothers worked in the woods; and I worked in the woods. I once counted how many axes there were in the house. There were twenty-nine. Does that answer your question, ma'am?"

"And what about fighters? Were there any fighters in your family?" she asked.

"My father wanted to be a catch wrestler, but there weren't that many opportunities for people living in small villages then. He fought at fiestas and other such events, and he was the best in our province. Until *I* started fighting, of course!"

His gold teeth made another appearance.

"What has been the most important day in your life so far?" the young man from the *Reno Evening Gazette* asked.

Dempsey got in first:

"Paulino can say what he likes, but he's not going to fool me. The most important day in his life was when he met a certain pretty young lady in Hollywood."

Everyone immediately thought of Clara Bow, although her days as a movie starlet were long gone. There was a rumour in Hollywood that they had been seen together after his fight with Les Kennedy.

"No, Jack's confusing me with another boxer," Uzcudun said. This time it was the journalists' turn to laugh. Uzcudun's rival, Max Baer, had a reputation as a Don Juan.

A New York newspaper had just published a photograph showing Paulino Uzcudun holding up three girls, one on each arm, with a third sitting on his shoulders, her bare thighs wrapped around his neck. He had confessed in the past to the fun he'd had the length and breadth of the United States with women who enjoyed "the horizontal position", and the unforgettable moments he'd spent driving along "the lovely Florida highways with some beautiful blonde, blue-eyed girl, of which there seems to be an inexhaustible supply".

But that wasn't the image he wanted to promote just then. Among the fans who would come to Reno on 4 July, the day of the fight, there would be a lot of Basque shepherds, resident on the West Coast. His fellow countrymen saw him as an equal, a sober, honest Basque woodcutter, and he didn't want to disillusion them.

"The most important day of my life was July 13, 1927, when I beat Harry Wills in Madison Square Garden," he told the young man from the *Reno Evening Gazette*. "There's never been a better one."

The journalists waited, without asking any further questions.

"I was paid eight thousand dollars for the Harry Wills fight," he went on. "For the next one, thirty thousand. How's that for progress?"

"How much are you being paid for your next fight with Max Baer?"

The question again came from the young man from the *Reno Evening Gazette*.

"Quite a lot," Uzcudun said, with a broad grin. As the Argentinian writer Roberto Arlt wrote, his smile was like an orang-utan's.

"Which has been your highest-paying fight?" the woman from the *Sacramento Union* asked. Dempsey reached out one arm and put his hand over Paulino Uzcudun's mouth. There was some laughter among the assembled journalists.

"If you don't let him answer, Jack, I'm going to tell everyone right now what you pocketed for your fight with Tunney," the man from the *Ring Magazine* said. He was a veteran reporter who spent long periods at training camps like Steamboat Springs, sending in two or three reports a week about upcoming fights. He knew all the secrets.

Dempsey put his hands together in a pleading gesture. Again there was laughter in the room.

"The fight I got paid most for was the one with Max Schmeling in the Yankee Stadium. I earned a hundred thousand dollars," Uzcudun said. There was a silence, followed by that orang-utan smile. "In other words, seven times less than Dempsey earned for his fight against Tunney."

Dempsey again made as if to cover Uzcudun's mouth. The journalist from the *Sacramento Union* raised her eyebrows.

"Those are astronomical sums of money. I'm not surprised Thomas Mann is so appalled," she said.

For almost a hundred years, since the days of Jess Willard up until Muhammad Ali, no sport has paid better than boxing, and Thomas Mann, who won the Nobel Prize for Literature in 1929, had, on more than one occasion, expressed his repugnance at this fact. It seemed completely unacceptable that famous boxers could earn more for a single fight than a German university lecturer could earn in a whole lifetime of work. This, however, was not the general opinion. Even among writers, the opposite point of view seemed to prevail. George Bernard Shaw boasted about his friendship with Tunney; Ernest Hemingway chose to write about boxing and had himself photographed as a prize-fighter; in Thomas Mann's Germany, Vladimir Nabokov had given a lecture about the fight between Uzcudun and Breitensträter in Berlin.

Jack Dempsey's business partner, Leonard Sacks, declared the press conference over. He thanked the mayor of Reno and other local institutions, as well as the Nevada casinos, who had helped organise the fight.

The journalists had already got up to leave, as had Dempsey, when the reporter from the *Sacramento Union* pointed at Uzcudun with her pencil.

"Aren't you afraid of Max Baer? They say he's a hard hitter."

Uzcudun laughed. She went on:

"Two years ago, he killed Frankie Campbell with just one punch. Remember?"

Leonard Sacks took it upon himself to answer.

"Ma'am, we all remember that unfortunate accident. Max Baer didn't fight for more than a year afterwards, and the only reason he came back into the ring was because he wanted to help Frankie Campbell's family. But this isn't the moment to remember such a sad event. We're on the eve of a really great fight, the best you could possibly get in the United States today."

"So far, no-one has knocked me out, and that's how it's going to stay," Uzcudun said.

Dempsey placed one hand on his shoulder.

"The risk of death is never far from heavyweight fights," he said, "and it will be there in this next fight too. For my part, I will try, as referee, to do things properly. What happened with Campbell and Baer was wrong, and should never have happened."

The press conference was over.

A REFLECTION ON THE IMAGE LEFT BEHIND BY PAULINO UZCUDUN

No-one lingers in the memory in all his or her complex biographical detail, and there are very few who become emblematic figures worthy of affection or admiration. Normally, the opposite happens. Most human beings leave behind them only a name and a few facts ("Hum-

berto Alba. San Juan de Puerto Rico, 1951 – Mekong Delta, 1973")
or else disappear completely, like the Congolese children slaughtered
by King Leopold II's mercenaries as if they were chimpanzees. There
is, however, a third fate, that of those who, when they die, leave a two-
sided emblem. This is what happened in the case of Paulino Uzcudun,
the most admired boxer in the Basque Country and in all of Spain.

On the day Paulino Uzcudun fought the Italian Erminio Spalla for
the European Heavyweight Championship on 26 May 1926, loudspeakers were installed in the streets of San Sebastián, so that people
could listen to the radio broadcast. According to one local reporter,
as soon as he was declared the winner, the fireworks that followed
woke up the handful of people who had already gone to bed. Shortly
afterwards, the new champion travelled to San Sebastián in a convertible Hispano-Suiza and was welcomed by more than a hundred
thousand people cheering him on, shouting "*Gora Uzcudun,*" "Long
live Uzcudun." The reporter rounded off his report by saying that
joy was universal and that everyone came out to greet Uzcudun: "the
bourgeoisie and the workers, left-wingers and right-wingers, the ladies
from the Yacht Club and the country girls who work as servants in
the city". To judge from the photographs, Paulino Uzcudun never
once stopped smiling, and his smile did not yet resemble that of an
orang-utan.

Picture cards bearing his effigy were printed, anthems and ballads
were written in his honour. That summer, as usual, the Court visited
San Sebastián, and King Alfonso XIII, accompanied by Princes Juan
and Gonzalo and many other important people, visited the champion's
birthplace. In their patent leather shoes they trod the fields and paths
strewn with cow and ox dung, and paid tribute to the woman who
had been "capable of giving birth to a fighter as strong as Paulino".
She thanked them for the visit and, since she could not speak Spanish
and could only express herself in Basque, her son translated her words.
She declared herself to be both happy and sad. Happy for her son's
success and sad because her husband was not there, for he had died
two years earlier and so never knew that his blood ran in the veins not
just of the champion of Guipúzcoa, but of Europe too.

One of the ballads written in Paulino Uzcudun's honour said: "*Kon-trariyorik emen ez eta zuaz Amerik'aldera; kanpeon zaude Europa'n eta, ekatzu hango bandera.*" ("With no more rivals left to beat, America awaits; you're European Champion now, bring us another trophy or two.") And that is precisely what happened. Before the end of 1926, the promoter Tex Rickard, "the emperor of boxing", invited Paulino Uzcudun to fight in the United States. After a stopover in Havana, Uzcudun made his first appearance in Madison Square Garden, beating Knute Hansen and Tom Heeney.

Months later, Tex Rickard suggested he fight Harry Wills, the Black Panther:

"Not even Jack Dempsey is willing to take him on. He doesn't want to risk losing to a negro. If you beat Wills, you'll be right up there with the great champions, among the best in the world."

Uzcudun accepted the challenge, and on the day of the fight, July 13, 1927, he demolished his opponent in the fourth round. Harry Wills, the Black Panther, fell backwards onto the canvas, his head almost out of the ring. Paulino Uzcudun accompanied him back to his corner like a solicitous nurse. Then he returned to the centre of the ring, lay down, and started performing gymnastics before flipping effortlessly back onto his feet, as nimble as a wild cat. Dozens of hats were thrown into the ring.

The newspaper reports of the fight stressed his solid punches, his agility, as well as his gentlemanly behaviour. Later on, both in America and in Europe, he would become known as "the Basque Woodchopper", an alias that would soon overtake previous nicknames: the Lion of the Pyrenees, the Spanish Bull, the Basque Colossus and so on. Gradually, his image became more fixed, one of the two sides of his emblem.

He became more and more famous. On June 27, 1929, he met Max Schmeling in the Yankee Stadium, and the following day, the *New York Times* sold 180,000 extra copies. The purse he received for each fight grew and grew. $18,000, $24,000, $30,000. Enough to buy twenty houses in the Basque Country.

The years passed, and his image acquired new adornments. Now people spoke of his courage and toughness. No boxer had yet succeeded in giving him the K.O. He had a jaw of steel, or, rather, wood, the jaw of a woodchopper, a direct descendant of Cro-Magnon man. As Emilio Fornet wrote in an ode: "Let no man deliver you a knockout blow, electric in the romantic storm, O neolithic skull emerging from the Basque cave!" The same idea inspired the sculptor Jorge Oteiza, who made a bust of him, giving him suitably primitive features.

He acquired a still more useful adornment. He was a victim. He had been treated unfairly, for, either because of their involvement in the betting industry or out of American patriotism, the fight organisers always managed to hand to other boxers victories that should, by rights, have been his. The gold teeth in his Cro-Magnon jaw were proof of this: they were replacing the teeth that a dirty boxer called Homer Smith had knocked out with a head butt. Even worse was what happened in the fight against Jack Delaney, who emerged from it as a new candidate for the world title. The referee disqualified Uzcudun when he looked set for an easy win. "American boxing is full of scandals," wrote a *Herald Tribune* reporter at the time, "but I can recall nothing worse or more scandalous, incredible and cynical than the referee's behavior in yesterday's fight between Uzcudun and Delaney . . ."

It happened again and again, and Uzcudun asked rather loftily: "What do I have to do to win a fight in the United States? Kill my opponent?" The Spanish press repeated the facts and revealed the reason behind such injustice. The promoter Tex Rickard had offered Uzcudun his support, as well as the opportunity to compete for the World Championship, but on one condition: he had to become an American citizen. According to the Madrid press, Uzcudun's response was blunt and to the point: "Nothing in the world would make me give up my Spanish citizenship." The news spread rapidly, and when haranguing their troops, military commanders held him up as an example to them all.

In 1931, when Jack Dempsey decided to become a promoter and put on a big fight in Reno, he immediately thought of Uzcudun and Max Baer. It was a great opportunity. Dempsey himself had promised that the fight would be clean, with no pre-fight fixes. Everyone was agreed on this, including the casino owners. "This is my first event as promoter, and I want it to be a great fight. That's why I'm going to referee it myself, and that's why it's going to be twenty rounds," Dempsey told Uzcudun, who accepted the challenge. He left New York and travelled to Steamboat Springs.

The fight took place on July 4, in temperatures of over thirty-eight degrees, and more than fifteen thousand people attended, from California, Utah, Oregon, Idaho and Nevada itself. One of the largest groups was made up of Basque emigrants to the American West. In the front rows sat the owners of casinos and various Hollywood actors and actresses, among them, the stars of the moment: Edward G. Robinson, Buster Keaton and the Marx Brothers.

The resin on the pine planks in the arena began melting in the heat, sticking to trousers and shoes. Meanwhile, in the ring, Max Baer and Paulino Uzcudun were doing all they could to get the fight over with as quickly as possible, afraid they wouldn't survive twenty rounds. "The boxers fought like wild cats," wrote the reporter from the *Nevada State Journal*. "They ignored all the rules of the ring in their eagerness to send their opponent sprawling onto the scalding-hot canvas."

In the sixth round, Uzcudun very nearly knocked Baer out; in the eighth, Baer cornered Uzcudun. From then on, the fight became very evenly balanced. Before they began the twentieth round, it was announced over the loudspeakers that the boxer who gained most points in the final round would be declared the winner. When the final bell sounded, Dempsey raised Uzcudun's arm. The spectators stood up and applauded the superhuman efforts of both boxers.

It was well-known that Max Baer had a bigger punch than any other boxer, and that even Max Schmeling had to be rescued from those pounding fists to avoid being killed. It was taken for granted, too, that he would be the next world champion, as happened in 1934, after his fight with Primo Carnera. If this is true, then what Uzcudun said over and over must also be true: he was on a par with the very best heavyweight boxers.

"The Basque Woodchopper, one of the best," was the headline in the newspapers the day after the fight in Reno. Uzcudun's emblem shone brighter than ever, and he tried to make this last by dictating a book, a kind of autobiography (*Mi Vida* (*My Life*), Espasa-Calpe, Madrid, 1934), in which he spoke about how he had been made a victim, about the fights that had been stolen from him, and he talked, too, about Al Capone, who had invited him to his house several times: "Capone lives the life of a king in Florida. He's a millionaire king, though, not one of those operetta kings who never have a penny. He liked me a lot, because he said I had balls, and because he had earned a lot from betting on my fights."

These two narratives did not quite fit. How could he be the victim of the Mafia who manipulated the fights and, at the same time, a friend of the most powerful Mafia boss? He seemed oblivious to such contradictions. All his failures were the product of dirty dealings on the part of his opponents; all his successes, on the other hand – beginning with Alfonso XIII's visit to his birthplace and ending with his friendship with Al Capone – were simply his God-given right.

In 1935, when he was thirty-six, he fought his last fight in America against Joe Louis, the Brown Bomber, fourteen years his junior. For the first time in his life, he was knocked out. He got on a boat and left the United States for ever.

Paulino Uzcudun died in Madrid on July 4, 1985. The journalist who wrote his obituary (Julio César Iglesias, *El País*, July 7, 1985) recalled that fight with Joe Louis, saying that a man is never the same once he's been knocked down. "Paulino Uzcudun did not die last Thursday in Torrelaguna. He died on December 13, 1935, fifty years ago, in Madison Square Garden in New York." The journalist perceptively described the change that took place in Paulino Uzcudun: the man who had been as strong as an oak had ended up becoming the felled tree.

He continued to inhabit the Olympus of champions, and his emblem remained untarnished. What did it matter if he was the felled oak or the woodchopper cutting it down! In both cases, he was still a woodlander: a prelapsarian man, brave and simple on the one hand, and, on the other, at worst, a King Kong, a primitive being who still bore traces of Cro-Magnon man and who, like the Great Ape, had never knowingly done any harm.

There were, however, the places Uzcudun frequented and which had little to do with oak trees and woods. The proof of this were the summer society columns published in the 1930s by *El Pueblo Vasco* and other newspapers: "Paulino Uzcudun and the heir of the Zuloaga family arrived yesterday in San Sebastián in a red sports car." "A large delegation from the Court attended yesterday's bullfight. They were accompanied by Spain's most famous boxer." The places he frequented, the friendships he cultivated, his neglect of the village where he was born, all indicated his detachment from the woods and forests that had shaped him; it was as if he were another person, as if Alfonso XIII and the two princes had carried off his woodchopper's soul.

The people who had known him since he won the European Championship noticed this change and their fondness for him cooled. They stopped singing anthems and ballads praising his name, and there were no more acts of homage. Some journalists attacked him. "Lately, we have often seen Paulino Uzcudun strolling in Alderdi-eder Park or along by La Concha beach," wrote one journalist, who signed himself "Azti". "That's all very well, but someone really ought to tell him that it's ridiculous to go skipping along, trying to imitate the aristocrats."

You might think that, in their innocence, children would like him, but they didn't. Not even those who had lived nearby and known him personally harboured fond memories of him. "We were always heaping him with compliments, organising receptions and parties, but he never brought us anything, not so much as a bag of sweets," wrote Inazio Maria Atxukarro in her book of memoirs *Irriparrezko printzak* (*Smiling Splinters*). "He was quite abrupt, both with children and with grown-ups. It just didn't occur to him to bring us any of those little things that give such pleasure to children. That's not so very strange, I suppose. Having come from nothing, he was interested only in greatness and the great."

When, on July 18, 1936, General Franco rose up against the Republic, thus triggering the Spanish Civil War, Paulino Uzcudun enthusiastically embraced his cause. Up until then, he had sought out the company of aristocrats and the bourgeoisie; from then on, his companions would be the military and, above all, the paramilitary, the Falangists who drew their inspiration from the doctrines of Hitler and Mussolini.

He soon found a prominent role in the new space created by the war. José Antonio Primo de Rivera, the founder of the Spanish Falangist Party, was in prison in Alicante, accused of conspiring against the Republic, and so, with General Franco's consent, the Falangists formed a commando unit of a hundred militants in order to free Primo de Rivera. Paulino Uzcudun wanted to be part of that unit and his comrades came to view him as a "champion of anti-communism".

The war continued. The fascist press often published photographs of Uzcudun. In one of them he is seen firing a machine gun. In full-face portraits, he is always wearing that orang-utan grin.

He started taking part in exhibition matches for the soldiers. On one occasion, in an encampment in León, fighting a much weaker opponent – who he kept poking fun at – an unexpected blow caused him to bite his tongue with his gold teeth. "Stitch it up! Stitch it up!" he told the nurse, when his mouth filled up with blood. As soon as the nurse had given him a couple of stitches, he went back into the ring and won by a knockout.

Rumours began to spread: that he volunteered to participate in firing squads, that he trained in prisons, using prisoners as sparring partners . . . The rumours reached the ears of children, and, in their fear – the same fear that had engendered various other bogeymen in the past – they created and drew in their notebooks a new image: a sack full of bones and skulls hanging from the ceiling, and, punching it, a boxer with the face of an orang-utan.

The drawing became Paulino Uzcudun's second emblem, and ever since then, it has stuck fast by the first one – that of the woodchopper – as surely as the shade sticks close to the tree. Inevitably, for ever, *ad aeternitatem*.

VIRGINIA CITY
MINING TOWN

Our Ford Sedan laboured up the hills to Virginia City, and the hostility of that bleak mining landscape awoke a voice inside my head:

"The human species does not know fear," the voice said, "and as with all the other animals, even insects, it is always moving forward, driven by a basic idea: I want to live and to endure! I want to stay in the world! Hosea and Ethan Grosh must have known fear – they were the brothers who discovered the vast silver deposits in Virginia City in 1857. Hosea would have known it when a wound became infected and he realised he had the symptoms of septicaemia, and Ethan when he was crossing the mortally cold Sierra Nevada; the miners working in the Yellow Jacket mine must have known fear when the fire from an explosion started to spread through the galleries, or Pierre Haran, the young man from Aldudes in Lower Navarre, when he went into a saloon to have breakfast and found a drunken gunman about to shoot him dead. But the species does not absorb these individual frailties, and new miners rush to take the place of the fallen, like zebras jostling for position on the banks of the river."

The voice was inside my head, and yet it seemed to belong to someone else, as if some magnetic force in the mountains around Virginia City had split my self in two, the half that spoke and the half that listened. I felt as if I were in a dream, and by the time I came round and returned to reality, Ángela was driving our car through the centre of town. It was an odd image: a vehicle from the year 2000 driving down a street flanked by wooden arcades. And yet the street looked more modern than the stereotypical towns in Westerns. Some of the houses were brick-built and rather elegant; others were whitewashed and had balconies and were genuine mansions. This was only to be expected: we weren't at the O.K. Corral or in Shinbone, but in Virginia City, which, in the nineteenth century, had been the richest place on earth.

There was no-one to be seen in Street C, the main street, although the car park nearby was almost full. We started walking, visiting the various places that were open, but they were all empty, devoid of life. Where was everyone? I didn't know what to think, and was hoping that the voice in my head might give me an explanation, as it had on our drive up Highway 341. The only sign I received was a kind of dull pain. I felt cold, even though the thermometer in the Visitors Centre said forty-nine degrees Fahrenheit, nearly ten degrees Centigrade.

THE SILVER QUEEN HOTEL

The hotel foyer was so plunged in gloom that, at first, we didn't even notice the person at the reception desk, a woman in her seventies wearing a long grey skirt and a black shawl. She came over to us and gave us a leaflet, which, among other things, described the hotel's chapel, ideal for weddings, and "the ghost tour" that the newly-weds could go on after their wedding party. Guaranteed thrills: night after night, the voices and evil spirits of the ghosts who haunted the peaceful bedrooms and corridors.

"I don't believe in ghosts," Izaskun told the woman.

"Neither do I, but you have to earn a living somehow."

Well, the woman didn't actually say those words, but her expression said it all.

"Our most famous ghost is a young woman," she explained. "She became pregnant and came to the hotel to meet her lover. He never appeared, and the girl killed herself. She's been haunting this house ever since. A lot of people have heard her weeping and moaning."

I remembered a song by Doc Watson about a girl who fell pregnant: "Oh, listen to my story, I'll tell you no lies, How John Lewis did murder poor little Omie Wise. Go with me, little Omie, and away we will go. We'll go and get married and no-one will know. She climbed up behind him and away they did go, but off to the river where deep waters flow. John Lewis, John Lewis, will you tell me your mind? Do you intend to marry me or leave me behind? Little Omie, little Omie, I'll tell you my mind. My mind is to drown you and leave you behind."

My mind would not rest. The Doc Watson song was followed by a childhood memory. I was walking with my father through a rural area called Upazan, and among the grass, I saw a deep hole, a chasm. My father said: "Listen." At the bottom of the chasm, more than sixty feet below, I could hear the sound of flowing water. A subterranean river. "Now look," my father said. "You see that house?" It was a white house with a red roof that blended perfectly with the green landscape. It was less than a mile away. "A girl who lived there fell pregnant. One night, she made supper for her parents and her siblings, carefully folded up her apron and said, 'I'll be right back.' But she never did come back. She threw herself into this chasm." I peered down and felt the cool air coming up from the deep earth and, again, heard the sound of the river. "She did it out of fear, because of the priests and the friars, who deliberately misled people. At the time, becoming pregnant out of wedlock was considered more shameful than the very worst of crimes. Ridiculous! We were so backward in this part of the country then."

The porch of the Silver Queen Hotel had supporting pillars, and from one of them hung ten or twelve dried rattlesnakes. Their eyes were big and black, but their mouths were what most impressed me. That was where the snake stored the venom that destroyed the red blood cells of its prey and drained it of oxygen.

I put my hand to my forehead and it felt hot. I was feverish.

Ángela was explaining something to Izaskun and Sara.

"When Dominique Laxalt visited the village where he was born, after forty years working as a shepherd in the Sierra Nevada, he took the rattles from various snakes with him as trophies."

A huge picture hung on the wall at the back. It was a portrait of the Silver Queen, a beautiful woman whose dress was made up of gold and silver coins.

"Baudelaire's giantess," I said, but the association made no sense.

"There are 3,262 silver coins and 28 gold ones," the woman said. She said this with a certain pride. For her, the hotel's main trophy was that picture, not the dried rattlesnakes.

Izaskun and Sara wanted to know where the gold coins were.

"On the belt," the woman said.

And the belt was, indeed, golden.

The voice in my head spoke again:

"Isn't it remarkable the lengths the species goes to in order to survive?" it said. "How did the rattlesnake develop in that way? What intelligence gave it the idea that it could move by crawling and store its venom in the roof of its mouth? Perhaps the same intelligence that placed a rattle on the end of its tail, knowing that survival sometimes requires us not to attack?"

There were no answers to these questions, only a buzzing noise, as if air were coming out of my ears.

"What's wrong?" Ángela asked.

"I need some fresh air. I'm going outside," I said. I felt dizzy.

In the street, five men were standing around their Harley-Davidsons, talking animatedly. They were all over fifty and all wore leather jackets, but no crash helmets, only scarves on their heads. The motorbikes, black and grey, looked as if they were made out of materials even more precious than silver. The engine of one bike was still running, its exhaust purring, a gentle, hollow sound.

I walked past the men. They were, in fact, discussing the exhaust. They were all wearing black cowboy boots with buckles on the sides.

Izaskun and Sara came running after me. The interesting places in Virginia City were apparently to be found in the opposite direction.

THE BUCKET OF BLOOD SALOON

We just had to push open the door of the saloon to find where all the missing people were: more than a hundred of them were sitting at small tables in front of a stage or else standing at the bar. As soon as we went in, I spotted a woman wearing a red hat: I noticed the hat first, but also noticed that, despite her age – she was over eighty – she was moving in time to the music played by the band on stage.

The musicians looked like real cowboys. They were wearing high leather boots, waistcoats, neckerchiefs and hats. They spoke with a pronounced Western drawl.

Ángela ordered a beer, Izaskun a bottle of water, Sara a Pepsi. I didn't feel like drinking anything.

The fiddle player in the band started telling a story: "A shepherd married a very refined, delicate young lady and took her to his encampment. In those days, you castrated sheep with your teeth . . ."

In short, the refined young lady offered to help him in this task and did so with astonishing skill. When he saw this, the husband looked down at his crotch and wondered: will my dangly bits be safe?

The other musicians accompanied the storyteller with chords on banjo and guitar. The audience roared with laughter. As did the old lady in the red hat.

There were three big steps from the bar down to the seating area, and I sat on one of them. I was shivering.

The band played another song: "In a cavern, in a canyon, excavating for a mine, dwelt a miner forty-niner, and his daughter Clementine . . ." The fiddle player urged on the audience, and the chorus rose up like a wave: "Oh my darling, oh my darling, oh my darling Clementine!" The old lady in the red hat got to her feet to sing. A lot of other people did the same.

A waitress came along and asked me to leave enough room on the steps. She was coming and going all the time, and I was in the way.

"I'm going outside. I don't feel well," I said to Ángela.

"Shall we all go?" she said to the girls.

Sara would have preferred to stay a little longer and only very sulkily agreed to leave.

WALGREENS DRUGSTORE

Back in Reno, we decided to go to the doctor, but that was hard to do at nine o'clock at night on a Sunday. We would have to call the insurance company, wait for instructions and find the dispensary they assigned to us. That would take too long.

"We could try Walgreens," Ángela suggested.

I agreed. That would suit me perfectly, a mixture of supermarket and pharmacy. It was also near the house.

The pharmacy itself was in one of the side aisles. When I described my symptoms to the clerk, she went over to a window at the back and rang a bell. The window was protected by bars far thicker than any in the Virginia City jail.

A young man in a white coat appeared from what, at first, looked like a laboratory, and came over to the counter. When I told him what was wrong, he asked me various questions: Did I have any problems with my heart? My kidneys? My liver? Any medical problems in the family? Could he take my blood pressure? He disappeared through the door as soon as I gave him my answers.

It took him ten minutes to prepare the medicine. The clerk at the counter gave me a dropper bottle. The instructions were on the label: "Ten drops mixed with water. Every eight hours."

"Fine," I said and nodded.

"A word of warning," the clerk went on. "This medicine is for you and not for your family. On no account must it be taken by children under the age of twelve."

Again I nodded.

Back home, I took the first dose. The effect was almost immediate. When I got into bed, a pleasant feeling ran through my body and silenced the voices in my memory-stuffed head.

MESSAGE TO L.
RENO, SEPTEMBER 9, 2007

A few days ago, I went into a saloon in Virginia City and saw something astonishing: an old lady of about eighty wearing a striking red hat and jigging about to a country-and-Western song. To me she seemed like a real heroine, a desperado pitting herself against the shadows of a death which, at her age, she must have felt was growing ever closer. She was, I felt, a Billy the Kid dancing and shooting at the treacherous Pat Garrett.

I've begun writing a poem inspired by that scene, *Clementine*. Here are the first lines: "Ever since eighty-year-old women started wearing red hats, Death simply hasn't been the same, Oh my darling, Oh my darling, Oh my darling Clementine!"

NOVEMBER 11.
VETERANS DAY

In Izaskun's class they didn't celebrate the day in any special way and ended the afternoon as they always did, by reading round the class. In Sara's class, though, they watched a war documentary, and she came home bearing a little book, the work of an association for war veterans.

The book was nothing very special, a few sheets of paper folded in half and not even stapled together. On the first page, which served as the cover, there was an outline drawing of a soldier, as well as the Stars and Stripes. The children were supposed to colour it in and then write their name underneath.

The second page was blank. On the third page was a drawing of a tank: "A tank, an armored combat vehicle." The exercise was easy enough. They had to add the vowels missing from two words: *turr_t* and *g_n*. According to the caption, the army was made up of soldiers trained to fight on land.

On the following page was an amphibious vehicle, much more sophisticated than the ones shown in the television documentary I had watched. On the next, a note about the work of coastguards and a drawing of a boat. This time the words to be completed were *st_rn* and *b_w*.

On the ninth page, the soldier from the cover reappeared. The caption read: "On Veterans Day we should honor and thank those who have fought in the United States Army defending our freedom."

Page twelve showed a drawing of an eagle along with these words: "In the United States, there are veterans from many wars: the First World War, the Second World War, the Korean War, the Vietnam War, the Gulf War, the Iraq War."

On page fourteen, there was a drawing of a plane and a note on the Air Force. On page sixteen, a submarine, and the children had to complete the word *peri_cope*.

Page seventeen was blank. On page eighteen, the Stars and Stripes again.

Page twenty, the last page, contained the date of Veterans Day,

November 11, followed by five words, all to do with the uniform of the soldier on the cover: _elmet, jacke_, ri_le, _ants and boo_s.

VETERANS DAY. NIGHT

Over supper, Sara said that she hadn't enjoyed the documentary they were shown at school, because it was all about war, with lots of explosions, and because the Americans always won. I read her a news item from the *Reno Gazette-Journal*. A soldier had died the day before in Iraq, in the province of Diyala, and his death brought the number of army casualties to 3,861.

MESSAGE TO L.

I was telling you about what I saw in the saloon in Virginia City, and how impressed I was by that old lady in the red hat dancing to the music. Well, according to Mary Lore, the old lady belongs to the Red Hat Society, whose aim is to "save women from universal boredom". Apparently it has thousands of members and draws its inspiration from a poem by someone called Jenny Joseph: "When I am an old woman I shall wear purple . . ." You can find it on the Internet.

When I saw that woman in the saloon in Virginia City, I thought she was acting independently, that she was Billy the Kid confronting life and the world, and I considered her a heroine. Being told she belonged to a society has tainted that image, and now the whole thing seems rather stupid.

NOVEMBER 14

ANOTHER ATTEMPTED RAPE IN COLLEGE DRIVE

When I opened the *Reno Gazette-Journal* in the morning, I found a report of another attempted rape. I didn't need to check the Internet this time to locate the scene of the attack, because it had happened in our street, "in a parking lot at 401 College Drive". The criminal was still very close to our house.

I mentioned this to Dennis when I went in to the university, and he found the report on the Internet.

"Hm, that really is close to home," he said.

I told him my concerns.

"Shouldn't the police send round a circular to alert the students?"

He adopted his usual pose, arms folded, hand on chin, and thought about this for about five seconds.

"I'll ask Bob," he said, sitting down at his computer and tapping at the keys.

There were no bottles on top of the filing cabinet.

"What happened to the spider?" I asked.

"Oh, he was clearly immortal, so I decided to give him back his freedom," he said, still tapping. "I left him up on the hill where that big cross is."

He was referring to the neon-pink cross on the other side of McCarran.

A message came up on his screen.

"Bob says that the police prefer not to say anything, so as not to spread panic among the students."

"That's the second attempted rape in a very short space of time," I said.

"And it won't be the last," Dennis said. "Rapists and paedophiles just have to do what they do. They only stop when they're either put in prison or killed."

I headed for my office. There were about forty students in the library, most of them staring at their computer screens, some of them asleep or about to fall asleep. All of them seemed perfectly calm. But were they? Somewhere inside them, was there not a tiny corner invisible to others, a glass bottle, and in that bottle a spider? Or was that just me? I couldn't stop thinking about the newspaper report. The criminal was prowling College Drive.

LILIANA

The municipal swimming pool was in a poor part of Reno, not that far from the university. It was about a hundred feet long and thirty feet wide; three of the four walls had no windows. In such an enclosed space, the smell of chlorine was positively suffocating. It was very echoey too, amplifying the swimmers' voices.

Oblivious to this unpleasant atmosphere, the ten or twelve children taking part in the swimming classes were doing their exercises in the water. The instructors were two athletic-looking girls. They would sometimes blow a whistle to attract the children's attention, like cowboys calling to their horses.

We used to see Liliana there every week. At first, we called her "the Russian flower", because she was pretty and because of her name. Then we called her "the silent Russian flower". Later still, "the depressed Russian flower". She seemed increasingly preoccupied. Sometimes, her son would call out to her from the pool in English, and she would respond softly in Russian. She was tall and blonde. She wore her hair in a short, boyish cut.

Only on the fifth or sixth week did she come over and talk to us. Her son also went to Mount Rose School, and she wanted to know what we thought of it. When we had exhausted that topic of conversation, she asked us where we were from. She was from Tver, a town about 125 miles from Moscow.

"Tver?" I said. "I was there once during the Communist era. It was called Kalinin then."

The bus taking us to Moscow had broken down on the outskirts of Tver, and we were obliged to spend the night at the roadside, hunched in our seats. The following morning, the first thing I saw on waking was a white goose peering at the bus. All the other geese, about a thousand of them, were some five hundred yards away, covering the spaces between three big huts with what looked like a piece of billowing white fabric. Now and again a tremor would run through the fabric, and some of the geese would fly up onto the roofs of the huts.

Liliana showed no surprise, as if she thought it perfectly normal to meet someone in Reno who had been to Tver.

"My town is very pretty," she said. Nothing more.

She was wearing a purple V-neck sweater. Around her neck, on a very thin chain was a Russian Orthodox cross. A gold ornament.

She asked us about birthday parties. She wanted to know if we had celebrated any birthdays since we had been in Reno. No, we hadn't. Our daughters had their birthdays in June and July.

"Misha's birthday was the day before yesterday," she said. "I decorated the whole house and made a cake, but none of his school friends came. We spent the whole afternoon alone. I've been living in this country for ten years, but I still don't understand Americans."

One of the instructors was holding Misha by his hands and pulling him through the water. Her colleague was making gestures with her arms, telling him to kick his legs. He must have been about seven.

"Have you come here to live?" Liliana asked us.

"No, we're just here for one year," Ángela said.

"If I had a good job in Russia, I'd go back. But I haven't, and so I have no option but to continue living with these people."

Some of the geese I had seen in Tver had managed to escape from the flock and fly up onto the roofs of the huts or onto the road. Liliana seemed incapable of making a similar effort.

"She's upset about her son's birthday, but she's not doing so very badly," Ángela commented when we left the swimming pool with Izaskun and Sara. "The diamond in that cross she was wearing certainly doesn't look like a fake."

NOVEMBER 20

THANKSGIVING DAY

People had originally started calling Mary Lore's husband "Mannix" because of his resemblance to the television detective of that name, and, thirty years on, the nickname still stuck, even though his bushy moustache and burly physique made him look more like a catch wrestler than a small-screen detective. And as Mary Lore told us, when she invited us to the celebration, he was always the one who cooked the turkey at Thanksgiving.

Earle, Ángela and I were sitting in the conservatory at the back of the house, drinking a glass of wine and waiting to be summoned to the table. Mannix joined us and told us his recipe for preparing the turkey or, as he called it, "the bird".

"Water, salt, apple juice, garlic, orange peel, butter . . ."

He counted off the ingredients on his fingers, and he needed the fingers of both hands to do this.

"It's the usual recipe, except I'm going to add some red peppers before serving. That's how they do it in Mary Lore's family, the way they serve chicken in the Basque Country. Caramelised red peppers are just delicious."

We could smell the caramelised peppers from where we were sitting.

"How much did our bird weigh?" Earle asked.

"Fifteen pounds. But don't worry, it'll be fine. It takes five and a half hours in the oven."

A teacher from the School of Journalism was playing the piano in the living room, and standing round the piano were Dennis, Mary Lore's niece – when we were introduced, she said her name was Natalie, French-style – and a male friend of hers, who wore round, intellectual glasses. Suddenly, they all started singing: The Beatles' "Let it be". The girls, who were watching television in a corner of the room, asked them to be quiet. Izaskun and Sara rather more vehemently than Mannix and Mary Lore's three daughters.

"The fireworks are starting," Earle said, looking up at the Reno sky.

Mary Lore opened the door into the garden, letting in the cold November air.

"Anyone who wants to see the fireworks can go outside!"

Ángela asked me to fetch the girls' coats, and I went out to the coat stand in the hall. The house was full of the smell of roast meat, which had taken over now from the smell of the caramelised red peppers. I also caught a tiny whiff of orange.

When I returned, I saw Dennis in the kitchen, crouched in front of the oven. I joined him. The skin of the fifteen-pound turkey had turned golden brown. The red peppers, which were dark red by then, filled two huge frying pans. On a small, crowded table were three tarts – two pumpkin and one chocolate – and ten or twelve different bottles of wine.

"Perfect!" Dennis said.

Ángela peered round the kitchen door.

"It's really cold outside," she said.

I handed her the girls' coats, and we went to join the others in the garden.

The rockets were being fired from the roof of the tallest casino, the Silver Legacy. Although the explosions were really loud, the twinkling lights were barely visible. There was too much ambient light and too much colour: the fuchsia, red and green glow from the casinos themselves.

"They should have turned off all the city lights. As it is, you can hardly see the fireworks," said a man I hadn't noticed before.

He had the air of an ascetic. He was very thin and his bald patch looked almost like a monk's tonsure. He held out his hand and introduced himself:

"I'm Jeff, Dennis's brother. I'm a typographer. I've been in bed up until now, resting."

I looked surprised. Dennis had never mentioned having a brother.

"I live in San Francisco," he said. "Besides, why *would* Dennis mention me? His real family are his electronic gadgets." He wasn't joking.

I thought that, had Earle been with us, he would have included spiders in Dennis's family, but Earle was at the other end of the garden with Mannix, Mary Lore and Dennis himself.

The more powerful rockets were being launched now. In the sky, in the half-dark, they formed cascades and flowers of light that expanded and changed like a kaleidoscope. The cascades of light were prettier than the flowers.

"The word 'typographer' is misleading, of course," Jeff said. "Most people think it means someone who works for a printing house, but it also means someone who is an expert in typographical fonts. I belong to the latter group."

"Interesting," I said.

Jeff wasn't even looking at the fireworks.

"Which font do you use when you're writing on your computer?" he asked.

"Garamond, Times, Lucida . . ."

"Yes, Lucida is a nice font."

Suddenly, it was as if the rockets were being fired out of a machine gun – the climax of the display. Two minutes later, Reno reverted to its usual self: a city of white lights, in which the Silver Legacy, Harrah's and the other casinos rose like cathedrals. The girls protested. They thought the display hadn't lasted long enough.

"I thought it would be prettier than that," Sara said as she came back into the house with Izaskun and Mary Lore and Mannix's three daughters. In the middle of the room, the table was ready, complete with hors d'oeuvres and drinks.

Jeff sat down next to me, Ángela opposite. Diagonally across to my left was Dennis, and to the right the teacher from the School of Journalism who had been playing the piano. Then came Mary Lore's niece Natalie and her intellectual-looking friend.

Mannix was standing at the head of the table, pointing to the hors d'oeuvres and naming them one by one:

"Tuna with avocado, rice with sun-dried tomatoes, endive salad with Gorgonzola, Spanish ham, Spanish chorizo, some hummus . . ."

Then he pointed to the bottles.

"Californian wine, Chilean wine, Spanish wine, French . . ."

"Is water still banned in this house, Mannix?" Earle asked. He was sitting to Mannix's left and to the right of Dennis.

"Anyone who wants water, lemonade or Coca-Cola can sit with the girls. And the same for anyone who wants pizza," declared Mannix, folding his arms and drawing himself up, like an actor pretending to be a wrestler.

"No offence meant, Mannix. And if wine must be drunk, then I'll drink it," Earle said.

The girls had sat down at the table in front of the television. Mary Lore was serving them pizza. It was supermarket pizza, heated up in the microwave.

"The bird is turning a really beautiful colour," Mannix said, returning from the kitchen. The living room was filled now with the smell of roast meat.

"What do you like about Lucida?" Jeff asked me as soon as we began eating. I had served myself a little tuna with avocado, and he had taken some ham.

"Oh, I like Garamond a lot too," I said.

Jeff took a notebook from his shirt pocket and began to draw various letters. He had a really nice pen, black with a gold nib.

"Garamond and Lucida look identical, don't they?" he said, showing me his notebook. He had written the letters F, H and T in capitals. "But they're not. The letters in Garamond are slightly broader, as you can see with the H. See? The H in Lucida is more upright. Now compare those two Ts. The two serifs on the arm are different – one is straight and the other leans slightly to the right. The serifs in Lucida are both straight . . ."

"Jeff, listen a moment. Everyone listen. I have an idea," Mannix said. He was again standing at the head of the table, hands on hips.

Jeff picked up his notebook and put it back in his shirt pocket. Ángela, Dennis, Earle and everyone else at the table stopped talking and listened. In the room, all that could be heard, very faintly, was the soundtrack of the film the girls were watching. It was probably "Ratatouille", I thought, which, at the time, was a particular favourite with Izaskun and Sara.

Mannix told us his idea.

"It would be a shame on a day like today, at a feast like this, if we ended up having separate conversations, so here's what I propose. We all talk about the same subject, but one at a time. One of us speaks, and the others listen."

"Have you chosen a subject?" Dennis asked.

"He's been worrying about it all afternoon, and, finally, inspiration struck," Mary Lore said. She had sat down now, to the right of Mannix and to the left of Jeff.

Mannix took an exaggeratedly deep breath, again imitating the mannerisms of a catch wrestler.

"Smells!" he exclaimed. "While I was in the kitchen, I thought of other subjects, love, money and suchlike, but when the bird began roasting in the oven, I knew what it had to be: smells! You have to say what your favourite smell is and talk about it to the others. We'll start on my left. You'll be first, Bob."

"Yessir!" said Bob.

Mannix poured us some wine, then raised his glass.

"Let's wait until the bird is served. Meanwhile, you can talk about whatever you like. Happy Thanksgiving supper! Cheers!"

We all joined in the toast and carried on eating.

"That gives us time to think," Jeff said.

Beginning with Bob, and following the order set by Mannix, I would be the seventh person to choose a smell. Jeff the eighth and Ángela the third.

The hors d'oeuvres, the sun-dried tomatoes and the avocado, the hummus and the Gorgonzola cheese, barely triggered any memories at all, or only of recent experiences, fragments from my life stored in the first or second layer of memories. On the other hand, the tuna, rice, ham and chorizo – or, rather, their various smells – penetrated deeper, and the four together, especially the peppery taste of the chorizo, reminded me of suppers shared with other soldiers in the barracks at Hoyo de Manzanares thirty years before, experiences buried in the seventh or eighth layer of my memories. But when Mary Lore and Mannix brought in the roast turkey and the caramelised red peppers, the threads of my thoughts transported me straight down to scenes from the twelfth or thirteenth layer, to the time when my mother subscribed to the *Reader's Digest*. In those days, the 1960s, my family used to gather for lunch at my aunt and uncle's restaurant to celebrate the feast of San Juan. Sometimes, as in Joxe Austin Arrieta's story, "Abuztuaren 15eko bazkalondoa" ("Table talk on August 15"), the conversation would be about the family's past history, with more or less veiled allusions to the Civil War; at other times, as in Bertolt Brecht's "A Respectable Wedding", the mixture of moods and alcohol provoked arguments as the meal progressed. But the meal was never what Mannix was hoping for now – or what Agathon had hoped for many centuries before him: an excuse for a good conversation.

Earle praised the food. The turkey was delicious, and the orange peel gave it an exquisite taste. We all agreed and, prompted by Dennis, applauded the cook.

"Enough of that nonsense," Mannix said, "let's begin with the smells."

"I'd love to be original," Earle said, "but I've chosen the smell that anyone living in Nevada would choose, and that's the smell of sagebrush."

I immediately remembered what Monique Laxalt Urza wrote in *The Deep Blue Memory*, about how the smell of sagebrush made her feel at home again when she returned to Nevada after a long stay in France.

"We invited Monique," Mannix said, "but she couldn't come. She says her brother's illness has become the family hearth around which they all gather."

"Which brother are you talking about? Bruce Laxalt? The poet?" I asked.

"Yes, he's very ill," Mary Lore said.

"We just bought his book in Borders," Ángela said.

Mannix held up his hands, indicating that the conversation should not go down that route. He looked at Dennis.

"It's your turn. What smell have you chosen?"

"The smell of the inside of a new car," answered Dennis.

Jeff leaned towards me.

"I knew he would choose a machine. He's always been like that. His fondness for insects is more to do with where he lives now. If he lived in San Francisco, he wouldn't feel like that."

Dennis told us about the memory he associated with that smell. When he was six or seven, his mother had bought a new Packard and immediately took him for a spin round the block. That had been a big moment for him. A moment of happiness.

Jeff was following this explanation with a distinctly distracted air. Before his brother had finished speaking, he took out his notebook again and wrote something down.

It was Ángela's turn.

"I really like the smell of rain on dry earth," she said.

She was referring to the small village in the Basque Country where she used to spend the summer as a child. There would always be a storm at some point during the August fiestas, when the earth in the square was at its driest. Her choice had to do with that period of her childhood.

"That would be a rare smell in Nevada," Mary Lore said. "It never rains here."

"And there are no fiestas in villages either," added Jeff.

The teacher from the School of Journalism spoke next.

"I choose the same smell Marilyn Monroe chose. Chanel No. 5. I'm serious. I love it."

There was laughter around the table. Jeff again leaned towards me.

"I knew he would make a joke of it."

The talk turned to Marilyn Monroe. The teacher at the School of Journalism explained that, in the actress's last interview, she had referred to Rilke's *Letters to a Young Poet*, and that it wasn't so very strange to think of her as a kind of poet. Had she lived longer, perhaps she might even have become a real poet, we would never know. He then went on to talk about Bob Dylan's lyrics, saying he deserved to win the Nobel Prize for literature.

Jeff's whole body shook with laughter.

"These university people crease me up," he whispered in my ear.

"She was married to Arthur Miller, remember," Mannix said. "They came to Pyramid Lake while they were making that Huston movie."

"'The Misfits'," the teacher from the School of Journalism said.

"I can never think of Monroe without thinking of Kennedy," Jeff said, out loud this time. "Marilyn showing off her tits and thighs and singing, 'Happy Birthday, Mr President,' and Kennedy in his hotel room, making time to screw her. I understand they helicoptered her in specially, complete with tits and thighs. Definitely one of the high points of our democracy."

A silence fell.

"I'm going to take advantage of this impasse and put the turkey back in the oven. It's getting cold," Mary Lore said, picking up the dish; and then the tension eased somewhat.

"Kennedy wasn't just a womaniser, Jeff. He was rather more than that, I think," Mannix said.

Jeff took a sip of wine.

"Oh, without a doubt. He nearly triggered a Third World War over that Bay of Pigs affair."

"I think we need to change smells," Earle said. "Chanel No. 5 is definitely not contributing to the spirit of Thanksgiving Day. I'm sure Natalie will suggest something more appropriate."

He winked at Mary Lore's niece. In her tight jeans and black tank top, she was the very opposite of Liliana, the young Russian woman at the swimming pool. She spoke with great energy and used her hands to express herself more eloquently.

"Did you know she's been made captain of the hockey team?" Mary Lore said.

This did not surprise me.

"I know exactly which smell to choose. I like the smell of liniment," Natalie said.

We all waited for an explanation, but she made a gesture indicating that she had nothing to add.

"I'm dying to know more, Natalie," Earle said. "The smell of liniment seemed so full of promise."

We all laughed, including Jeff.

Mannix, Dennis and Ángela began clearing the table of empty wine bottles, the little plates of hummus, the bowl of grated Gorgonzola, the pans of red peppers, while Mannix hoovered up the crumbs with a mini-vacuum cleaner.

The threads of my thoughts once again reached down to the layer of memories from forty years before, and I was back in my aunt and uncle's restaurant, at a table decorated for the feast of San Juan. They had one of those tabletop hoovers too, a present from our French relatives, as were the bottles of Legrain champagne and the Duralex plates. There was wine as well, and cider too, and to eat, fried hake served with slices of lemon, and roast chicken rather than turkey, but the red peppers were the same. The atmosphere, though, was sad and full of foreboding: the life of José Francisco, my aunt and uncle's autistic son, was set to end tragically.

Ángela noticed my thoughts were elsewhere and asked me to "rejoin" the party. Earle, Dennis and Mannix agreed.

"My mother wept the day Kennedy was assassinated in Dallas," I said, as if that was what I had been thinking about. "She believed that Kennedy, like her, was a good Catholic, who had never broken the seventh commandment."

"How absurd!" Earle said.

That was what I thought too, but it hurt me to hear those words on someone else's lips.

"She was a subscriber to *Reader's Digest*, which is where she got her view of Kennedy. My aunt was quite a different matter. She barely knew how to read at all. She probably didn't even know who Kennedy was."

Jeff gave an approving thumbs-up.

"We are all children of our age, aren't we?" Earle said. "You judge others too harshly, Jeff."

"He thinks an older brother's most important role in life is to pick holes in other people's arguments," Dennis said, trying to make a joke, and for the first time that evening, Jeff smiled at him.

Mary Lore brought in the dish with what remained of the turkey and sliced it up with a knife.

"We still haven't finished with the smells," Mannix said. He was walking round the table, serving everyone more turkey. We all had seconds, apart from Ángela.

Then Mannix addressed Natalie's boyfriend.

"Your turn."

"I like opening a new book and sticking my nose in among the pages. On the other hand, I hate the smell of old books. They often stink of cigarettes, especially if they've been in someone's personal library. I speak from experience. The shelves in my dad's study were crammed with books, and he was an inveterate smoker."

"Thank you, Mr Scholar," Mannix said.

"I like the smell of new-mown grass," I said.

"Well, I like the smell of dogs' paws," Jeff immediately added. "That will doubtless seem like an odd choice, but it's a really nice smell. Michael Ondaatje says the same in one of his books, and I agree."

He took a sip of wine.

"I choose the smell of freshly baked bread," Mary Lore said.

We all sat looking at Mannix.

"While I've been listening to you all, I've changed my mind five or six times," he said. "I like the smell of roast turkey, and I like all the smells that you chose too, rain on dry earth, new-mown grass, sagebrush . . . all of them! But I'm going to choose the one that occurred to me while we were watching the fireworks: the smell of spent gunpowder! That brings back my childhood when we used to let off firecrackers."

"I still prefer the smell of dogs' paws," Jeff said. "The smell of gunpowder is the smell of war. That must be the predominant smell in Iraq at the moment. Although, when I think about it, the deadly substances they use now are probably odourless. We've progressed. We've got better at killing."

He poured himself some more wine and, before drinking, raised his glass as if in a toast.

"The only person who's at war today, Jeff, is you," Mary Lore said.

"I'm going to bring in the desserts, and see if we can make peace," Mannix said. Earle went with him into the kitchen, and they returned bearing a pumpkin tart and a chocolate tart.

Mary Lore brought more plates and placed one before each guest.

"Do your girls like chocolate?" she asked Ángela.

"They love it."

"Fine, I'll give the girls half the chocolate tart. And Jeff, you divide up the rest of the tart. You deserve to be punished for being so contrary."

Mary Lore took the tart over to the children's table, and Jeff started slicing up the other half with the same degree of concentration as when he had drawn those letters for me. Each slice – a perfect isosceles triangle – was the same as the previous one and the following one. He put the first slice on Mannix's plate.

"I gladly accept this as a sign of peace," Mannix said, winking at Earle and Dennis.

Jeff's hands moved very coolly and calmly. He put the slices exactly in the middle of each plate. I asked him for a slice of the pumpkin pie, because I didn't think I'd ever tried it before.

"Are you sure that's what you want?" Jeff said.

"Is the chocolate tart better?" I asked.

Jeff cut a triangular slice of pumpkin tart in half, then did the same with a slice of chocolate tart, and placed the two halves on my plate.

"Wow, I bet if we measured them, they'd be exactly the same size," I said.

He smiled.

"Remember, Garamond and Lucida may look the same, but they're not."

Mannix was standing up, his glass in his hand.

"At the risk of repeating myself: Happy Thanksgiving!"

Mary Lore brought in the coffee and filled our cups. The smell of coffee was pretty good too.

"Oh, and another thing," Mary Lore said. "If you want to smoke a cigarette with your coffee, there's no need to go out into the garden. We don't want anyone to freeze. You can smoke in the conservatory."

"Tonight, I'm going to smoke," Earle said.

"Me too," Ángela said.

"I'm up for it. Only don't tell my trainer," Natalie said.

Jeff and I were left alone at the table. Earle, Mannix, the teacher at the School of Journalism, Natalie, her boyfriend and Ángela went out into the conservatory; Mary Lore and Dennis had joined the children at their table. The film had ended, and they were playing Monopoly.

Jeff again took his notebook from his shirt pocket and showed me the sentence he'd written on one page: "The quick brown fox jumps over the lazy dog."

"It doesn't mean anything," he said, "but it's the sentence we typographers use most, because it contains all the letters of the alphabet, and when we're trying out a new font, it gives us an overall impression. There are some fonts, though, like Braggadocio, for example, that are fine for labels, but unsuitable for a longer text."

With slow, precise, unhesitating strokes, he "drew" the sentence on the paper: "The quick brown fox jumped over the lazy dog."

"This is Braggadocio," he said, when he had finished.

"May I ask you something regarding my own language?" I said. "It has lots of Zs and Ks. And a lot of As too. What would be the best font to use for that?"

"Having lots of As is normal, but when choosing a font, you'd have to bear in mind the Z and the K."

He leaned back in his chair and closed his eyes. I imagined his mind as a space in which thousands of vowels and consonants were constantly churning about. Occasionally, like a sky filled with fireworks, there would be cascades of words, kaleidoscopic flowers made of Zs and Ks.

Jeff took his time. He thought for almost a minute.

"You'd have to start with Oldrich Menhart," he said at last, sitting up and opening his eyes. "He designed it for the Czech language, but I think it would suit your language as well."

He opened his notebook again and drew some Menhart Ks and Zs, upper case and lower case. They seemed to vary a lot, and I commented on this.

"Yes, in a way, you're right," he said. "The Menhart font did evolve over time, but it still bears his mark."

The teacher from the School of Journalism was playing the piano again. "Imagine". The guests who had gone out into the conservatory to smoke came back in and started singing along.

Sara came over to me. She was wearing her coat.

"Are we going home soon? It's not that I'm tired, I just want to see if the raccoon has come back to the garden," she said.

"What made you think about the raccoon now?" I asked. "We haven't seen him for about two months."

Sara didn't answer and went back to the table where the other girls were still playing Monopoly.

"She was probably reminded of the raccoon by the movie they were watching, 'Ratatouille'," Jeff said. He handed me a card. "Here's my email address. Why don't you send me a short text in your language? I'll set it in Menhart font and send it back to you."

I said goodbye to Jeff and went over to the children's table. It was very late. Two o'clock in the morning. Like Sara, Izaskun and Ángela wanted to go back to the house.

JOSÉ FRANCISCO
(A MEMORY)

My cousin José Francisco Albizu died in San Sebastián hospital on August 12, 1967. Three weeks before, he had swallowed some nails and various bits of metal, which had perforated his pharynx and his stomach. He was fifteen at the time.

On one of her visits, my mother asked him:

"Why did you do it, José Francisco? What made you swallow those horrible bits of metal?"

My cousin responded with a smile, his second smile, the one that appeared on his face shortly after he began taking the medication prescribed by the psychiatrists, a mere rictus, rather than a smile; he did not respond with his first smile, his childhood smile, a remote smile that always reminded my mother, quite rightly, of the "Mona Lisa".

"We will never forget his smile," the priest at the funeral said.

He presumably meant José Francisco's childhood smile.

Whether it was his first or his second smile, José Francisco could never hold it for long. His whole body was constantly in movement; his head bobbed back and forth, like the head of a bird or a chicken; he twisted from side to side; he waved his arms about like someone trying to shoo away a swarm of mosquitoes.

I have a photograph taken the year he died: six boys standing on a bridge, next to the restaurant owned by my aunt and uncle, José Francisco's parents. I'm the oldest. I must be about sixteen or seventeen, and I'm wearing my hair Brylcreemed into an Elvis Presley quiff, in imitation of an Elvis imitator, a school friend called Luis at Colegio La Salle. I'm looking straight at the camera, as are three of the other boys. José Francisco, on the other hand, is looking away, as if searching for something in the cornfield or in the shrine in the background. But there's nothing there. The shrine, a small stone building dedicated to San Juan, is closed.

The restaurant, a renovated inn-cum-tavern, also acted as a boarding house, and normally, during the week, the guests sat down to eat at the big table in the kitchen. It was a place in which "good humour reigned supreme", as I heard the village priest say once. However, he must have been referring to José Francisco's childhood. Afterwards, the atmosphere changed. My aunt never seemed happy. Nor did she seem sad either. She had the intense gaze and the stern face of a landlady, which is what she was, because she was the one who ran the restaurant, and she spoke very little. She sometimes quarrelled with her son, but always indirectly, addressing the people having lunch or supper at the table, using them as a chorus:

"José Francisco is a very bad boy. He hits his mother and makes her sad."

She had a beautiful voice, firm and clear.

The chorus could have responded:

"Woman, that boy is the kind of child the Spartans would have hurled off a cliff, but he's your own flesh and blood and, if necessary, you would conceal him from the civil guard if they came for him. And yet he hits you. Why resign yourself to your fate? How much longer are you going to put up with being mistreated?"

However, the guests who sat at the kitchen table did not know how to speak in that tragic tone, and so said nothing in response to my aunt's complaints.

You could never grab José Francisco's arm or push him or get in his way. He would think you were going to hurt him and would react with anger, punching and biting, and it could take two or three men to subdue him. Sometimes, he did fall out with other people and would then inflict harm on himself, banging his head on a wall or rolling around on the ground until he bled.

We all knew that José Francisco could be dangerous. Both to himself and to others. His mother, my aunt, found this hard to accept. She treated him as if he were perfectly normal, and if he disobeyed her orders – "Go to the chicken run and bring me some eggs" – she would put this down to naughtiness or obstinacy or laziness. One day, she got angry with him and threatened him with a broom handle, and José Francisco pushed her so hard that he hurled her backwards against the kitchen wall. My aunt ended up on the floor with a broken rib.

At first, until José Francisco was five, the family thought he was deaf and dumb, but doubts soon arose. It seemed that the problem was not just with his hearing and his vocal cords. There was something else, probably some mental deficiency, although, given his appearance – he was a tall, fair-haired boy with green eyes – this was hard to believe. And then there was that *Gioconda* smile of his.

When he was seven, they took him to Madrid. My uncle knew an admiral in the Spanish navy, to whom he had acted as aide during military service, and thanks to him, they were able to have José Francisco admitted to a clinic run by a doctor who "knew all about the mind". Later on, I discovered, from a receipt my mother kept, that the doctor was called López Ibor, and the clinic, Mirasierra. He was not perhaps the worst option in post-Civil War Spain, where most sinister psychiatrists – with Antonio Vallejo-Nájera at their head – publicly defended the supposed link between Marxism and a lack of intelligence, or the intellectual atrophy that was said to afflict all women from birth; but at any rate, it turned out to be a wrong decision. My aunt did not speak Spanish and could not go with her son to Madrid; nor could my uncle, because, quite apart from helping out in the restaurant, he worked as a truck driver six days a week; as for my mother, even though she had studied and was a teacher, she was nevertheless rather unworldly and would have been completely at a loss in a big city and among psychiatrists. Given the circumstances, the family knew almost nothing about the treatment given to my cousin, only that its purpose was to draw him out of his silence and teach him to speak.

José Francisco spent nearly two months in Madrid. He did not learn to speak, or, rather, he learned just one word: "fasten".

The word sounded strange in our world, because, as in the case of my aunt, most people in the village knew very little Spanish. As an example of our linguistic situation, I remember what happened the day the first television set was installed in my aunt and uncle's restaurant. They didn't put it in the kitchen, but quite high up on a shelf in the dining room, and all the girls and boys from round about sat down to watch a Tarzan film that was just beginning: "Trek to Terror". The film opened with a voice loudly repeating the title: "The Trek to Terror!!!" The boy sitting in front of me turned round: "*Zer da 'trek'?*" he asked. "What does 'trek' mean?" As soon as I had explained, another four or five heads turned to me: "*Eta 'terror'? Zer da 'terror'?*" "And 'terror'? What does 'terror' mean?" In that atmosphere, knowing the word 'fasten' only emphasised José Francisco's oddness.

José Francisco had always been obsessed with fastening things. If someone approached him with the buttons of his jersey or shirt undone, he would get upset and insist on doing them up. If he saw the neighbours' dog running loose, he would grab it by the collar, drag it over to its kennel and chain it up again. In the morning, as soon as he got out of bed, he would rush to the shoe cupboard and tie all the shoelaces together. He used to do so silently, but after he came back from Madrid, he would shout: "Fasten! Fasten!"

When José Francisco turned fourteen, my aunt and uncle decided to send him to San Sebastián, to a residential school for children with special needs. By then, there was a name for his illness.

"Apparently, he's autistic," my mother told us, after going with my aunt to see the doctor. "And the school specialises in caring for such children."

My father remarked laconically:

"I don't know why they waited so long."

My mother said that they already had a date for his enrolment: June 25.

"I suppose that means there won't be any family lunch," my father said.

He was referring to the lunch my aunt always prepared on the eve of San Juan, as part of the fiesta held at the shrine near the restaurant.

But there *was* a lunch. My aunt didn't want that year to be an exception. About midday on June 24, twenty-five or so relatives, mostly from outside the village, were gathered in their various groups: the men, holding glasses of white wine, were standing round the radio, listening to the broadcast of the pelota match between Azkarate and Atano X; the women were wandering about near the shrine, which had been decked with flowers for the occasion; we, the adolescents and children, were sitting near the weir at the watermill, a short distance from the restaurant, looking at the postcards of pop singers brought by our French cousin Didi, who lived in Hendaye.

The dining room filled with voices when we sat down at the table, and everything seemed to indicate that we were going to enjoy the same celebratory lunch as we had in previous years, undimmed by José Francisco's imminent departure. The table – made up of five normal-sized tables – had been dressed beautifully by my aunt. On the white linen tablecloth the fine Bidasoa plates were arranged in two parallel rows, and between them, forming a more or less homogeneous line, were the soup tureens and the serving dishes: fish soup, Russian salad, ham, croquettes and asparagus. In between the serving dishes and the tureens were little bunches of flowers. "They were left over from the shrine," my aunt told anyone who made jokes about such "luxurious touches". Among the flowers stood the gleaming bottles of cider brought up from the river where they had been cooling.

At first, while we were enjoying the fish soup and eating the ham, croquettes, Russian salad and asparagus, the conversation followed its usual quiet, banal course, interrupted only by some of the men arguing about something that had happened in the match between Azkarate and Atano X. Then the next course arrived – fried fish and roast chicken with red peppers – and one of José Francisco's uncles began to protest at the decision to send José Francisco away to a residential school. The pleasant atmosphere vanished at once.

"What are they going to do to him? The same thing they did to me?" he said, picking up his plate and bringing it down hard on the table.

He had chosen hake to eat, and a piece of fish fell onto the tablecloth. His face was scarlet.

His brother, José Francisco's father, turned to him and said:

"Be quiet. The last thing we need is you getting all worked up!"

Miguel ignored him and continued shouting:

"I don't need to die in order to find out what hell is like! I found out when I was in the insane asylum!"

"Oh, no, here we go: the same old story!" said José Francisco's father, folding his arms.

"What are you talking about, Miguel?" my mother said. "No-one is sending José Francisco to an insane asylum. He's going to a school for children with special needs."

Miguel wasn't listening and he continued to protest until my aunt called to him from the kitchen door.

"Miguel, I need your help. I'm not sure how this new oven works."

He immediately fell silent and walked meekly over to the kitchen.

A quarter of an hour later, they both returned, accompanied by Estepani, the woman who helped in the kitchen, each of them bearing a chocolate soufflé.

"Would anyone like cheese as well?" my aunt asked. We all said no.

"Have you calmed down now?" my uncle asked his brother.

Miguel was too busy eating the fish still on his plate to respond. My aunt and Estepani returned to the kitchen, where José Francisco was having his lunch, because he never ate with everyone else.

The weir by the watermill was surrounded by hazel trees, and we, the younger members of the family, escaped there once we had devoured the chocolate soufflé. Our French cousin Didi continued to do most of the talking. He was the star of the group, because he was French and because of the way he looked. His hair was "long as a girl's", and he wore flowery shirts. The one he was wearing then was green with purple roses.

Didi talked to us about a new singer who had just released a record in France. His name was Antoine, and he'd had a huge hit with a number called "*Les Elucubrations*", in which he made fun of the French rock star, Johnny Hallyday. Hallyday had responded that same week with a song entitled "*Cheveux longs et idées courtes*" – "Long on hair, short on ideas". Didi preferred Antoine. He was more modern. In his song, he said that you should be able to buy the *pilule* – the Pill – in your local Monoprix supermarket.

Antoine, Johnny Hallyday, Monoprix, pilule . . . Those unfamiliar names and words plunged into my mind like the hazelnuts that tumbled into the waters of the weir at the mill. At night they plunged still deeper, and, the following morning, I ran to find my mother. Accompanied by my older brother, she and my aunt were going to San Sebastián to take José Francisco to his new school.

"Could you buy me this record?" I asked.

I wrote the name down on a piece of paper: Antoine, "*Les Elu-cubrations*". We had an old, refurbished Telefunken record player at home, a present from Miguel, who owned the local repair shop for electrical goods, and I was dying to hear that song.

"You won't forget, will you?" I said.

My mother got angry. They were going to San Sebastián in a taxi, and the residential school was nowhere near the town centre. Besides, it wasn't going to be easy leaving José Francisco there. It would take time. It wasn't like dropping off a parcel. She was still in a bad mood after the previous night's argument with Miguel.

"Would *you* buy it for me?" I asked my older brother.

"No way," he said.

I was most put out – or peeved, as we used to say then – but I was determined to follow the path Didi had shown me, and two days later, after both my mother and my brother had said no, I went to San Sebastián on the bus on my own and did the rounds of the record shops. I couldn't find "*Les Elucubrations*" because it hadn't yet been released in Spain, but I found a magazine, *Fans*, intended for lovers of pop music. I opened it and there were Antoine and Johnny Hally-day face to face. Antoine with his long hair and his huge dark glasses, Johnny with his Elvis Presley-style quiff.

In the weeks that followed, my head filled up with names gleaned from *Fans*, names I had never heard before: Françoise Hardy, the Beatles, the Animals, Los Brincos, the Kinks, Jefferson Airplane, the Troggs, Donovan, Los Sírex, Herman's Hermits, Michel Polnareff, the Mamas and the Papas . . . At the same time, my hair – how to comb it and even how long to grow it – became my main preoccupation.

The village fiesta held in the second week of July was fast approaching, and I noticed in the programme, along with the names of the bands who were going to play at the dances, a call for floats and car-nivalesque characters. I decided to have a go. I would buy a pretend guitar and a wig that resembled Antoine's head of hair, and I would ask Didi if I could borrow one of his flowery shirts, which were hard to find in San Sebastián. Dressed like this, I would appear in the parade and observe the effect my new appearance had on others.

The day arrived, and it was an unmitigated disaster. Immediately in front of me was a young man dressed in tails and riding a kind of penny farthing, and he garnered all the looks and comments from the waiting public. Besides, hardly anyone knew who I was meant to be, because no-one had heard of Antoine or any other pop singer. The worst response, though, came from the few who did know. They sensed that, unlike the other participants in the parade – pirates, clowns and so on – I took my disguise seriously. One of them, the village's only university student at the time, waited until I drew alongside him, then shouted:

"Doesn't he look good! So modern!"

His companions, who were all about twenty years old, laughed so loudly that even the young man on the strange bicycle turned to look at them. I realised then that the apparent compliment was, in fact, a mocking insult directed at me, a country hick trying to conceal his true origins. As soon as I was out of his sight, I left the parade and went home.

"You just can't resist playing the fool, can you?" said my older brother when I told him what had happened. He only went out during fiesta time to watch the boxing matches or the cross-country races. Otherwise, he sat on our back balcony, reading; this time it was a book by Dostoyevsky.

"Oh, shut up!" I said. He laughed and showed me the title of the book: *The Idiot*.

"*You're* the idiot!" I said, but he merely laughed again.

Luis, a friend from school, used to phone me sometimes, and we would arrange to go into San Sebastián to visit the record shops. He could afford to buy as many records as he liked because his father was an army colonel, stationed in the Loyola barracks, and had a lot of money. I usually bought only one a week. The first record I took home with me was not Antoine's "*Les Elucubrations*", which had still not been released, but Scott McKenzie's "San Francisco".

My friendship with Luis was reinforced by those tours of the record shops, and one day, he invited me to the dance that he and his friends organised each Sunday. He explained that about thirty or so boys and girls got together and played music by Elvis, the Kinks, the Beatles, the Rolling Stones, the Beach Boys, the Everly Brothers and many others. He had a Philips stereo record player that could really blast the music out.

"Where do you hold these dances?" I asked.

"Opposite the train station in Loyola. You know the place."

It was an annex to the barracks, a stable alongside a paddock for horse-jumping. When the train was late, we Colegio La Salle students often had to kill time at the station, and we would amuse ourselves, as we stood on the platform, watching the soldiers trundling barrow-loads of hay around or cleaning out the stables, or we would watch a rider, a girl, going over the jumps on a horse that had a white star on its forehead. I did indeed know the place.

"Yes, we hold the dances in the stables, although, of course, we take the horses out first," Luis added. It was a joke, which I failed to get.

He patted me gently on the back.

"Of course we don't hold it in the stables, stupid. There's a house behind the stables. The only one in the area. Come on Sunday at about half past five and ring the bell. A girl will open the door."

The following Sunday, I arrived in Loyola at five o'clock, not half past. Initially, I hung about the station, pacing up and down the platform; then, I headed off in the direction of the school, only to walk back again to the point where the path met the walls of the barracks; finally, when it was just three minutes to half past five, I crossed the tracks and went into the paddock.

There were three soldiers sitting on a porch, smoking. The air was thick with the smell of manure and livestock. I heard a horse snort and whinny briefly, and remembered the horse with the white star on its forehead and the girl who rode it, the girl we all watched from the platform when we were waiting for the train.

One of the soldiers was holding a small blaring transistor radio in one hand. That Sunday afternoon's football match must have been a very close thing because the commentators were shouting for all they were worth. Where were the girls and boys who went to the dances? Where was Luis? It seemed odd that there was no-one around.

I went over to the soldiers.

"How do I get to the house?"

The three soldiers stared at me. They were eating bread and canned tuna and mussels, using some planks as an improvised table. On the radio, two commentators were discussing a penalty.

"You can't pass without permission from the sergeant," said one of the soldiers, whose head was completely shaven. His fingers were sticky with the orange-coloured sauce from the mussels, and he was busily licking them clean.

"The colonel's son invited me," I said.

"Well, the colonel himself invited *us*!" said the soldier, and his two colleagues burst out laughing.

Apparently grown weary of the commentators' shouting, the soldier slammed one hand down on the radio to turn it off and offered me the bottle of wine that was cooling in a bucket.

"Go through the stable and you'll see the house straight ahead. But you'd better have a drink first. You need to get up your courage before you meet the girls."

The other two soldiers laughed again. They clearly knew about the dances.

I declined their offer of a drink, thanked them and walked briskly away. I heard them laughing behind me, and then, once again, the hysterical voices of the sports commentators on the radio.

The stable was made up of two rows of stalls and a central walkway. The stench of manure and livestock was even stronger there. The smell of manure was slightly sour; the smell of livestock – although there were only horses in the stalls, not cows or donkeys or chickens – was slightly sickly.

A noise made me turn round. A horse was peering over the door of one of the stalls. It had a white star on its forehead. It observed me quietly.

Far from the soldiers, the silence in the stable was absolute. I went closer and spoke to the horse.

"I've seen you being ridden by that girl," I said.

Then I became aware of someone else in the stable, smoking a cigarette. I caught the whiff of tobacco first, then I saw the smoke, and finally I saw the smoker.

"Ah, the student who talks to horses," he said. Then he came towards me, holding out his pack of cigarettes.

It was a brand I hadn't seen before. He went to the same school as Luis and me, but he was a year ahead. Initially, I could only think of his nickname, Hump, a reference to his hunchback. His chest and back bulged out, and he had one shoulder lower than the other. He was tall and very thin.

I took a cigarette. He lit it with a mother-of-pearl lighter.

"Let's get out of here. Horses don't like the smell of Virginia tobacco."

"Plus there's a lot of straw around," I said.

I suddenly remembered his real name: Adrián.

"There's the house," he said, going ahead of me down a neat gravel path that led into a small wood.

The house was like a rather run-down version of the one in the school grounds, its walls painted dark yellow and with white blinds at the windows. There were cracks in the walls, and some of the windows had come off their hinges. Withered climbers hung from the balcony.

When we reached the door, we saw another path, at the end of which, less than a mile away, we could see the school and its adjoining house.

"Yes, the houses are identical," Adrián said, as if he had read my mind. "They once belonged to the same family. Then they shared them out, giving one to the school and one to the army."

He took a drag on his cigarette and looked me straight in the eye, as if expecting me to say something. My thoughts, however, were elsewhere.

"Have people already arrived for the dance?" I asked.

Adrián rang the bell, which jingled merrily. Then he turned and set off back to the stables.

I could hear the song being played inside. "Ticket to Ride" by the Beatles.

"Aren't you coming in?" I asked Adrián, who was already some way off.

"No, I want to have a word with the horses first," he answered, without turning round.

I didn't know what to do with my cigarette end, so I threw it down on the ground and stubbed it out in the gravel.

A girl opened the door.

"Hi, my name's Cornélie," she said, holding out her hand. She had a strong French accent. She was fair-haired and was wearing glasses with turquoise-coloured frames. She beckoned me in.

"Where are you from?" I asked. "Ticket to Ride" was playing at such a high volume now that we had to shout to make ourselves heard.

"From Lyons. My father's the French consul."

She took off her glasses and waved them around to indicate that I should follow her.

The room where the dance was being held was packed with people. Next to the record player, three boys were playing air guitar, and singing the words exactly as they sounded on the record: "*Shee's gotta tikit to ra'a, shee's gotta tikit* . . ." The air was filled with cigarette smoke.

Cornélie was just about to explain something, but Luis grabbed my arm and dragged me off to meet the people who were, according to him, going to be my "rivals". Five minutes later, I was standing next to the record player again, trying to memorise the names of my supposed rivals: Miracoli, Vergara, Ernesto, Micky, Dublang, López, Álvaro, Miguel Ángel . . . Luis introduced me to the boys studying at Colegio La Salle by their surnames, and those studying at other schools by their first names.

The record player stopped, and so did the dancers. I looked at the records, of which there were many.

"Careful now, don't get them mixed up!"

Vergara and López were by my side. They were not in the same year as me, but I knew them because they were members of the school's cross-country team. They both came from rich families.

The records were divided into three piles. Vergara placed the palm of one hand on each pile in turn, as if they were packs of cards.

"These are to be played from six until seven; these ones from seven until eight; and these ones from eight o'clock on."

He again patted the three piles of records.

"Fast, medium fast, slow."

"I see, so every record has its moment," I said, accepting the role of disc jockey. I felt comfortable next to the record player.

A lot of the groups and singers were new to me. Most came from England or America – Black Sabbath; Crosby, Stills and Nash; Roy Orbison – but there were French and Italian singers too: Claude François, Adriano Celentano, Bobby Solo . . .

I saw Adrián come into the room. He took off his maroon jacket and hung it on the coat rack. His grey-and-white floral waistcoat was very baggy, but not enough to conceal his bulging back and chest.

"I'd start with 'Pretty Woman'," he said, coming over to the table and choosing the Roy Orbison record from one of the piles.

I followed his advice.

"Play a couple more tracks, then try 'Mrs Robinson' by Simon and Garfunkel. If you agree, of course. Forgive me interfering."

He spoke very politely.

"There's nothing to forgive," I answered, adopting the same polite tone. "I don't honestly know which songs to choose."

"No, it's not that easy. Some records have fast and slow tracks. How about putting this one on next?"

He was holding a record by the Mamas and the Papas. It was one I knew. Luis had bought it when we were on one of our record-buying trips.

When "California Dreamin'" began to play, Adrián offered me another of his cigarettes.

I took one and he lit it with his mother-of-pearl lighter, then lit another for himself.

We moved from the first pile of records to the second. Around eight o'clock, the curtains were drawn, and the room was left in semi-darkness. Luis came over to us.

"It's time to start playing the slow songs," he said.

He sorted through the third pile and handed me a record by another singer I hadn't heard of: Bobby Vinton.

"Play the first track: 'Blue Velvet'."

Then Adrián said he had to leave, and shook my hand.

"See you again."

"You never change, do you, Adrián?" Luis said to him. Then he turned to me: "You know Adrián, don't you? He's a real artist. Everything he does, he does well. Last year he won the Coca-Cola essay competition – for the whole of Spain! This year, he came top in the regional art competition, but he won't take part in the most important competition of all. He keeps well away from girls."

Adrián put on his jacket and waved goodbye from the front door.

"It must be dreadful to have been born with a hunchback like that," Luis said. "But he's a real artist and he really knows his music."

"Yes, I could see that."

Cornélie came over to us. She took my arm.

"Aren't you going to dance? You can't spend all evening just being the D.J."

I could feel myself blushing.

"My last train leaves at ten past nine," I said.

Cornélie whispered in my ear:

"We've got lots of time."

I thought I could detect, as well as her perfume, a faint whiff of the sickly smell I had noticed in the stables.

"Take that record off, will you, and put something nicer on," she said to Luis.

"Françoise Hardy?"

"No, Bobby Solo."

"*Se piangi, se ridi*?"

"Yes."

Cornélie led me to the other side of the room and put her arms around my neck. I placed my hands on her waist.

*

My hair had become a matter of vital importance to me. Most of the boys who went to the dances sported a Beatle cut; Luis did too, having got over his quiff-and-Brylcreem phase. In my case, it was more difficult. The problem was that because I had curly hair, it tended to go all frizzy, a look I didn't like at all. When I went to San Sebastián, I would investigate not only the record shops, but the barber's shops too, hoping to find a barber who could give me a modern hairstyle.

On one of those occasions, I met my mother in the square where I caught the bus back to our village. She had just been visiting José Francisco, and immediately started talking about him. My cousin's behaviour at the residential school was exactly as it had been at home. He would gather together all the shoes from all the bedrooms and tie them up – "Fasten! Fasten!" – sometimes tying more than ten pairs together at a time. The most worrying thing, though, was his tendency to self-harm. Sometimes, he would have terrible rages, and the nurses would have to lock him up in a padded room.

The river that ran parallel to the road was usually pretty filthy because of the effluent from the paper mills. On that day, as I could see from the bus window, the waters were covered with a layer of white foam. My mother looked out at the foam and started softly reciting a poem: "Our lives are rivers that flow down to the sea, to death." The only poem I had heard her recite until then was a prayer that she said every night before going to bed. "It is not the heaven you promised me, my God, that moves me to love you . . ." and somewhat alarmed by her mood, I did not dare bring up the subject going round and round in my head. Apart from getting a fashionable hairstyle, I wanted a new record player. The Telefunken we owned was very old and the sound was poor.

A week later, while we were having supper, my mother gave more details about José Francisco. He was not at all well. The doctors at the residential home didn't know quite what was wrong, but he was very poorly, so weak he could barely stand.

"And he's so pale," she said. "He doesn't seem to be in pain, but he looks dreadful."

"Is he going to die?" my youngest brother asked.

"I think so," answered my older brother. He sometimes went with my mother to visit José Francisco and was familiar with the situation.

"Please, don't talk like that," my mother said.

"You know I always speak my mind," my older brother said.

As usually happened whenever the subject of José Francisco came up, my father mentioned Miguel. He thought they were connected in some way.

"Miguel isn't normal either. Everyone knows that. How long did he spend in the insane asylum? Almost six months, wasn't it?" he said. "Who knows, without the treatment they gave him, he might never have recovered. What did they call what they did to him? I know it involved putting a sort of helmet on his head."

"Electroshock therapy," my older brother said, and as soon as those words were out of his mouth, my aunt suddenly appeared. She knocked twice on the door and came into the kitchen.

"I've just had a telephone call," she told my mother. "José Francisco's condition has worsened. They've taken him to hospital."

Electroshock therapy. The expression entered my mind and joined the new lexicon I had begun to build with words like Antoine, *pilule*, Monoprix, etc. I thought that if I learned to play the guitar and formed a band, that is what I would call it. I could even imagine the photograph: four boys, three on guitar and one on drums, and on the bass drum that word: Electroshock.

The following morning, I went to see Miguel in his workshop. I wanted to talk to him about the record player and ask if he had a newer one, but he wasn't there. I soon found him. He was in the restaurant kitchen, along with Estepani and about ten men; Estepani was standing, stirring the pots; Miguel was leaning against a pillar. His face was very red, as it had been during that San Juan lunch. His voice sounded dull and flat, though.

"What did we gain by sending José Francisco to Madrid?" he asked. José Francisco's internment had really shaken him.

All the customers were eating the same meal – fried eggs and bacon with tomato sauce. They weren't looking at Miguel.

"He spent two months in Madrid surrounded by strangers, and all the boy learned was that one word 'fasten'. What was the point?"

The chorus, the customers, could have said:

"And what's the point of you getting so upset about it, Miguel? You can't turn back the sun the way you can the hands of a clock. There's no returning to the past. Fate has spoken, and you have to accept that."

But no-one said anything. The chorus, the ten men sitting round the table, continued eating their bread, bacon, tomato sauce and fried eggs in silence.

"Think of the hours that boy spent with me in my workshop," Miguel said. "Hours and hours," he said in answer to his own question. "And how often did he try to attack me or harm himself? Never."

This looked as though it was set to be a long monologue. I withdrew discreetly.

The new names no longer plunged into my mind like the hazelnuts sucked down by the waters of the weir, but like the detritus swept along in a landslide. Now, the names came not only from *Fans* magazine or from radio and television programmes. Some, like Katia, Candy, Maribel, Juana, Bárbara and Cornélie, came directly from reality. They were the names of some of the girls who went to the dances. Many of them had fair hair and dark complexions. When they danced – when it was the moment for "*Se piangi, se ridi*" or other slow numbers – each would put her arms around her partner's neck. In Cornélie's case, she would take off her glasses and rest her head on my shoulder.

A new boy started coming to the dances, Aguiriano. Like Vergara and López, he belonged to the school's cross-country team, and he soon became my travelling companion on the train back home. He came from a village even smaller than mine.

"You're lucky. You get to dance a lot and with girls who like to slow-dance too," he said to me one Sunday night, on our way to the station. "I have a terrible time. Vergara can't get any of the girls to dance with me, and I have to spend the whole evening manning the record player. It's a real drag. And now that Adrián doesn't come any more, I'm going crazy with all those records to choose from. I never know what to put on."

He was a tall, gangly youth, who wore his hair unfashionably short, like the soldiers. His clothes weren't exactly trendy either.

He shrugged.

"It's because of my acne," he said. "I've tried all kinds of creams, but none of them works."

"Do you fancy one of the girls, then?"

"Oh, all of them," he said at once.

He gave detailed descriptions of Katia, Candy, Maribel, Juana, Bárbara, Cornélie and all the other girls, as if he had compiled a dossier on each of them. When it came to Cornélie – we were on the train by then – I realised I was feeling tense. Suddenly, I really cared what Aguiriano thought. Judging from his descriptions of the other girls, he obviously didn't waste his time when standing by the record player. His descriptions were spot on.

"Now Cornélie may not look it, because of those strange glasses of hers, but if you ignore them, she's actually the prettiest of the lot. I've had a good look at her when she takes her glasses off, and she's really pretty. And she may be small, but she has a really athletic body."

"Yes, you're right, she has."

"I don't mean she's muscular, not at all. Whereas Maribel, for example, has really big, bulging calves. Not Cornélie though."

"Yes, I see what you mean."

Aguiriano said something else, but we went into a tunnel at that point and the clatter of the wheels drowned out his voice. I thought, however, that it had something to do with me.

"What did you say?"

"That you're lucky there too. Cornélie is always after you to dance with her. She pretends she's not sometimes and flirts with López, but only to make you jealous."

"You don't miss a thing, do you?" I said, laughing. I was delighted.

"Well, I need to do something to pass the time! It's pretty dull spending four hours standing next to the record player."

Aguiriano got off the train two stations before me. I was sorry to say goodbye to him.

"And now it's nearly two miles to my house!" he sighed.

"Cheer up," I said. I felt euphoric and infinitely superior to poor Aguiriano, who couldn't attract a single girl.

"I don't mind really. I usually run all the way home as part of my training."

"How long does it take you?"

"Twelve and half minutes, more or less. But that's because I'm wearing street clothes and ordinary shoes. Otherwise, I'd do it in under twelve minutes."

The train had stopped. The moment he stepped onto the platform, Aguiriano broke into a run.

The Sunday dances had me hypnotised. Katia, Bárbara, Cornélie, Elvis Presley, the Beatles, Antoine, Bobby Solo, Françoise Hardy . . . The names sparkled like bits of glass gleaming in the water.

At home, on the other hand, the sole topic of conversation was José Francisco. My mother went to visit him every day. Then, at night, she would give us the latest news from the hospital. We knew now what was happening to him – that he had swallowed nails and bits of metal. We knew, too – or came to know – that the internal bleeding would not stop and there was no way they could operate. Suddenly, in the first week of August, my mother lost all hope and stopped talking about him. My older brother grew increasingly sombre and also stopped talking about him. My father went to the hospital. My aunt and uncle closed the restaurant. The following Saturday, August 12, the lines from the poem I heard my mother recite on the bus became reality: "Our lives are rivers that flow down to the sea, to death."

A lot of people went to the funeral. From where I was sitting in the second row of pews, to the right of the altar, I watched the people in the front row to see who was crying and who was not. My aunt wasn't crying, my uncle was; my mother was crying, my father wasn't; my older brother wasn't crying, my younger brother was; Miguel wasn't crying, although he sat throughout the service with his head bowed and his eyes closed. At one point, the priest made that comment about how we would never forget José Francisco's smile.

A single candle stood on the altar, and its flame flickered and grew still, bent and then straightened, then bent again. Higher up, the saints and virgins on the retable gazed languidly heavenwards. Still higher, at the top of the retable was a white plaster dove, its body pierced by golden rays. The image of Cornélie came into my mind. Because of her glasses, no-one would think she was the prettiest girl at the dances, but Aguiriano was right, she was much prettier than she seemed at first sight. And it was true, too, that she liked to stay close to me.

The cemetery was at the top of a hill, and the funeral cortège began heading up the slope at the same slow, grave pace as the tolling bell. Once there, when we were about to enter the graveyard, we cousins were called upon to carry the coffin on our shoulders. I was at the back, behind my older brother and alongside Didi. Shortly afterwards, all the family, those who used to gather together to celebrate the feast of San Juan and many more, formed a circle round the dug grave, and the priest began to say the prayer for the dead. I again watched to see who was crying and who was not: my uncle was; my aunt was; my mother was; my father wasn't; Miguel was. And even more surprising, Didi and my older brother were both crying too. As for my younger brother, he did something very odd indeed: he jumped down into the grave, from which he was immediately removed.

There was a scrapyard not far from the cemetery, and we began to hear a loud clanging, like the sound of a hammer striking an anvil, ruining the peaceful atmosphere created by the church bell. The priest frowned and fell silent for a moment, but the noise only grew louder, and he hurriedly finished the prayer. My aunt and my uncle each picked up a handful of earth, kissed it and threw it onto the coffin. The rest of us did the same. The gravediggers approached then and began filling in the grave.

Everyone went down the hill to the restaurant, and I went with them, but, first, I stopped off at my house to phone Luis and ask him for Cornélie's number.

"About time too," he said when I told him why I was phoning. "You've finally cottoned on!"

"What do you mean?"

He said exactly what Aguiriano had said to me in the train, as if they had come to an agreement on the matter.

"You might not think so, because of her glasses, but she's the prettiest girl at the dances."

Luis's words galvanised my whole body, and the tingling feeling grew still more intense when I made the second call and heard Cornélie say at the other end:

"I thought you would never phone."

Her accent was more marked than usual, as if she had been speaking French up until the moment before I called. Her father, I remembered, was the French consul.

"Where shall we meet?" I asked.

"Wouldn't you like to meet Mademoiselle?"

I didn't know what she was talking about.

"I'll give you a clue," Cornélie said. "She has a white star on her forehead."

"You mean the horse?"

I remembered the scene I had watched so often from the station platform: a girl going over the jumps on a horse with a white star on its forehead.

"So you're the horse-rider."

"Right. And you're the boy who used to look at me, the student who came by train from his village," she said and giggled. "Fortunately Luis studies at Colegio La Salle too. Otherwise, I would never have got to meet you."

"I'm surprised."

"I'm not surprised you're surprised." And she laughed again.

"I have to go now," I told her. "We've been at a funeral. A cousin of mine died in really tragic circumstances."

"Really?"

"Yes, I'll tell you about it later."

I felt relieved. One of the problems with Cornélie is that I didn't

147

know what to talk to her about. José Francisco's death would help on our first date.

The people who had walked down from the cemetery were all gathered in the dining room and kitchen of my aunt and uncle's restaurant. I wanted to sit next to Didi, but he was sitting at the kitchen table between Miguel and my older brother, drinking soup and listening to the priest, who was trying to explain God's behaviour to all those present: why did He allow Evil to exist, why did He allow a life like the one José Francisco had led, why did He allow such a death or indeed any death? As usual, the chorus did not respond. They continued drinking their soup, their eyes fixed on their white soup bowls.

I left the restaurant, intending to go home again, but I met my mother and my aunt standing by the shrine.

"Have you had your soup?" my aunt asked.

I told her I hadn't, and she took my arm.

"We're going to have ours now. Come with us."

We made our way slowly back to the restaurant.

We went into the kitchen. The priest had stopped speaking and, like everyone else at the table, seemed to be concentrating on his plate of beef stew with peppers and eggs. Before I sat down, I bent over to speak to my mother.

"I have to go to San Sebastián tomorrow."

"In the morning or the afternoon?"

"In the afternoon."

She nodded and handed me the bowl of soup my aunt had brought over.

THE MAN AND THE ECHO

The man asks the chorus: "Would you say that this young fellow, indifferent to the slow agony and subsequent death of José Francisco, had a heart of stone? I don't think so. At that point in his life, at seventeen, he was following the dictates of Eros and responding to the primordial impulse that had been lying dormant until then in his body. Was

148

it perhaps a victory over Thanatos? Life must go on, that is the law. One generation follows another. Indifference, which is part and parcel of being young, is essential to that process. What should he do? Let himself be weighed down by José Francisco's death? But why grant Death such power?"

The man asks this over and over, but the chorus does not respond.

AGUIRIANO
(A MEMORY)

The four cross-country runners from Colegio La Salle went out training together. They would set off towards Loyola train station, down streets and along the main road and, from there – crossing a bridge and skirting round the barracks – they would come to some allotments. Then, after following a path by the river which led, eventually, to some bare, marshy land near the Escuela Universitaria de Guipúzcoa, they would change direction and head back across country to their point of departure, the small house in the school grounds. A total distance of about four miles.

Training took place in the autumn and winter months. Four days a week, Monday, Tuesday, Wednesday and Thursday, they would be allowed to miss their afternoon classes, French, Spanish literature and other such secondary subjects, and become "harriers", but only until March 21, once the Junior Championship in Guipúzcoa had taken place. This signalled the end of the season, and they would then go back to being normal students. Their names were López, Ganuza, Leblanc and Vergara.

Their trainer was Santiago Oroz, or Don Santiago, who had been the gym teacher at the school throughout the post-war years. When the runners set off, he would follow them with his binoculars from the balcony of the house in the school grounds and, if someone happened to be with him – the Prefect, José María, or Don Ramón, the priest who said Mass in the chapel – he would provide a commentary, as if he were a radio commentator.

"Vergara's in the lead, followed by Leblanc and Ganuza, with

López bringing up the rear. But López has put on a spurt now and has taken the lead from Vergara. Come on, López!"

He was mad about cross-country running and about all long-distance races – 1,500 metres, 5,000 metres, marathons – and his dream, which he even included in his prayers, was to discover an athlete like Paavo Nurmi, Alain Mimoun or Emil Zátopek, to have God place a similar prodigy in his hands before he died, and to be able to read in *El Diario Vasco* or *La Voz de España* something similar to what Emil Zátopek was quoted as saying in a Prague newspaper: "I owe an enormous amount to the trainer I had at school. I think of him every time I win a race."

On many afternoons, while his wife was listening to the latest radio serial, he would sit in his armchair and imagine himself at school again, alongside Prefect José María and Don Ramón, excitedly following the runners doing their training.

"That new boy can really move! He makes López and the others look like real slowcoaches. He's a locomotive! A new Zátopek!"

He would close his eyes and conjure up these chimerical figures: the new runner powering along the muddy path by the river, López thirty yards behind him, Vergara and Leblanc perhaps fifty yards behind, and Ganuza, poor Ganuza, who hadn't even made it into the top sixty in the Junior Championship, was still lost in the allotments somewhere. Sometimes, when he managed to prolong his fantasy, the images in his mind altered, and he would see himself running, he, Santiago de Oroz, cross-country champion of Navarra in 1934 and 1935, Spanish champion in 1936, just months before the start of the Civil War. And then, during the war – and although he would rather not remember what happened, he often did – the mortar exploding, leaving a piece of metal in his head, the operation at the Military Hospital, and, finally, his return to the land of the living, but with a piece of platinum permanently lodged in the side of his head.

"You seem miles away. Are you alright?"

This was his wife's perennial question whenever she found him sitting daydreaming in his armchair, eyes closed. She was twelve years older than him and had been his nurse in the Military Hospital before she became his wife, but as often happens with couples who meet in time of war, they were not a perfect match. They had different tastes, different interests and very different temperaments. Fortunately – that word "fortunately" frightened him sometimes – she had grown quite frail with age and was quite content to listen to radio serials and repeat that same question: "You seem miles away. Are you alright?"

"Daydreams hurt no-one," he would say, and that was enough for his wife to leave him alone.

And yet he, too, was affected by time. He wasn't frail and had all his wits about him, but he was a failure. He found it hard to accept that word, "failure", but why deny the truth? And the truth was that, despite having been the gym teacher at La Salle for more than thirty years, he hadn't discovered a single truly exceptional runner, no human locomotive à la Zátopek, or even anyone to compare with such Spanish champions as Antonio Amorós, Fernando Aguilar or Mariano Haro. Besides, things would become even more difficult in the future, because now there were some marvellous runners from Africa, athletes like Abebe Bikila or Mamo Wolde, who seemed to come from another planet, who flew over the muddy track and crossed the finishing line without so much as a speck of mud on them. They were birds, butterflies. He had seen Abebe Bikila run in the Zarautz marathon, had followed him for the entire distance in the organisers' convertible car, feeling a mixture of joy and sadness, an urge both to laugh and to weep. Bikila ran so beautifully, keeping his arms close to his chest, and taking long, straight, regular strides, long, long, long strides, so utterly different from the other runners! In Zarautz, he came in five minutes ahead of his nearest rival, the Spanish champion, Carlos Pérez. And Carlos Pérez was certainly not your average runner; his record in the marathon was 2:22:45. After seeing Bikila run, Don Santiago had returned home feeling deeply troubled, unable to talk to anyone, overwhelmed by emotion.

"I don't know why you go and watch these races. They don't do you any good," his wife said when she saw him sitting in his armchair, eyes closed.

"I thank God for having given me the chance to see Abebe Bikila run," he answered.

There was a long gallery at the school that gave onto the recreation area. Prefect José María used to walk from one end to the other during the morning break, in order, he said, "to take the air" and to perform three other tasks: first, to keep an eye on those who had been kept in as punishment and make sure they were doing the work they had been set; second, to observe those playing sport down below and see if anyone showed unusual talent; third, to check in the newspaper for any reports of handball matches, especially those involving his favourite handball team, Salleko.

He was a heavily built man, and the older students called him "Hippo", short for "hippopotamus". He had a big head of curly hair, moist green eyes and creamy white skin.

In his welcoming speech, he would tell the new students: "The first word you should learn in this school is 'Salleko'. Along with Madrid Athletic and Granollers, they're the best handball team in Spain! Two years ago, we came second in the League. Last year, we were third."

The team was very dear to his heart, because they spread the name of the school throughout Spain and because he had personally discovered some of the star players when they were still only adolescents, having spotted them from the gallery during break-time in the recreation area.

"Perhaps one of you will turn out to be a really good player and make us league champions."

The new students would listen, smiling and slightly embarrassed.

When he reached the end of his speech, he would speak more gravely.

"Lastly, one very important thing. The matter of my name. Everyone here calls me 'Hippo', which is fine. I even rather like it, but . . ."

He left that "but" hanging for a few seconds.

". . . don't let me hear *you* using it. If I'm within earshot, refer to me either as 'Prefect' or as 'Brother José María'. Do you understand?"

All the new students, without exception, nodded.

Once a week, Don Santiago and the Prefect would patrol the gallery together, along with Don Ramón the priest, and would use this time to review the sporting situation. In January 1968, during their first conversation after the Christmas holidays, the future looked rather grim. Salleko was having a very erratic season and was only fifth in the League; as for football, Real Sociedad had improved slightly after a disastrous start – when they were beaten 9–1 by Real Madrid – drawing with Barcelona in Camp Nou, but they were still very low down the table. And there were no new developments in the hand pelota stakes, for it seemed certain that the final would be between Atano X and Azkarate.

The talk shifted from professional sport to amateur, and they began discussing cross-country running.

"What are we going to do about this year's Junior Championship, Don Santiago?" the Prefect said. "It's only a couple of months away."

He leaned on the balustrade, looking down at the recreation area.

About fifty students were playing football. Another ten were on the pelota court. The others, scattered around the recreation area, were eating their break-time sandwich. It appeared, at least at first sight, that no-one was smoking.

"I'm feeling a bit depressed about it really," Don Santiago said. He, too, had gone over to the balustrade and was gazing down at the recreation area, without looking at anything or anyone in particular.

"What's wrong, Don Santiago? Do you think the Jesuits are going to win?"

"Certainly not!" Don Santiago exclaimed. "They won't even make the first ten."

"Won't ours either?"

"López might, but I'm not sure. He's been very slack lately, almost as slow as Ganuza."

"I think our cross-country team needs some new blood," the Prefect said, putting his arm around Don Santiago's shoulder. He was smiling broadly.

"Who did you have in mind, José María?"

The Prefect pointed to one of the students playing football.

"Aguiriano. The long-legged boy in the navy-blue jersey."

Don Santiago studied him closely. The boy cut rather a gawky figure, but he had a good, long stride. And he was strong too.

"He runs from the station to school every day," the Prefect told him. "He arrives five minutes ahead of the students who come on the train. He's a good lad. From a village too, not from the city, like López and the other rich kids. Why not put him in the team, Don Santiago?"

"He's not exactly a graceful mover, José María."

The Prefect again put his arm about his shoulder.

"Remember Zátopek. He was the ugliest runner in the history of athletics, and yet he was one of the best ever. People called him "the Czech locomotive"."

Don Santiago took another look at Aguiriano.

"He's certainly strong."

"Why not give him a go?"

"Alright, I will."

They went down into the recreation area to talk to Aguiriano.

Once the runners reached the station and turned to the left, they found themselves at the rear of the barracks, where they were out of range of Don Santiago's binoculars, and all of them – López, Leblanc, Vergara and Ganuza – would then take the opportunity to have a rest. They would stop running and walk instead, until, at the end of a long wall, they again came within range of the binoculars.

When they reached that point on Aguiriano's first training day, he was surprised to find that his companions had stopped running. He looked back, ran round in circles a few times, then, not knowing what else to do, continued on. López shouted to him:

"Where are you going? Stop!"

The rest of the group began shouting at him. Was he stupid or something? What was he doing, going off on his own like that?

Aguiriano hesitated. He disliked any kind of cheating and couldn't understand their attitude. Besides, it frightened him. If Don Santiago found out and reported back to Hippo, the Prefect would be terribly angry. And he didn't want that. Hippo was very good to the poorer students from the villages. On the other hand, he didn't want to fall out with his fellow runners, certainly not on the first day.

They began to run slowly. Aguiriano and Ganuza went ahead, with Vergara, López and Leblanc about five yards behind.

Vergara spoke loudly enough for them all to hear.

"It's our fault. We didn't explain the rules. That's why he didn't understand what was going on."

"Rules? That's the first I've heard of any rules," Ganuza said. "I thought we were just skiving."

Vergara told him to be quiet and ran to catch up with Aguiriano.

"Those are our rules, you see. Up until the first of March, we take it easy and keep the training as light as possible. We have a bit of a rest when we reach the barracks, then take it in turns to be the leader . . ."

"If we do it often enough, Plati thinks we really are putting our all into it. An optical illusion," Ganuza said.

This was the first time Aguiriano had heard Don Santiago's nickname, "Plati". It wasn't particularly ugly, but he knew he would never use it. The thought of that piece of platinum lodged in Don Santiago's head set his teeth on edge.

They left the wall behind them and headed down the path by the allotments. A hundred yards further on, they would be back in full sight of the binoculars. They continued jogging slowly along, almost at walking pace.

"So no overdoing it until the first of March, Aguiriano," Vergara said. "We all stick together, right? From then on, though, and up until the championship, it'll be full steam ahead and every man for himself."

"You talk too much, Vergara," López said from behind. He seemed annoyed.

"He's worried," Vergara whispered to Aguiriano. "Up until now, he's been the best in the team, but now that you've joined, he's feeling a bit nervous."

"The day you beat López, I'll be a happy man," Ganuza said. "He's always making fun of me. Do you know what he calls me?"

Aguiriano shook his head. He found his companions frankly alarming.

"He calls me 'Sixty-seven'. Good morning, Sixty-seven, Good afternoon, Sixty-seven. Because that's where I came in last year's championship."

"Don't you two get on?" Aguiriano asked.

Ganuza lowered his voice: "No, not really."

"Don't exaggerate. It's not that bad," Vergara said. "We're all part of the La Salle team."

"Binoculars on the horizon!" Leblanc shouted, and they all speeded up.

February was cold and rainy, and the training sessions were getting harder. The five runners would return to school covered in mud and always in the same order: López first, Aguiriano second, then, some way behind, Vergara, Leblanc and Ganuza. They were working as a team, respecting the pact they had made – stopping when they reached the rear of the barracks and taking it in turns to be the leader over the last mile or so – and they were all making an effort to create a positive atmosphere, even López; one day, he brought along some liniment and shared it with them all; on another, he brought a camera to take a picture of the team.

Aguiriano felt he was steadily improving. He really enjoyed being a cross-country runner, although he did sometimes feel a little awkward, especially in the showers, when López and the others stripped off outside the cubicles, and he couldn't help seeing their bottoms and their private parts; however, Leblanc – the most silent among them, but also the most sympathetic – told him:

"No need to be embarrassed, Aguiriano, this is normal among sportsmen. You wouldn't expect us to get showered fully dressed, would you?"

Vergara was also friendly, possibly the friendliest of them all, and one day he took Aguiriano to one of the Sunday dances and introduced him to lots of pretty girls. But there was something else too, something that helped him feel at ease in the cross-country running team. During their training runs, when they were heading towards the barracks, or along the muddy path by the river, with López in front and him behind, he had the feeling that he could easily, almost effortlessly, overtake him. Could he be the best runner in school? A little voice in his head was telling him that he was.

Towards the end of February, there was heavy snow, and a new idea alighted imperceptibly in his mind, like another snowflake. López was good and last year had come eighth in the championship. If he was better than López, how far could he go? He once asked Vergara about this, as discreetly as he could:

"What goal do you think I should set myself?"

"I think you should always set yourself the highest goal possible," Vergara said.

The students who travelled on the train used to make fun of him because of his habit of running from the station to school, but then they weren't sportsmen, they were smokers, people whose vice had been punished more than once by Hippo; and yet, despite that, he did make friends with one student called "Lawrence", who had an incredible memory for sporting records. After Aguiriano joined the cross-country team, Lawrence would sometimes sit next to him and fire questions at him as if he were a quizmaster:

"What was Alain Mimoun's winning time in the Melbourne marathon?"

Aguiriano would happily join in and give the answers, although these were usually wrong. And yet he always got Zátopek's times right. Zátopek was his idol.

"What was Zátopek's best time over ten thousand metres?"

"Twenty-eight minutes, fifty-four point two seconds!"

Lawrence always used to say "winning time" or "best time", and Aguiriano adopted these terms too.

The second day of March was a Wednesday, colder even than in February, and, at first, Don Santiago watched from inside the house; however, five minutes later, he was out on the balcony, oblivious to the cold, amazed at what he was seeing through his binoculars: Aguiriano was in the lead as they ran along the icy bank of the river, a good ten yards ahead of López, fifteen yards ahead of Vergara and Leblanc and forty or fifty yards ahead of poor Ganuza. What Aguiriano lacked in style, he made up for in speed.

"Come on! Come on!" Don Santiago shouted, his breath forming a cloud in the air. As if he had heard these words, Aguiriano accelerated and increased his lead still further.

Don Santiago was reluctant to go home. He would have liked to stay on at school until late and share his thoughts about the upcoming championship in the light of that last training session and the new hierarchy in the team; however, his preferred companion, the Prefect, was away on retreat, and so he had to take his ideas to bed with him. As he lay dozing in the darkness of his bedroom, he imagined Aguiriano running hard along the frozen river path, with the others being left ever further behind.

When the Prefect returned to school and came to watch the runners doing their training, Don Santiago received him with a broad smile on his face.

"You look very pleased with yourself, Don Santiago," the Prefect said. "Had some good news?"

"You'll see for yourself in a moment, José María."

They waited until the five runners had covered the first part of the course, from the school to the station and from the station to the barracks. Then, when they reached the allotments, Don Santiago picked up his binoculars and began to follow them.

"Take a look, José María," he said after a while, handing him the binoculars.

"Our village boy can certainly run!" the Prefect said. "What an improvement! He's showing López a clean pair of heels, alright."

"Keep watching, José María, keep watching."

The runners had reached the path along by the river.

"If I wasn't seeing it with my own eyes, I wouldn't believe it. He's put on a spurt now and is even further ahead. There's more than ten yards between him and López," the Prefect said.

"La Salle has found its runner, José María!" Don Santiago cried. "All thanks to you."

He was filled with the same emotion he had felt on the day he watched Abebe Bikila run, a mixture of laughter and tears. Reality and dream were now running along the same track.

That night, back at home, his wife looked at him very hard and said:

"Santi, tell me honestly: have you started drinking again?"

"No, I haven't. I'm just happy, that's all."

"If you *have* started drinking, that's your lookout. Don't forget you've got a piece of platinum in your head. Taking to drink again is the worst thing you could do."

The nightmare also had its place on the track, but no matter. In his own way, *he* was a locomotive too. Like Zátopek and like Aguiriano.

Don Santiago could not stop talking about Aguiriano, whether walking up and down the gallery with Don Ramón, in the chapel after Mass, or at meetings with the other teachers. La Salle finally had a runner who could well become junior champion of Guipúzcoa: Aguiriano.

He went to see the head teacher.

"We've had an outstanding handball team for some years," he said, "but from now on, we're going to be big in athletics too."

The head teacher offered to help. They would organise a bus for those students and teachers who wished to go to the championship and cheer on Aguiriano.

"He already has a lot of fans, I believe," he said. "I hear them urging him on during the training sessions."

It was true. Some teachers allowed their students to skip the last class in the afternoon so that they could go and watch the runners training. At the end of the four-mile circuit – with Aguiriano a long way out in front, followed by López and Vergara, and, much later, by Leblanc and Ganuza – his fellow students would greet him with genuine fervour.

On March 14, a week before the race, all the team members apart from Aguiriano appeared at the door of the Prefect's office.

"Take a seat," he said when he saw them.

They obeyed and sat down, eyes fixed on the floor.

"What's going on?" the Prefect asked, but he already knew. He knew the moment he saw them. Suddenly, everything fitted, and the variables of the equation became clear.

"It was all a joke," Vergara said, without looking up. "We were just having him on."

The Prefect said nothing. He wanted a full explanation.

"We didn't mean any harm," Vergara went on. "Aguiriano seemed such an innocent and took the sport so seriously. We decided to play a trick on him and let him win."

"He's not really that good," Leblanc said. "About my level really."

Vergara looked up, but still without meeting the Prefect's eye.

"We wanted to stop, but, by then, it was too late. Aguiriano is convinced now that he's a great runner."

López pulled a sad face.

"We didn't set out to do it," he said. "It happened almost by accident."

This was the only way of avoiding punishment, by alleging that there had been no evil intent, that it had all been a joke. If they lost points for bad behaviour, they wouldn't be allowed back to school for a month.

The Prefect asked them about the running times. Aguiriano had lopped a whole minute off the time they normally took to complete the circuit. That was what had fooled him.

"Where does that minute come from?" he asked.

"Well, before, we always used to take a rest and walk the part of the circuit that goes behind the barracks. That's what makes the difference," answered Vergara.

"We weren't actually walking," Leblanc said, correcting him. "We were just running a bit more slowly."

Ganuza decided to intervene.

"That's the thing, you see – what started out as a joke somehow took on its own momentum."

The Prefect felt for the crucifix he usually kept in the pocket of his cassock. He had his right hand pressed to his forehead, shading his eyes. Lord, here I am again, he thought, bending over the desk. As he had just returned from a retreat, that "again" could have been merely descriptive, but it was more like a sigh, a groan.

He squeezed the wooden cross until it dug into his hand.

"Excuse me, Brother José María, but I have to go to the toilet," Ganuza said, getting up, then immediately sitting down again.

The office was filled with a whitish light. The Prefect was looking at the four runners without actually seeing them. The voice he could hear inside him demanded all his attention. It was his own voice, but it sounded odd to him, as if it were speaking in a vacuum: "This is what we're going to do. When the race starts, the four of you set off at a fast pace, taking Aguiriano with you. One or two hundred yards in, when you reach the first muddy bit or the first obstacle, you, Vergara, trip him up from behind, so that he falls over. Then, when he's on the ground, you all pile on top of him so that he can't move. If he does get up and continue running, you had better start looking for another school. He has to lose the race, you understand, but it has to be by accident."

The hand clutching the cross still hurt.

"And what if we break his leg?" he heard a voice ask. The question set the whitish light in the room vibrating.

He thought the question had come from Ganuza, and could not help but smile. It was absurd for Ganuza to ask such a thing. He would get left behind as soon as the race began, with no chance of stopping Aguiriano.

"Better a broken leg than have the school exposed to ridicule," another voice said. The Prefect thought it was the voice of the spiritual director of the retreat he had just been on. "That would shame everyone in the school, especially Don Santiago."

The whitish light in the office suddenly vanished, and he could see the four boys clearly. Each of them was looking at a different spot: Vergara at the floor, as he had been from the start; López at the ceiling; Leblanc at the window; Ganuza at the calendar on the wall. He took the crucifix out of his pocket and shifted it from hand to hand. He was weighing up the idea that had just occurred to him.

"What nonsense," he told himself.

Free from that initial dazzle, he could think properly again. The idea of tripping up Aguiriano made no sense at all. More than a hundred runners took part in the junior section of the championship, and, with all those other runners jockeying for position, it would be very hard for Vergara, López and Aguiriano to remain together during the first hundred or two hundred yards. Besides, what would the school gain from it? Because, of course, the interests of the school came first. If they tripped Aguiriano up, he wouldn't be the only one to fall – lots of other runners would fall too, and later everyone would learn that it had been the fault of the La Salle students. And if anyone found out it had been deliberate, then the federation would intervene. To make matters worse, López and Vergara were the sons of industrialists, and if the news got out, their fathers would demand an explanation from the head teacher, a weak man, who would be incapable of doing a decent job of defending La Salle.

He looked at the boys. His eyes felt bleary, as if he had just woken up.

"On your feet," he said, putting the crucifix down on the desk. He got to his feet as well and walked to the door of his office.

The four boys all reacted differently. Vergara stood up at once and went over to the door, where the Prefect was standing. López got up too, but did not move. Leblanc and Ganuza stayed seated.

The Prefect opened the door.

"Line up here, all four of you," he said and drew an imaginary line in the air.

Vergara and López were quick to obey. Then Leblanc joined them. Ganuza remained on his chair, head bowed.

"Ganuza, come here!" the Prefect said. Ganuza finally obeyed and went and stood next to the others.

Ganuza received the first slap. Leblanc the second. Vergara the third. The fourth, given to López, was the hardest.

"Now get out of here!" he told them, and they trooped out of the room, each with his hand pressed to his cheek. Ganuza was crying.

When he was left alone, the Prefect began pacing back and forth, from the door to the window, from the window to the door, ten paces there and ten paces back. Outside, the sky was grey and over-cast; near Loyola station, the railway lines glinted in the dull light; the tiles on the barracks roof were an orange colour. Beyond that, the sky and the mist mingled to form a seamless curtain. The hills were invisible.

He spent a long time pacing his office. At one point, he picked up the crucifix and put it back in his pocket.

He heard a metallic whistle and went over to the window. Don Santiago was walking along the gravel path to the pelota court, followed by a line of thirty or more new students aged thirteen or fourteen. In two years' time, possibly sooner, they would walk along that same path, not in an orderly line, but throwing pebbles and hurling insults at each other and calling Don Santiago "Plati".

They called Don Santiago Plati and him Hippo, but it wasn't the same thing. In Don Santiago's case, it was a superficial matter, a way of showing their disdain for him. That was clear, even to the students themselves. However, those who called him Hippo would not be able to say – certain things took years to understand – to what extent they were driven by hatred or love or fear. And in a way, that was normal. There is a place in the heart, a nucleus, where all our feelings are jumbled up together. More than that: all our feelings came from that same original mix, and hate, love and fear were, originally, all the same, as were the bird and the reptile. How odd: the snake and the swallow, the swallow and the snake, were completely interchangeable, as were hate, love and fear.

He sat down at his desk. He felt a headache coming on, a pulsing in his temples. His green eyes grew wet with tears.

He felt like protesting to God. Why now, just when he had returned from retreat? Why shatter the peace he had found there?

He could not hold back his tears then, and he covered his face with his hands.

"Don Santiago, we were wrong about Aguiriano. I know this will be a bitter blow to you, but I have to tell you the truth."

That is what he would say to him when he next saw him. Then he would wait ten seconds before going on, so that Don Santiago's heart had time to assimilate those first few icy drops.

"I'm entirely to blame, Don Santiago. I was the one who suggested Aguiriano in the first place. I was the one who mentioned Zátopek.

You were deceived too, but that's because they tricked you. Do you know what they do during their training sessions, Don Santiago? Do you know what they've been doing up until now? The little reptiles stop running as soon as they're out of range of your binoculars. That way, it's impossible to calculate how long the run really takes. You'll just have to accept the fact that La Salle won't be taking part in the Guipúzcoa championship. I'll talk to the head teacher and tell him to cancel the school trip and the bus."

He shook his head angrily. No, these were misguided, childish thoughts. He would say nothing of the sort to Don Santiago. He wouldn't cancel anything. Things had gone too far. The federation would never understand. Nor would the parents' association. Besides, the bus company would demand a cancellation fee. And then there was the matter of the head teacher. He knew nothing about sport and distrusted all kinds of sporting competitions. He used to say: "*Mens sana in corpore sano*, yes, but what matters most is the mind." What he cared about was having the school do well in the Coca-Cola essay competition or win prizes from the Artists' Society of Guipúzcoa, and he was thrilled to have a champion in the school, Adrián, who also happened to be the biggest smoker in the school's entire history. If the championship went badly, if there was a scandal, Don José María could kiss goodbye to the money he had requested for refurbishing the handball and basketball courts. The head teacher would channel the money into some other activity. No, he would say nothing. Let whatever happened happen.

It was nearly half past eleven in the morning. He pressed the button on the wall of his office to sound the bell. Then he went down into the recreation area and walked over to the spot where López, Vergara and the others usually gathered. When they came down, he would call them over and, putting a finger to his lips, would say:

"Remember, not a word of this to anyone."

A couple of weeks ago, after the Thanksgiving supper at Mary Lore's house (she's the director of the C.B.S.), our youngest daughter wanted to go home as soon as possible to see if the raccoon had returned to the garden. She must have a sixth sense or something, because when we arrived at College Drive and went out onto the porch at the back, there were the raccoon's two yellow eyes. We hadn't seen him for months.

It's very cold here at the moment. Every morning it's minus seven, minus four or minus eight. Sometimes it snows, but not much. Perhaps it's hard for our raccoon to find food in these conditions, and perhaps he's come back to our house because of our daughters' subversive hearts, for they ignore all the warnings about not feeding wild animals and are always leaving biscuits for him next to the hut.

I had no such premonitions during supper, but the caramelised red peppers troubled my head – and not my stomach, as they do with many people – and I've spent two weeks writing about the memories they awoke in me, including memories of Adrián and those two rich kids from the cross-country team, López and Vergara. Do you ever hear from them? I haven't seen them since.

We went to Borders today and I happened upon a book of photographs entitled *The Way We Were*, published by the University of Toronto. The book tries to draw a comparison between the fate of the Canadian soldiers who fought in the Second World War, in particular those who took part in the Normandy invasion, and that of people nowadays or a few years ago. For example, there's a black-and-white photograph of the beach at Dieppe, taken in 1944: dozens of dead soldiers lying on the sand in postures no living being would ever adopt. Tanks on fire. Half-sunken landing craft marooned on the shore. Then, on the next page, a photograph of the same Dieppe beach, but taken in the 1980s: a family enjoying the sun, a couple sitting under a sunshade reading magazines, children building a sandcastle. In the sea, a group of young people playing in the waves. After leafing through the book, I thought: What we call "fate" is all a matter of timing. Everything depends on which thicker line crosses our thinner line. Of course, it's easy enough to accept that truth in Reno. It wouldn't be so easy if I was in Iraq or Afghanistan.

Since coming back from Borders, I've been reading Bruce Laxalt's poems. I learned at the Thanksgiving supper that he's very ill, and the text on the back cover confirms this. He says that in 2003, he was diagnosed with motor neurone disease. One of his poems, a love poem, is actually called "Diagnosis Day": ". . . Our eyes meet warily on an unbargained-for shore. In yours, I see the days after. You in mine the days before. And then, in each other's, the day itself, on which our futures will meet and part."

An anecdote to conclude my record of our visit to Borders. As I was looking at *The Way We Were*, I was approached by a beggar apparently taking refuge from the cold. He pointed to himself and said: "Vietnam, Mekong Delta." For some reason, I responded by giving him the thumbs-up. He reacted by giving me the thumbs-down and saying: "No, it was terrible. We lost!"

DECEMBER 15
MISSING DOG

I was walking down Washington Street after taking the girls to school, and I stopped to read a notice attached to the lamp posts. "Missing dog. His name is Chetos and he's eleven months old. He's a pit bull with a blue nose. He's very sweet and gentle. We miss him and want him back. He's wearing a red collar, with no chip. Please get in touch."

The notice affected me deeply. I know it was a banal event, and yet I couldn't stop thinking about it all day. *Missing dog. His name is Chetos . . .*

DECEMBER 17
CONVERSATION

At around ten in the morning, Dennis sent me a link, adding: "The spider is getting closer."

I clicked on the link and up came the online edition of the *Reno*

Gazette-Journal reporting another sexual assault. It had taken place near the university. The victim was a twenty-two-year-old female student. The attacker had forced her to get into his car and give him oral sex.

I went to Dennis's office. He told me Earle had been talking to the police chief on campus.

"They're really worried. The attacker seems to be a professional rapist."

I didn't understand what he meant by a "professional rapist".

"Apparently, he prepares carefully for these attacks," Dennis explained. "He obviously knows that to get his D.N.A. all that's needed is a single hair, and so he shaves his pubic region."

I didn't know what to say.

"Oh, and I have a message for you from Jeff," Dennis said, tapping at his keyboard. "I'm forwarding it to you now. He's asking you to send him a text in Basque so that he can set it in a particular font, Menhart, I think."

"That's right. I promised him I'd do that at the Thanksgiving supper."

"Just send him the text and that will be that," Dennis said. Then he looked out of the window and said in a different tone of voice: "In a way, Jeff is lucky. His whole life centres around fonts. They create a barrier between him and the world."

"We were thinking of spending the Christmas vacation in San Francisco," I said. "Perhaps I should tell Jeff. It would be good to see something other than the usual tourist sights."

Dennis put his hand to his chin.

"No, don't do that," he said at last. "Jeff wouldn't be a very good guide to the city. As you saw at Thanksgiving, he doesn't know how to behave around other people. Besides, he finds children annoying."

He looked up and smiled.

"So you're off to San Francisco. An excellent idea."

"How about you? Are you going anywhere?"

"Bob wants to go to Tonopah to visit a mine, and I'm tagging along."

"Sounds interesting," I said. "I bought a book about the history of boxing, and it mentions Tonopah as a place where Jack Dempsey fought when he was world champion. There must have been a lot of money in the town then."

"It's a military installation now. They don't live off gold and silver any more, but uranium and plutonium. It's a test base for bomber pilots."

He again changed the subject.

"Be careful on the drive to San Francisco. Crossing the Sierra Nevada at this time of year can be problematic. Be sure to check the weather forecast."

"We will," I said.

"And another thing," he went on. "When you're in San Francisco, don't leave the girls alone. There will be plenty of spiders around there too. There's a plague of them in America. Maybe that explains the success of *Lolita*."

DECEMBER 23
ON THE WAY TO SAN FRANCISCO

From Reno to San Francisco is over two hundred miles, fifty of which are through the Sierra Nevada, at an altitude of over six and a half thousand feet, regardless of whether you take the I-80, passing through Truckee, or the US-50, which skirts round Lake Tahoe, or travel by train. Potentially, it's the most dangerous stretch, because of the mists and sudden gusts of wind; then, as you approach the first Californian city, Sacramento, the journey becomes really pleasant.

Earle advised us not to bother with the train, because it came all the way from Chicago and was almost always delayed.

"I wouldn't recommend going via Lake Tahoe either. It's the prettiest route, but we're in December now, and the road is quite an empty one. Best take the I-80 – that way, if it snows, some truck is sure to come along to rescue you and your fragile little Ford."

The words "fragile" and "rescue" emerged from his lips with a certain emphasis.

In the days before the journey, I kept a close eye on the website showing the temperatures near Lake Tahoe. On December 20, the maximum was 5 degrees C, the minimum minus 9. The following day it was even colder, with a minimum of minus 12 degrees. On December 22, on the eve of our trip, the minimum was minus 7 and the maximum, at midday, was 6 degrees. The forecast for the 23rd wasn't too bad. They predicted a rise in temperatures and clear skies. There was only a 0.5 per cent possibility of precipitation in the form of rain or snow. I told Ángela.

"Reading Scott's diaries has marked you for life," she said. "We're going to San Francisco, you know, not the South Pole."

Ángela's sense of humour was becoming more and more like Earle's.

We left Reno at ten o'clock in the morning. As forecast, the skies were blue, and the thermometer in our house read 35 degrees F, about 2 degrees C. When we got onto the I-80, we sat back in our seats; the girls plugged the D.V.D. player into the car's cigarette lighter and Ángela and I began drinking the coffee we had bought at the gas station in Virginia Street. It was such a joy to feel the bright sunlight in our eyes, and to leave behind us the spider prowling around our part of town.

We drove up the first hills and reached the frontier between California and Nevada. The border patrol guards only checked vehicles carrying plants or animals, and so we went straight through, only stopping for a moment. The traffic lights indicating the risk of snow were green.

For us – although perhaps not for the inhabitants of six hundred thousand years ago – the physical world is always, or so it seems, something secondary, a mere support, the surface we need in order to sow corn or plant potatoes or to supply an industry or, seen from a very different angle, a ductile material that changes according to our moods, becoming sad when we are sad – O grey sky! – or happy when we are happy – O ray of sun! But that vision, which is there in the myth – "Adam, you are the centre of creation" – and which you find in the gentler landscapes of Europe, is untenable in Nevada, where the mountains and the deserts proudly proclaim their power: "Here we are, violent beings; we are not at your mercy, you are at ours." Perhaps that is why the Paiute and the Washoe Indians call nature Manitou, considering it to be a god, something remote and alien.

We became aware of the sheer force of the Sierra Nevada as soon as the I-80 began to climb, but for some miles we were aware, too, of the protection afforded us by the road. We were on one side, along with the other cars and trucks; the precipices, rocks, snow, steep slopes and mountain peaks were on the other, kept at bay by the metal fences.

That feeling of safety, of being protected, only lasted until we reached Truckee. From that point on – where some vehicles took the exit for the town and others took the exit heading for Lake Tahoe – the precipices, rocks, snow, steep slopes and mountain peaks installed themselves firmly in the car and in our minds, leaving no room for anything else. We all fell silent, even Izaskun and Sara, who, up until then, had been pestering us to let them watch a film.

At an altitude of six and a half thousand feet, every stretch of the road was different. First it turned to the left, then to the right, then to the left again, went down, rose up, and so on and on. It was flanked on both sides by rows of pine trees, most of them damaged in some way; quite a few lay fallen on the snow. In the distance we saw dozens of gleaming white mountains. Further off still lay the open sky and a great bright space: the Pacific Ocean.

"In 1856, a group of more than a hundred people, the Donner Party, tried to follow this route, hoping to reach California, but they met with terrible weather and lost their way."

Ángela was talking to us about the history of the Sierra Nevada, but it seemed to me that it was the Mountain itself speaking through her.

"Forty-three people died of cold and hunger. Did you see the sign for the Donner Pass a moment ago? It's there because of those people who lost their lives."

An eagle glided across the clear blue sky.

"In 1956, two Basque shepherds died in this same area. They got caught in a snowstorm and couldn't escape. They were found dead alongside the corpses of the two thousand sheep they were tending, who had also frozen to death. A real feast for the vultures!"

The Mountain was sending Ángela ever more sombre messages.

"The stories of some of the Basque shepherds who worked here are truly remarkable. Dominique Laxalt, the Barinaga brothers, the Bidarts, the Eiguerens . . . Not all of them had such luck though. The other day, in the microfilm archive, I found a report published in 1914 in the *San Francisco Star*. It was about three Basque shepherds who returned to France to fight in the Great War. They almost certainly ended up being gassed at Verdun."

"What a dumb thing to do!" Izaskun said in English from the back seat. After just four months at Mount Rose School, she spoke English fluently.

"Some priest probably persuaded them to go back," I said.

I had in mind a play by Piarres Lafitte, "*Egiazko argia*", "The True Light", written as an attack on those who fled across the Pyrenees into Spain to avoid being sent to Verdun or Salonika during the First World War. The protagonist, who has left his dying wife to go to the front, and who, once there, loses his sight after being gassed, suffers a crisis of faith. In despair, he tries to commit suicide and, not content with that, he has the audacity to criticise God, France and, worst of all, the priesthood! In the end, though, thanks to a seminarian called Domingo and his own desire not to deprive a son of his first communion, he regains his faith and, sobbing, makes a statement that deserves to be included in an anthology of the stupidest things ever said in literature: "I am blind, Domingo, but, like all Basques, what illumines me is the true light, the light of faith."

We started to descend, gently at first, then faster, losing more than three hundred feet a minute. Along the sides of the road, poplars had replaced pine trees.

"Yes, it probably was the fault of the priests," Ángela said. "They put pressure on the young emigrants, making them feel guilty for having abandoned their mothers in the villages where they were born, and urging them to go back. Not always in order to send them to war, of course. Many small villages in the Basque Country were left with almost no young men, and they wanted to put that right."

"They had another reason too," Izaskun said. "The priests were terrified of sex, and thought that, in America, the young men would get a taste for visiting brothels."

Children may not have the keen hearing of dogs, but they're not far off. What Izaskun had just said was a fragment of a conversation Ángela and I had once had in the kitchen at College Drive while Izaskun and Sara were sitting out on the garden porch reading.

The bends in the road seemed more like ramps now, and suddenly, after descending another few hundred feet, the Mountain finally released us. The precipices, rocks and snow, the steep slopes and mountain peaks left the car. Our minds could begin to think about other things.

"When are we going to watch the film?" Sara asked, trying to make the most of the new situation.

There was a service area by the roadside, with a gas station and a restaurant. Ángela drove in.

"First, we're going to stop and have a sandwich."

From the car park, we could see the plain of Sacramento. I was thirsty and took out a bottle of water from the car boot before going into the restaurant. I couldn't drink it, though, because the water had turned to ice. A souvenir of the Sierra Nevada.

SAN FRANCISCO

The walls of the corridors in the Hotel Rex were adorned with literary quotes. The one in the space between the doors of our two rooms was by Jack London: "I would rather be ashes than dust! [. . .] I would rather be a superb meteor, every atom of me in magnificent glow, than a sleepy and permanent planet. The proper function of man is to live, not to exist . . ."

"I like it," Izaskun said.

"*I* don't," I said as best I could, trying to manhandle our heaviest suitcase into the room.

The thermometer in the hotel read 61 degrees F, about 16 degrees C. There was only the gentlest of breezes. The sky was blue. The sun was clear and undimmed by mist. We took a tourist boat around the bay and passed under the Golden Gate Bridge.

"The first European ship to cross this strait was the *San Carlos*, in 1775," said Ángela, who had been reading up about the first men to explore California. "The captain was Juan Manuel de Ayala; the pilot was Juan Bautista Aguirre; and the chaplain was Vicente de Santa María. All of them Basques."

"How cool!" Izaskun said.

"In the diary kept by Vicente de Santa María, he recorded some words from the language spoken by the natives of the bay. They called the sky *carac*. The sun *gismen*."

Carac was as blue as it had been first thing in the morning; the rays of *gismen* glittered on the mirrors of the cars crossing the Golden Gate Bridge.

TELEPHONE CALL TO MY MOTHER

The signal in the hotel was excellent, and I could hear my mother's voice as clearly as if she were in the next room. She sounded very cheerful.

"I'm phoning you from San Francisco," I said. "We've come to spend Christmas here. What about you? How is everyone? How was Christmas Eve?"

"Well, what can I say? Your brothers prepared a lovely supper. First, we ate . . . oh now, hang on, what was it? Ah yes, croquettes, first, croquettes, then prawns, then pâté, and then . . ."

"Sounds delicious. We didn't bother with a special meal."

"And asparagus! We ate asparagus too. And then . . ."

"Was it fish perhaps?"

"Wait, now what was it?"

When the silence went on for too long, I began talking:

"We've just had breakfast and we're about to go for a walk. Yesterday, we visited Chinatown. We were really surprised to hear everyone speaking Chinese. We went into one shop and couldn't make ourselves understood at all. They only spoke Chinese. A very strange place. Sara and Izaskun found it a bit frightening."

"Where did you say you are? In China? I thought you were somewhere else."

"Listen, the girls are calling me. They want to go on a tram."

"Fish stew!" my mother exclaimed. "That's it, we ate fish stew!"

"Good."

"Oh, it *was* good, but I went to bed immediately afterwards. Besides, those brothers of yours are always talking about politics. I tell them politics is a dirty word, but it's no use, they won't stop. It's so boring."

OUT AND ABOUT

In the morning, we went to Sausalito, but found it rather dull. There was no-one in the streets and no-one to be seen on the yachts in the harbour either. At two o'clock, we caught the *Golden Gate* ferry back to San Francisco.

In front of the bench where Sara and I sat down, there were two serious-looking, middle-aged men.

"The way people write about literature nowadays is completely metafactual," I heard one of them say. "It depends almost exclusively on biographical or anecdotal details."

They were wearing black jackets and white shirts with Mao collars, and they were Spanish. I imagined they taught at some college in California.

"What do people remember about Raymond Chandler? That he always used to stock up on whisky before starting a novel. And Allen Ginsberg? That he wrote 'Howl' when he was high on marihuana, Benzedrine and who knows what else. With Kerouac it's more or less the same. Plus the fact that he wrote *On the Road* on a roll of paper, not on separate sheets."

"That's what they used to say about Juan Benet. That roll of paper caused great consternation in literary circles in Madrid."

Ángela and Izaskun were standing at the prow of the ship, beckoning to us to join them. We didn't hesitate.

In the afternoon, we strolled along the Embarcadero and visited the aquarium: squid, sharks, jellyfish, turtles and fish, thousands of fish. Outside, at Pier 39, we saw sea lions dozing and lolling about in the sun. Occasionally, they would roll casually, lazily into the water. The tourists would laugh and take photographs, thousands of photographs.

As we were leaving the pier, we passed the two Spanish teachers again.

"To give another example: what do people know about Borges, apart from the fact that Perón appointed him a chicken inspector?"

I didn't hear the answer, but I imagined it would be "Nothing".

ALCATRAZ ISLAND

Izaskun tapped Ángela on the arm when the voice on the headphones explained that the island of Alcatraz was given its name by Captain Juan Manuel de Ayala, "the first European to cross the strait now known as the Golden Gate'. She remained in the same ebullient mood while we were visiting the other parts of the prison too: "Oh, I know who Al Capone was. I read about him in a book." "Ah, yes, I know that story about the prisoner who kept birds." Sara, on the other hand, seemed frightened. She held on to my hand as we walked past the rows of cells.

"Is this where they've put the man they arrested in Reno?" she asked. There were mannequins in some of the cells, and she eyed them warily.

"Who do you mean?"

As I suspected, she answered: "The fat man with the round head. The one who was in Tacos."

She wasn't wearing headphones, and I took mine off.

"This prison is a museum," I explained. "There haven't been any actual prisoners here for ages."

This wasn't quite true. I had just found out, through my headphones, that Robert Kennedy only closed the prison in 1961. Not that long ago really. Sara seemed reassured though. She still clung on to my hand, but not quite so tightly.

I remember L. telling me once that, during his time in prison, he found everything unbearable, but worst of all was the noise: people rattling the bars, the footsteps of the prison guards, the prisoners' shouts, the sirens, the warnings over the loudspeakers, the shrill whistles . . . That day in Alcatraz, all that could be heard were the tourists' murmured comments. A snob would have said that this was no better than all those other prison noises, but I found them infinitely preferable.

We walked along a gallery to one of the biggest attractions, the cell of prisoner AZ85, Al Capone. Above the door were two photographs of the Mafia boss, full face and in profile.

"Paulino Uzcudun's friend," I said, but Ángela and Izaskun still had their headphones on and didn't hear me.

"I'm bored! When are we going to leave?" Sara asked.

"Five more minutes and we're done," I said. I was beginning to get bored too.

"What is completely unacceptable is him manipulating half the department staff just to give a job to one of his cronies," I heard someone say behind me. It was the two Spanish teachers again. They had changed the subject, but not their tone of voice.

"The trouble is there are lots of people in the department who don't have tenure yet, so they're not going to do anything to stop him. They couldn't care less who he brings in, his best buddy or the Holy Mother herself."

Heading for the exit, we found the souvenir shop and went in to buy some postcards. One of them, an old sepia photograph, showed a group of prisoners. The caption read: "Hopi prisoners on the Rock." On the display table there was a book bearing the same image. The back cover explained that the Hopis were opposed to the cultural changes being forced on them by Washington and they refused to allow the government agents to take their children to remote white schools; to settle the matter, nineteen chiefs were arrested and imprisoned in Alcatraz for a year.

In the mountains, the snow came down as far as the edge of the road and was so blindingly white that we all had to wear dark glasses. The music we'd been listening to until then, the compilations of songs by Jefferson Airplane and the Mamas and the Papas that we had bought in San Francisco, seemed incompatible with the new landscape and, in the end, we turned it off. The mountain was silent, the snow was silent, and we had to respond to that silence with our own.

We stopped in Truckee and walked down the main street, which was full of shops selling winter sports gear. We went into a stationery shop and, as usual, bought some postcards, one of which showed a railway tunnel, one of several that cross the Sierra Nevada.

"The sixth tunnel was the most difficult to build," the note on the back of the card said. "It took more than two thousand Chinese workers eighteen months to dig, from 1866 to 1867."

I leafed through the magazine of the Truckee-Donner Historical Society. According to the heading on one article, Truckee had one of the biggest Chinatowns in the West, but this was completely destroyed during the violent anti-Chinese riots that took place towards the end of the nineteenth century.

When we went back to the car park, I saw a rather faded poster on the noticeboard. It showed a photograph of Charles "Coogan" Kelly, the snowboarding champion murdered in Reno at Halloween; it was announcing a celebration of his life that had taken place a month before.

DECEMBER 31
BACK IN COLLEGE DRIVE

At around ten in the morning, heavy snow began to fall in Reno. Izaskun and Sara set about making a cake; Ángela decided to transfer all our San Francisco photographs onto the computer; and I started reading the books we had bought at City Lights just before we left. Ginsberg's *Howl and other Poems*, Kerouac's *On the Road*, and an autobiography by Bob Dylan, in which he praised Kerouac for mentioning unfamiliar places with strange names, like Truckee.

Around eleven o'clock, attracted perhaps by the smell of the cake in the oven, the raccoon came and perched on the kitchen windowsill, and, for a moment, we all stopped what we were doing to take a closer look. It was part-dog, part-cat, but its eyes were colder, wilder.

TELEPHONE CALL TO MY MOTHER

"Another year over."

"I know. I can't believe it," my mother said.

"Yes, time passes so quickly, we hardly notice it. Here we are at the end of 2007."

"I know. I can't believe it."

"What are you having for supper tonight? What have my brothers cooked for you?"

"Oh, something or other. And your other brother, you know, your older brother, he bought me a huge bunch of flowers. I've put it in the kitchen. I don't know what kind of flowers they are, but they're almost every colour under the sun: white, pink, yellow, red, speckled . . ."

"Ángela wants to speak to you, and so do Izaskun and Sara."

"There are purple ones, pink ones, yellow ones . . . It's just incredible how many colours there are in that one bunch. He's got a real thing about flowers, your brother. Incredible really. I dread to think how much he spends on them!"

NEW YEAR'S EVE

Around seven o'clock in the evening, we heard someone stamping his feet on the porch to shake the snow off his boots. We opened the door, and there was Dennis. He was wearing a waterproof red cap and a very nice raincoat the same colour.

"I've come to eat cake," he said.

"Just like the raccoon," Sara said.

"Yes, he's the one who told me about it. It's true, you know. I talk to the raccoons. It's telepathy."

"I don't believe you," Sara said. "You could smell it."

Izaskun sighed loudly.

We were going to have supper at Bob Earle's house, and Dennis was carrying a big Tupperware container in a paper bag.

"I've made Mexican-style roast chicken. You'll love it. And you'll love this even more!"

He produced a D.V.D. from his raincoat pocket: "Pirates of the Caribbean 3: At World's End".

"It's the new one!" Izaskun and Sara cried in unison.

Dennis gave them the thumbs-up, then turned to me:

"Before we go up to Bob's house, we have to send an email to my brother. He insists on you sending him a text in Basque so that he can see how it looks in Menhart font. As I said, Jeff thinks only of fonts. Even on New Year's Eve."

I had completely forgotten about it. I hesitated.

"It will only take us a minute," Earle said. "Just choose a text and that will be that."

In the end, we sent him two texts: a page from the essay on Basque immigration that Ángela was writing, and the beginning of something I had written about Paulino Uzcudun.

SUPPER

The supper menu: to start, imported ham that Earle had bought in Tom's Food Boutique, aubergine salad from Mary Lore and prawn croquettes prepared by C., Monique Laxalt's friend. The main course: Dennis's Mexican-style roast chicken and roast beef stuffed with Philadelphia cheese prepared by Mannix in Earle's kitchen. For dessert: ice cream and the cake made by Izaskun and Sara. To drink: Californian wine, Sierra Nevada beer, Gatorade and water.

The dish that received the most plaudits was Mannix's roast beef.

"There's no mystery to it," he said. "It's the easiest thing in the world. First, take your cheese and mix it with mustard, parsley and black pepper. Then, make a few cuts in the meat – taking care not to slice right through it – and fill the cuts with the cheese mixture. Melt the butter in a frying pan to brown the meat a little, then stick it in a moderate oven, 150 or 160 degrees, and in less than half an hour it's ready."

"You're an artist, Mannix," Earle said. "Any time you want to use my oven, feel free!"

"All the ovens in the world are my friends."

We raised our glasses for the first toast of the evening. Izaskun and Sara went to fetch C.'s dog, which was in her car, parked out front. He was a border collie, about four or five years old. His name was Blue and he was completely drenched.

"He didn't want to come in at first and started running about all over the place, and then he started eating the snow," Sara said.

C. went into the kitchen and returned with a bowl of water.

"He's probably thirsty."

Blue started drinking as soon as she put down the bowl.

"Bob, have you got an old towel I can use to dry Blue off?"

"Yes, take one from the bathroom."

Five minutes later, Izaskun and Sara were lying on cushions in front of the television, watching "Pirates of the Caribbean 3". Blue lay curled up between them. Mannix and Mary Lore's daughters were having supper with their grandparents that night.

DESSERT

C. called Monique Laxalt to wish her a happy New Year and to ask how her brother Bruce was. Then we all had a quick word with her, although Earle and Mary Lore spoke to her for several minutes.

"It's not so long ago that Bruce was playing squash with me. Now he can't even raise a cup to his lips," Earle said.

Mannix shook his head.

"It's just terrible."

C. chose a book from Earle's library and went and sat on the sofa. It was a copy of Bruce's *Songs of Mourning and Worship*.

"We have that book at home too," I said.

C. was looking for a particular poem.

"It's called 'Christmas Letter'," she said and began to read out loud:

"Where are you today, old friends still-living and this long year's / New-wandering ghosts, as we pause to take our moment of rest?/

At Beth's family's table in Oregon you must be, David, far from / the Nevada pond where you scattered dear Helmi's ashes in July."

"I remembered the title and thought I might read the whole poem to you," C said. "But it's too sad. We can't start the New Year with a poem like that."

She continued reading silently

"But these last lines are perfect," she added and passed us the book so that we could read it for ourselves.

"A squall hit the island a bit ago, one of the storms / That have mercifully broken the drought. The cisterns are all overflowing again, / The sky having given back purified the water it had taken from the sea."

"Yes," I said, "that link between time and water is really good. New Year, new water in the cisterns."

Dennis was standing before us, holding two bags of popcorn. He said to Ángela:

"Shall I give these to Izaskun and Sara?"

"Go ahead," Ángela said.

He went straight over to where the girls were watching the film. They both held out their hands to take the bags. Blue looked up expectantly, but immediately rejected the piece of popcorn Sara offered him.

VICTOR AND THE SNOW
(A MEMORY)

Ángela and I were driving from Bordeaux to Montpellier along a mountain road, when the engine started sputtering and losing power. Slowly and with some difficulty – not to mention anxiety – we managed to labour up a few more hills and round more bends before reaching the next village. We read its name on a rusty sign: SAINT-SERNIN-SUR-RANCE.

There was a garage at the entrance to the village, and we parked outside with what Ángela called "the engine's last gasp". Then, when I started explaining the problem to the mechanic and said the word "power", he countered with the word "pistons", as if this were some kind of question-and-answer session.

"It could also be the spark plugs. Anyway, come back in three hours," he said.

He was a nice man. He glanced at the clock on the wall and asked if we wanted to spend the night in the village. If we did, he could recommend somewhere clean and reasonably priced. It was nearly four o'clock.

At the time, the autumn of 1992, Ángela and I were living about eighty miles from Montpellier in a village called Brissac, or, to be more precise, about four miles outside that village, in Mas de la Croix, a farmhouse with rooms for people who wanted a quiet place to work. Ángela was translating Faulkner's *The Sound and the Fury* into Basque, and I was writing my novel *The Lone Man*. If we set off at seven, we would be home by ten.

We said thank you, but, no, we wouldn't be needing anywhere to stay and decided to go for a stroll around the village.

The late afternoon light, neither strong nor weak, made the shapes of the mountains stand out clearly against the unsettled sky, but the landscape itself was not particularly attractive. The woods thinned out around the village and a lot of the hillsides were thick with scrub. The only pretty houses were those in the older, possibly medieval quarter. Many of the roofs were tiled with dark grey slate.

We followed the road and came to a stone-and-brick monument that seemed to depict an animal. However, on closer examination, we saw that it wasn't an animal at all, but a human being, a boy crouching on all fours, his hair like a mane. The plaque said: "*Ici fût chassé l'enfant sauvage dit Victor de l'Aveyron.*" "This is where the wild boy known as Victor de l'Aveyron was caught." It gave a date too: 1799.

I was so moved by this discovery that I rushed to the local shop and bought a book of postcards and a small forty-page guide. Then I took photographs of the street in the old part of the village where the boy had been imprisoned; I even picked up a few pebbles from the street as souvenirs.

Ángela was surprised to see me behaving as if Saint-Sernin-sur-

Rance were a place dear to my heart, and to be honest, it wasn't. My excitement had to do with a book that had given me much food for thought, a book written by Dr Jean Itard about the boy who had been "caught" in that village: *Mémoire et rapport sur Victor de l'Aveyron*.

Friends to whom I gave the book to read were hard pushed to understand why I thought it so important. I tried to explain by telling them about the school I went to as a child in Asteasu, not that any of my classmates had been wild children exactly, but there were what we called *betizuak*, "truants", children who almost never went to school and who seemed quite different from us. Perhaps I associated the story of Victor de l'Aveyron with the *betizuak* of my childhood, and that was why it affected me so deeply. And yet I wasn't sure that was the real explanation.

Victor de l'Aveyron: a boy who had grown up outside society and who shared certain characteristics with the animals. He couldn't speak. He didn't feel cold or heat as humans do, and was capable of going from a warm kitchen to the bank of a frozen pond and staying there for hours. He didn't get ill and never caught a cold. He didn't feel pain either. His senses were dulled.

Dr Itard's attempts to educate the boy lasted for seven years. His aim was to teach him to speak and transform him into a human being through language, but Victor made no progress. He couldn't learn the names of things. When he heard the word *livre*, "book", he thought this meant a particular book, the one the doctor had used as an example; he couldn't comprehend abstractions. He remained mostly inactive, sitting for hours on end by his bedroom window, rocking back and forth.

There was one exception to this.

"One winter morning," Dr Jean Itard wrote in his diary, "after a heavy fall of snow in the night, he woke with a cry of joy, left his bed, ran to the window and then to the door, running from one to the other in a state of great impatience and excitement, until, still half-naked, he escaped into the garden; there he gave free rein to his joy, uttering loud, piercing shrieks, rolling about in the snow, gathering it up by the handful and finally eating it greedily until he could eat no more."

Snow interrupts the wheel of time, it intervenes like some extraordinary event in the midst of a long series of very ordinary events; that is where it derives its power. We're all aware of its impact, children especially. But Victor de l'Aveyron? Where did his euphoria come from? What lay behind his reaction? There was the snow on the one hand, and, on the other, a wild child, *un enfant sauvage*. And in between? Nothing. Not a single idea or influence, no associations with a Brueghel landscape or an ancient Chinese poem. No memories connecting snow with childhood Christmases or anything of the sort. Just two sides, two extremes: the snow in all its power, and the innocent and, if you like, empty spirit of Victor. And yet, he shrieked with joy.

I once heard the philosopher Agustín García Calvo say that emotion was impossible without some pre-existing idea, and that, for example, we would feel no strong emotion when confronted by the death of our father or our mother if we did not already understand the concepts of "father" and "mother". However, Victor's reaction to the snow casts doubt on the universality of such a statement.

JANUARY 6
DENNIS AND THE SWAN

The swan was idling about near the edge of the Manzanita Lake on campus. When it noticed us, it straightened its neck and put its head on one side, fixing us with watchful black eyes above an intensely orange beak; then it suddenly lost interest and paddled off to the opposite shore.

Apart from the swan gliding across the water, there was no other sign of life on the campus. No students, no police either, although one of their vehicles was parked nearby, beside the School of Mining. The ducks, thirty or forty of them, were sitting hunched on the grass, ready to go to sleep. It seemed extraordinarily quiet for six o'clock in the evening, but, as Ángela said, some days in Reno were like that.

"Look, there's Dennis," Sara said.

He was about twenty yards from us, wearing his red cap and raincoat.

"Where are you off to? The ice rink?" he asked, coming over to us.

"We went there the other day. Izaskun slipped and fell," Sara said.

"He didn't ask you that!" protested Izaskun.

Dennis spoke to Ángela.

"How about having another go?"

"Yes, why not? We have time."

"I agree," Izaskun said. "We're not like those ducks, who go to bed at six o'clock in the evening."

The open-air rink was on the bank of the Truckee river, near the monument to the Fallen Soldiers. We headed off down Virginia Street and, as we passed over the I-80, a trailer truck painted with the Stars and Stripes greeted us by honking its horn. It sounded as loud as the siren on an ocean liner.

"The spirit of Christmas is still alive!" Dennis cried.

"The trouble is we've got to go back to school on Monday," Sara said.

JANUARY 7
A VISIT TO THE PAIUTE MUSEUM

We set off in our Ford Sedan and drove to Pyramid Lake via Highway 447. We reached Nixon and parked in front of the Paiute Tribe Museum & Visitors Center at the entrance to the town.

There wasn't another soul to be seen. The only presence – a somewhat surly one – was the wind. It tousled our hair and battered the flag on the mast. The nearest desert peaks looked grey-brown in colour, while those further off were white.

The museum building itself was beautiful, made up of irregular geometric shapes and covering an area of no more than about 3,200 square feet. According to the sign, it was the work of the Hopi architect, Dennis Numkena.

Of all the documents and artefacts on display, I was particularly taken with two photographs. The first was of the warrior Numaga; the second of the educator Sarah Winnemucca, who was the author of the first book to be published in America by a Native American Indian (*Life Among the Piutes*, Boston, 1882), as well as being the leading advocate for the rights of the Paiutes.

In the display devoted to the twentieth century, several of the images seemed to have been taken from documentaries about the Second World War: a Paiute working a field radio; Paiute soldiers standing next to a road sign bearing the name NORMANDY; a larger group saluting the Stars and Stripes.

Before leaving the museum, we bought a copy of the latest edition of Sarah Winnemucca's book. There was still no-one else around, and our Ford Sedan was still the only car in the car park.

"Nixon doesn't seem like a very lively place," Ángela said. "We'd be better off driving to Sutcliffe and having lunch at the Crosby Bar."

I took the wheel and asked Ángela to read us a passage from the book.

"I was born somewhere near 1844, but am not sure of the precise time," she began. It was wonderful to hear Sarah Winnemucca more than a century later speaking through Ángela, and to be there with Izaskun and Sara listening to her words as we looked out at the turquoise-blue lake and the ochre-and-white desert, the Paiute territory that Numaga had fought to defend.

"I was a very small child when the first white people came into our country. They came like a lion, yes, like a roaring lion, and have continued so ever since, and I have never forgotten their first coming. My people were scattered at that time over nearly all the territory now known as Nevada. My grandfather was chief of the entire Paiute nation, and was camped near Humboldt Lake, with a small portion of his tribe, when a party travelling eastward from California was seen coming. When the news was brought to my grandfather, he asked what they looked like? When told that they had hair on their faces, and were white, he jumped up and clasped his hands together, and cried aloud: "My white brothers – my long-looked-for white brothers have come at last!"

"I don't want to hear this story," Sara said.

"Why not?" I asked.

"Because it will be sad," she said.

Ángela looked at me. Sarah Winnemucca's story probably would be sad.

We arrived in Sutcliffe and went into the Crosby Bar. The waitress from Idaho greeted us warmly. She was wearing a badge with Obama's face on it.

"We're definitely going to win!" she said. "He's going to be the next President of the United States!"

JANUARY 11

THE SOLDIER DAVID J. DRAKULICH

The news appeared in the *Reno Gazette-Journal*. A twenty-two-year-old soldier, David J. Drakulich, who had been in the army since 2004, had been killed in Afghanistan.

There were statements from members of his family. His father: "Four years ago, he said, 'Dad, I'm going to be an airborne ranger.' I was floored by that. He was fearless. He knew what he was doing."

His mother: "He loved his country, and joined in order to serve. We loved him very much."

His sister: "He went straight to heaven. I know that."

According to the same article, he was part of an extended Nevada family of lawyers, teachers and real-estate agents. He had planned to attend college when he returned from Afghanistan in April.

His father was shown holding a framed photograph. It was a montage. In the foreground was a picture of his son in dress uniform; in the background, the same boy coming down in a parachute.

JANUARY 12

THE LETTERS

"Bob, there's a letter from Obama here. He's going to visit Reno again and would like you to attend the meeting."

"You keep it. I've got two more here, and another one from Hillary Clinton."

JANUARY 14
BARACK OBAMA SPEAKS AGAIN

We went to the university basketball stadium to hear Barack Obama. His usual supporters, mostly under twenty-fives, were there again and also present was his main campaign slogan: *Change! Change! Change!* It was impossible to miss, because it was everywhere, not in every conceivable colour – the only acceptable political colours in America are the red, white and blue of the flag – but in every possible size, even obscuring the insignia of the Wolf Pack, the university basketball team. *Change! Change! Change!*

Barack Obama appeared along with his heartbreaker smile, his white shirt and his black suit. The warmth in the stadium was almost palpable, like threads reaching out to him from the four or five hundred supporters present; invisible threads, far finer than those a spider weaves in the branches of a bush, but strong enough to raise their candidate up to the skies.

"How far can Barack Obama go?" one interviewer asked Obama's opponent Hillary Clinton. "I think the sky's the limit. Some day, anyway," she said.

However, the supporters gathered in the Wolf Pack stadium, the ordinary workers who applauded him and laughed at his jokes, the students who watched, mesmerised, the harmonious movements of his water-divining hands, did not want to wait, they wanted that "some day" to come right now, in 2008. *Change! Change! Change! Obama for President!*

The meeting, though, was not quite the same as the one held three months before in the Grand Sierra Resort. The most obvious difference – apart from the tight security, which had been almost non-existent then and was now on a par with airport security – was the participation of Obama's wife, Michelle, who talked about being black and about the race question. The most subtle difference was the visibility of the campaign's logo which was everywhere now and which – as I had thought the first time – probably took its inspiration from the Japanese flag: at the bottom, blue and white horizontal lines representing a sea and, emerging from that sea, a white sun;

around the sun a blue semicircle, the sky. The rising sun.

I imagined David Axelrod, the chief strategist behind Obama's campaign, wondering if they should back up the logo with the song "The House of the Rising Sun" – Doc Watson's version for the West Coast and Eric Burdon and the Animals' version for the East Coast, but they couldn't possibly have done that. After all, the House of the Rising Sun, like Mustang Ranch, had been a brothel.

JANUARY 18
HILLARY CLINTON AT THE GRAND SIERRA RESORT

More than a thousand people were at the Grand Sierra Resort, all looking for a place where they could see and hear Hillary Clinton during her first and only campaign visit to Reno. There were about a hundred seats set aside for the elderly, and a large empty space for those of us who would have to stand throughout the event.

Initially, we stood on one side of the hall, behind the disabled area, but this proved problematic, because we kept getting in the way of the people arriving in wheelchairs. So we moved closer to the stage, where the Nevada militants taking part in the campaign were gathered – Hillary Clinton's chorus.

A woman came over to us and said:

"If you like, you can go up on stage."

One small leap and we had joined the chorus, like Hillary militants. The spot reserved for the speaker, the podium where she would stand, was just in front of us, about six feet away. We could also see the entire hall and the thousand heads in the audience. A privileged position.

At first, it looked a bit like the annual general meeting of all of Nevada's teachers and social workers, organised by some honourable association with rather limited means. There were no special effects; a few spotlights; two enormous flags, but not made of satin as they had been at Obama's meeting in another hall in the same Grand Sierra Resort. There were just two exceptions to that otherwise discreet atmosphere: the television cameras and a large square red carpet bearing the candidate's first name, "Hillary". But there weren't that many cameras or journalists, and the red carpet was quite small given the size of the venue. "I will know what awaits you when I see what you're wearing," says a very old Persian poem. To judge by the decor, we were looking at a loser.

There wasn't much hubbub or excitement. A couple of young people – because not all young people were Obama supporters – were handing out posters that bore the campaign slogans: SOLUTIONS FOR AMERICA, HILLARY FOR PRESIDENT. The message on the T-shirts was different: READY FOR CHANGE.

An announcement over the loudspeakers explained that the candidate's flight from Las Vegas had been delayed, and the room filled with a murmur of voices. I looked at the people in the front row: seven out of ten women looked like feminists to me. The men, all of whom were getting on in years, bore the stamp of progressives from the 1970s.

"For once, the sociologists are right," Ángela said.

The sociologists did, in fact, say that the people who would vote for Hillary Clinton, winning her the Democratic nomination and the Presidency, would be feminists and elderly progressives. Plus the Hispanics, because, for them, Bill Clinton had been the first President who could speak Spanish.

The murmurs grew like a bubble, then burst whenever anything happened. Not that much did happen. Someone brought on a lectern and it seemed – at least to the many people who briefly stopped talking – that the candidate would arrive at any moment, but she didn't. A little later, an elegantly dressed Afro-American woman ran across the stage and, again, people stopped and looked; but as Cervantes says: "*Fuese y no hubo nada*", she left and that was that. It was five in the afternoon. The candidate was now an hour late.

Two musicians sat down on the stage in front of the chorus. One of them, wearing a scarf and a beret that made him look French, would occasionally address the audience:

"Hillary Clinton's on her way! Hillary Clinton, the first female President of the United States!"

Her supporters responded by waving banners and applauding. They were impatient, but not angry.

"Why don't you play something?" someone shouted.

The two men played a couple of folk songs, and a woman standing in front of the disabled area translated the words into sign language. Two men went over to her, as if to talk to her, but instead they merely removed the lectern they had placed on the podium a few minutes before.

The two musicians were playing their fifth or sixth song when the applause and the shouts suddenly grew louder, almost drowning out the music, and everyone present stood on tiptoe, looking intently at the spot where Hillary Clinton would appear. Two banners showing the intertwined flags of America and Turkey rose up above all the others: TURKISH AMERICANS WITH HILLARY. The musicians stopped playing. Camera flashes filled the room with bursts of light. Hillary Clinton walked briskly onto the stage, stopping a couple of times, just long enough to greet someone she knew among the chorus. When she stepped onto the podium, she applauded the people applauding her. Another gesture typical of 1970s progressives.

She was wearing a black suit and a pale blue, round-necked top. The retired general who accompanied her onto the stage made a very persuasive introductory address: he had known Hillary for a long time and knew how capable she was. A woman was finally going to be elected to the White House.

Hillary Clinton began her speech quoting a politician from the past and then talked about the new generations. Whenever we talk about change, we must be sure to think of our children and grandchildren, because it is their future that lies in the balance. She went on, briefly but calmly, to set out the main themes of her campaign: education, the war, the plight of war veterans and the health system.

"How many of you know someone who has no health insurance?" she asked those present. Hundreds of arms shot up. "And how many people do you know who are having problems with their insurance company?"

Again, hundreds of arms went up.

A woman fainted and collapsed. Someone handed Hillary Clinton a bottle of water, and she asked them to give it to the woman who had fainted.

"The same thing happened to me in a museum in Florence, while I was looking at Michelangelo's 'David'," she said.

The remark, the reference to Europe and to a classical work of art, seemed appropriate somehow. Of the two rival candidates, Barack Obama was the romantic choice, and she was the classical or, if you like, the pre-romantic choice, like Michelangelo.

Political candidates all over the world are always aware of what their critics say about them and their work, and Hillary responded to one such criticism when she resumed her speech.

"They say my health plan wasn't any good. Of course it wasn't! I know that! That's why I've spent fourteen years thinking about how to make it better!"

She spoke in more bitter tones when she mentioned the people who accused her of being in cahoots with the political lobbyists in Washington. Weren't her rivals as "Washingtonian" as she was? For example – she didn't name names, but she didn't need to because they were there in the newspapers – who had supported Obama in Nevada? A well-known lobbyist.

She was a great speaker. The other candidates, and especially Barack Obama, may have garnered more applause, but she garnered more silence, more respect. The people at the Grand Sierra Resort understood the depth of her words and listened intently. "I'll know what awaits you when I see what you're wearing . . ." But things don't always happen as they do in poems. Judging by what she was wearing, Hillary Clinton looked like a loser, but after her speech, no-one gave her clothes a second thought.

"Reality is what matters," I once heard the Hellenist Rodríguez Adrados say. That, in essence, was Hillary Clinton's message. Given the choice, better a classical president than a romantic one.

LUNCH AT HARRAH'S CASINO

I went to Harrah's Casino with Dennis and Mary Lore, and Earle led us into the members' dining room. It was a very elegant setting: wood-lined walls, carpets, lamps, mirrors. The eighty-something man sitting at a table to one side was wearing a black velvet suit and a gold Certina watch on his wrist. The food was on display, like in a self-service place, but it was served by a waiter.

Before sitting down, we went to the poker room, and one of the men playing cards got up from the green baize table to greet us.

"This is my little brother," Earle said, introducing us. "As you see, he plays poker. A true Nevada man."

We all shook hands.

"Were you winning or losing?" Earle asked him.

"As a true Nevada man, I will make no comment," his brother said. Then he said goodbye and went back to the poker table.

Over lunch, the conversation was all about the political events that had just taken place in Reno, the visits by Barack Obama and Hillary Clinton, and it soon became clear that Mary Lore and Dennis held very different views. Mary Lore was in favour of Hillary because she was a woman and because she had a track record in government; Dennis was in favour of Obama, a breath of fresh air in the rather tawdry world of American politics. Earle followed the discussion with a faint smile on his lips, but did not offer his own views.

I told them about the woman who had fainted during the meeting, and about Hillary Clinton's reaction, describing what had happened to her once in Italy.

"What did she actually say about Italy?" Earle asked.

I gave him the details, and he burst out laughing.

"Loads of rich Americans fall into a dead faint in front of a Michelangelo sculpture. It's the glamorous thing to do. It's not like fainting in a gas station on Virginia Street."

"Obama never comes out with stuff like that," Dennis said.

Mary Lore didn't like this comment.

"No, of course, Obama prefers to quote Martin Luther King. For some reason, he always calls him 'Dr King', so as to look like his disciple, I suppose, and win votes."

"At any rate," Earle said, "Hillary's fainting fit would have been very brief and barely perceptible to other people."

"Are you saying she lied at the Grand Sierra Resort?" asked Mary Lore, who was getting angry now.

"I'm going to tell you something that will amaze you," I said, interrupting. "Unless I'm very much mistaken, I actually witnessed Hillary's fainting fit on a trip I made to Italy with my mother, ten years ago."

The waiter came over to us. Earle and I ordered coffee, and Mary Lore and Dennis green tea.

"I'm going to smoke a cigar while I hear this second tale from Italy," Earle said, placing a slight emphasis on that word "second".

The waiter named half a dozen brands of cigar. I only recognised one of them, "Cohiba".

"Bring me a small one. You choose," Earle said.

Five minutes later, the coffees and teas were on the table and Earle was smoking his cigar. It smelled very good.

"So you were there when Hillary fainted in Italy, and with your mother too," he said.

"Yes, I think so. Rather a lot of things happened on that particular trip."

"Why don't you tell us about it? We're in no hurry," Dennis said. "Nor are you, I believe. I met Ángela at the university earlier on. She was about to take Izaskun and Sara to a school party."

It took me fifteen minutes to tell the story.

"You should write it down," Mary Lore said when I'd finished.

"I already have," I said.

Earle got up and so did we. We waved to the players from the door to the poker room.

"What a very enjoyable lunch," Earle said as we emerged onto Virginia Street.

JOURNEY TO ITALY
(A MEMORY)

There were forty-two of us, thirty-eight pensioners and four young or semi-young people, and we were all travelling to Italy on a bus. The circumstances were, to say the least, rather complicated, since we were not all of the same nationality; we were, in alphabetical order, from Barcelona, Guipúzcoa and Madrid. Charles de Gaulle once asked with a sigh: "How can you govern a country that has two hundred and forty-six varieties of cheese?" I wondered: "How can you govern a Confined Space forty feet by eight feet by nine feet filled with three different nationalities?" This was, however, a purely rhetorical question. We were at the beginning of the trip – with Cannes behind us and Monaco ahead – crossing a part of France blissfully free of tunnels, and the route was very pleasant.

However, once we left Ventimiglia, we entered Italy, where the tunnels awaited us. When we came to the twentieth tunnel, the Catalan nation uttered its first complaint:

"Aren't we ever going to stop?" asked Eugeni, a retiree. "These seats are so cramped, we'll be too stiff to move."

The guide in charge of the Confined Space was a young man, who was accompanied by his new wife. He clearly had very acute hearing and, although he was sitting in the first row of seats, and Eugeni was halfway down the bus, he was ready with an immediate response:

"These tunnels can get very wearing, Eugeni," he said, picking up the microphone. "I've been through them hundreds of times, and I know what it's like, but the tunnels will come to an end soon, and then we'll find ourselves in one of the most beautiful places in the world."

His wife followed up these words with:

"*Eugeni, et ve de gust un albercoc?*" And she held up one hand to show him an apricot. Eugeni replied affirmatively and the apricot was passed from hand to hand down the bus.

The driver was made of stern stuff and put his foot down on the accelerator, but the tunnels were made of still sterner stuff and went on and on. The atmosphere in the Confined Space grew more strained, and it was not long before the first conflict between nations broke out.

"Of course, if we hadn't been held up for so long in Barcelona . . ." grumbled a white-haired gentleman from Madrid, also sitting halfway down the bus.

"Yes, it's because we were held up in Barcelona that we now have to drive on without making a single stop," said the fair-haired woman beside him, doubtless his wife.

"I suppose you'd have us all start the journey in Madrid!" retorted Eugeni, the most dynamic element in the Confined Space. "Madrid! Madrid! *N'estic fart de Madrid!* I'm sick to death of Madrid!"

The *madrileños* remained undaunted.

"You can say what you like about Madrid. We're from outside the city, from Tres Cantos."

We, the members of the Basque Minority, said nothing.

Someone blew into the microphone a couple of times. It was our guide, the newly-wed, the husband.

"Forget about Barcelona and Madrid! We're in Italy!" he cried. "We're fifty miles from Genoa and there are no more tunnels. To celebrate, I'm going to play some Italian music: Adriano Celentano's *Azzurro!*"

The song immediately reached into all four corners of the Confined Space.

We, the members of the Basque Minority, approved of his choice of song. "*Azzurro*" has always been one of my favourites.

"The gentleman from Madrid was right in a way, don't you think?" my mother said, sitting beside me. "We did spend far too long in Barcelona."

I quietly agreed with this concession to Centralism, but the moment belonged to Adriano Celentano: "*Azzurro, il pomeriggio è troppo azzurro e lungo per me . . .*"

To our left, beyond the fields full of polytunnels, the Mediterranean resembled thick blue ink, *azzurro*. On its waters, like dark specks, we could see the fishing boats; in the sky, like yellow specks, a scattering of about ten stars. Night was coming on.

"Have you seen the sea?" our guide asked when Adriano Celentano had fallen silent. "Well, carry on enjoying the view while you listen to this next song."

Once again music filled the Confined Space: "*Sapore di sale, sapore di mare . . .*"

196

"I wouldn't be surprised if that young man was a psychologist, because he coped brilliantly with the situation," my mother said. "If I was younger, that's what I would study, psychology. When I was young, I liked chemistry best, but now I prefer psychology."

"Sorry to keep bothering you, and I'll shut up after this," said the guide, the newly-wed, the potential psychologist. "But you really need to know what the words of this next song mean: '*Se piangi, se ridi, io sono con te . . .*' It means: 'Whether you're laughing or crying, I'll be there with you.' It's a lovely song, my friends. Close your eyes and listen!"

The voice of Bobby Solo emerged from the loudspeakers: "*Se piangi, amore, io piango con te, perchè tu sei parte di me . . .*" Over the sea, the stars were growing brighter in the sky, but the fishing boats had vanished.

I got up and walked down the aisle to the most private place in the Confined Space and, as I did so, I observed the atmosphere in the different rows of seats. All the nations were sitting quietly now, eyes closed and either asleep or half-asleep. The only exception was a woman from Madrid, who had a strange face, as if carved out of stone. "*Se piangi, se ridi, io sono con te,*" sang Bobby Solo again, but she cared little for the singer's feelings.

"What a rubbishy song!" she said when our eyes met. Her voice was made of stone too, a kind of metal-plated stone. She sounded as if she came from Lavapiés or some other old quarter of Madrid. I smiled faintly and moved on.

I found it hard to go to sleep, and started looking out of the window. The lights of Genoa were not far away. I remembered a poem written by a man born in that city, Eugenio Montale, unforgettable lines that I first came across when I read them in Francisco Ferrer Lerín's Spanish translation: "I would have liked to feel rough, elemental as the pebbles you tumble about, pocked by salt, a timeless shard, witness to a cold, persistent will." As I recalled the poem, I could feel the sea close to me and imagine the wet pebbles the waves were depositing on the sand – one, two, three – and then I fell asleep.

*

The longest section of the journey was over, and the forty-two members of the Confined Space were standing in the Piazza del Duomo in Pisa, feeling happy and contented. The sun had taken the place of the melancholy stars; the blue sky had taken the place of the night. Before us, on the young grass, stood three white marble buildings. The one nearest us was *il campanile*, the most famous tower in the world.

"*Quina meravella, Déu meu!*" Eugeni exclaimed.

"Absolutely marvellous!" agreed the *madrileño* from Tres Cantos.

There was nothing more to be said, and the rest of us stood in silence.

Then came that stony, metal-plated voice:

"What a disappointment!"

These words pierced the silence like a dagger,

"What a disappointment!" the voice said again. I recognised the accent. It was definitely from Lavapiés.

Most of the members of the Confined Space turned round.

"It looks good in photographs, but it's no great shakes in the flesh, so to speak," the woman said. We travellers from the three nations looked at each other, dumbstruck.

"Let's go!" said someone briskly. It was our guide, the newly-wed, the potential psychologist. "The tower has 294 steps. Let's climb up to the point where Galileo used to stand."

Eugeni shook his head.

"I'm not sure I can climb that many steps. I'm not as young as I was . . ."

"If Galileo Galilei could do it, why shouldn't you, Eugeni?" said our guide encouragingly.

A member of the Basque Minority suddenly broke away from the group and trotted over to the foot of the tower.

"How do we get there? Through here?" she asked. Needless to say, it was my mother.

"Yes!" responded another member of the minority, running after her. Needless to say, that was me.

Most of the members of the Confined Space joined us, and, after a few moments, we were all at the spot chosen by Galileo for his experiments.

"He would stand here and throw different objects out of the window: objects made of steel, wood or gold," explained the guide. "He assumed that the heavier objects would hit the ground first, but that wasn't the case. They all landed at the same time."

We looked down at the ground below, but saw no objects, whether of steel or wood or gold. We did, however, see the Stone Woman. She was sitting on a bench made of the same material as her.

The following day, we stopped in Lucca to take a look around and have some lunch. It seemed a lovely, cheerful city, but, as our guide pointed out, it lacked any exceptional buildings or works of art, and so it would be best if we explored it on our own, with no fixed itinerary. Nevertheless, the group stayed together initially because Eugeni asked the Stone Woman a question, and no member of the Confined Space wanted to miss her answer.

"What have you got against the tower of Pisa, may I ask?"

That was his question.

"Look, Señor Eugeni," began the Stone Woman in her heavy Lavapiés accent. "I have nothing against the tower itself. But let me ask *you* a question: Have you ever seen a film?"

Setting aside for a moment our divergent identities, the *madrileño* couple from Tres Cantos stood up for the Catalan representative.

"Oh, come on! Do you really think there are no cinemas in Barcelona?"

The Stone Woman replied in a cold and even more metallic voice:

"There are lots of cinemas in Barcelona. I know that. If you're interested, there are nearly two hundred and twenty cinemas in the whole province, and nearly seventy in the capital. But that isn't what I meant. What I was asking Señor Eugeni was if he had ever seen a film being made."

The bells of Lucca began ringing very loudly, interrupting the conversation. When silence was restored, the Stone Woman continued her argument:

"Because *I* have. I've worked in the film industry all my life and have been on many film shoots. And do you know what? It's all a great big lie. You see a shipwreck on the screen, but that shipwreck has been created by the director with a toy boat in a washing-up bowl. And they have a particular way of photographing the tower of Pisa, so that when you . . ."

I was intending to stay and hear her out, but the other member of the Basque Minority, needless to say my mother, was heading briskly off to some indeterminate part of the city, and I felt obliged to follow her.

We reached Florence in the late afternoon, and our guide advised us to make the most of what was left of the day to visit the city on our own. We, the Basque Minority, chose to go for a stroll along the banks of the Arno, knowing that the following day we would visit everything else – the squares, the churches, the museums – along with the other nationalities from the Confined Space.

We walked a couple of miles along one bank and the same distance back along the other. There was a breeze blowing, and I thought I could hear or feel, like a still gentler breeze, Dante's famous line: "*Tanto gentile e tanto onesta pare la donna mia* . . ."

We returned to the hotel at around midnight. While we were waiting for the lift, we noticed two shadows in the foyer. It was the newly-weds, our guide and his wife. They were sitting in a corner, facing each other and looking very down in the mouth. Suddenly, the man made an abrupt gesture, and the gesture the woman made in response was equally abrupt.

"I think they've had an argument," I said.

"Couples nowadays have no patience with each other. That's why there are so many divorces," my mother said.

On the sports channel, they were showing a replay of the game between Fiorentina and Sampdoria. It was a hard-fought match. Passarella, who played on the left wing for Fiorentina, was limping so badly that he asked to be replaced and withdrew to the sidelines. The substitute who came on in his place was a member of the Basque

Minority – my mother, needless to say. She came from behind with the ball, but just as she was about to enter the opposition box, a Sampdoria defender, the Stone Woman, needless to say, planted herself in front of her, saying in her strong Lavapiés accent: "Stop right there!" I woke up sweating. The television was on. Sampdoria were winning 2–0.

The following morning, our guide took us to the cathedral and had us stand outside the Baptistry of St John, before the Gates of Paradise.

"This is the work of the great Lorenzo Ghiberti. There isn't a more beautiful door anywhere in the world. Observe the details on each panel."

Some members of the Confined Space went to have a closer look, but the group was fragmented. Some were looking over at the cathedral; others, especially my mother, were already walking towards the campanile.

"What do you think, Eugeni?" our guide asked.

"Well, I left my glasses in our hotel room, but it certainly looks like a lovely door," Eugeni said.

Those of us still standing near the baptistry looked inquisitively at the Stone Woman. She held our gaze for five long seconds. Then she sighed. Then she summarised her thoughts:

"They look rather like picture cards. Nothing very special at all."

I looked up at the sky and saw a head wearing a green scarf peering down from the top of the campanile. It was, needless to say, my mother.

Galleria degli Uffizi, Ponte Vecchio, Piazza della Signoria, Santa Croce, Le Cappelle Medicee . . . We visited all those places and more in our five- or six-hour tour; but the forty-two members of the Confined Space felt oppressed, as if beneath the weight of a heavy stone slab, and the most weighed down of all were Eugeni and the man from Tres Cantos.

"What will that miserable woman say now?" the man from Tres Cantos kept muttering, while Eugeni's constant refrain was: "I can't see a thing without my glasses."

When we were in the Uffizi Gallery, standing before Leonardo's

"Annunciation", our guide finally reacted. He said to Eugeni rather tetchily:

"Look, give me your room card, and I'll go and fetch your wretched glasses!" Then, turning to the rest of the group: "Let's meet in twenty minutes' time at the exit. We still have two marvellous things to see: Fra Angelico's frescos and Michelangelo's magnificent 'David'."

"*Molt bé*," Eugeni said, cheered by the prospect of recovering his glasses. Meanwhile, our guide disappeared down the steps of the Uffizi.

"I wonder where his wife is. I haven't seen her at all today," my mother said.

Contrary to expectations, the day went downhill after this. In the Convent of San Marco, standing before another "Annunciation", this time by Fra Angelico, the Stone Woman spoke again. She waited until most of the members of the Confined Space had stopped speaking and our guide was ready to give us a brief talk about the painting, then she gave her succinct opinion:

"A bit old hat, don't you think?"

Her scornful remark dropped like a rock into the waters of a pool.

"Why didn't that woman stay in Lavapiés?" the man from Tres Cantos said.

"I think the angel's wings are really lovely," Eugeni said, now with his glasses on.

"Yes, they're beautiful. Like the wings of a butterfly," my mother said.

However, it wasn't easy to forget those stony, metal-plated words, and we slouched irritably off to the Galleria dell'Accademia to see Michelangelo's "David".

The white marble sculpture was in a small room. It was very hot, and when the forty-two members of the Confined Space entered, the temperature rose a couple more degrees. The physically oppressive atmosphere only increased the irritation most of us were feeling, especially the man from Tres Cantos, whose cheeks were already scarlet, his gaze sombre, his chin jutting forwards. A confrontation seemed imminent. Then suddenly, a woman looking at the sculpture fainted and fell to the floor. There was something of a commotion and – by one of those mysteries of the human mind – all the members of the Confined Space forgot their problems and relaxed.

Three burly men helped the woman to her feet. She was small and blonde and was wearing a Stars-and-Stripes badge on the lapel of her jacket. Was it Hillary Clinton and her bodyguards? I didn't have the chance to confirm this, because another matter demanded my attention. Public Enemy Number One, namely, the Stone Woman, took advantage of the silence filling the room to state her opinion:

"It's so much smaller than in the photographs!"

Our guide turned pale, but did not faint.

"He doesn't look at all well," my mother said. "Besides, his wife hasn't been seen all day. That would be the last straw if they were to split up having only just got married!"

And she laughed gaily, in the way conservative people of a certain age do laugh at the foolishness of the young.

When we returned to the hotel, we found his wife sitting in an armchair in the foyer, reading a magazine. When her husband, our guide, arrived, they exchanged an affectionate kiss.

"That's a relief!" my mother said.

At this point in the journey, after Pisa, Lucca and Florence, my mother was gripped by an anxiety that went way beyond the problems of modern marriage.

"We've seen some really beautiful things, haven't we?" she said as we were making our way back to our room.

"And there'll be more to see in Rome," I said.

"As far as I know, we don't have such fine sculptures and paintings in the Basque Country. And to tell you the truth that makes me a little sad."

"This place is unique in the world. Even Americans have to come here to see Michelangelo's sculptures," I said, going off at a slight tangent.

As we went round a corner, we came face to face with our guide and his wife. They had come up by the stairs. They were positively glowing and had their arms about each other's waists.

"In Rome, we'll see the '*Pietà*', Michelangelo's masterpiece," remarked our guide, the husband, the keen-eared one.

"I don't think they're going to split up," I said to my mother. "Not at least on this trip."

We were standing before the "*Pietà*". The body of Jesus lying across his Mother's lap, his right arm hanging limply down, his head fallen back; his Mother, head bowed and reaching out with her left hand. The shapes that Michelangelo had carved out of a block of white marble from the Alps.

It was still very early, and the members of the Confined Space were almost the only visitors to the basilica of St Peter's. The silence was broken only sporadically by a whisper or the sound of heels click-clacking over the marble floor. Even the organ was quiet. We were all looking at the sculpture. Intently, or, rather, expectantly.

And yet there was no scornful comment, no rocks, no daggers, no sharp remarks, only the murmur of someone struggling to get her words out:

"But this . . . this . . ."

It was the Stone Woman. She couldn't find the words to express her feelings. Something was holding them back. We gave her time to say what she had to say.

"This," she cried at last, "is utter perfection!"

Suddenly, the organ music flooded the basilica. It wasn't a hallelujah, but a graceful melody, worthy of the birds fluttering about in the vaulted ceiling.

"*L'art ha triomfat!*" Eugeni exclaimed.

"Yes, victory!" said the *madrileño* from Tres Cantos.

"All's well that ends well," added my mother.

Most of the members of the Confined Space thought that the visit to the basilica and her emotional response to the "Pietà" would bring the story of the Stone Woman to a close, but as the newspapers say, it wasn't over yet. A still bigger surprise awaited us. It happened when we left Rome and went to Assisi, birthplace of St Francis.

The basilica of St Francis of Assisi is on the top of a hill from which you can look down over the countryside for miles around. That summer, the fields were yellow; the olive trees, planted in neat rows, were green and leafy; the distant forests black. It was a sunny day.

We visited the church and the tomb, we studied the frescos by Giotto and Cimabue, and we went out into the atrium. It was nearly dusk, and the sun was already low on the horizon. Our guide – the newly happy husband – jumped up onto a parapet and called us to order. A young monk, a very skinny fellow, did the same and stood by his side.

"I've asked Giovanni for a favour," our guide said. "With his help, we are all going to recite the "Canticle of Brother Sun", which St Francis composed in this very place. Giovanni will give us the Italian, and I will read the words in Spanish. I have the translation here."

Travellers from other Confined Spaces joined our group. Most were Italians. In the end, there were eighty of us standing before Giovanni and our guide.

"*Altissimu, onnipotente, bone Signore . . .*" began Giovanni, pressing his two hands to his chest. Yet again, the first lines of the song reached the ears of believers and non-believers alike.

As if it were a litany, the Italians who had joined our group repeated each line. Then our guide read us the translation:

Laudato sie, mi'Signore cum tucte le Tue creature, spetialmente messor lo frate Sole [. . .] Laudato si, mi Signore, per sora Luna e le stelle . . .

"Be praised, my Lord, through all Your creatures, especially through my lord Brother Sun [. . .] Be praised, my Lord, through Sister Moon and the stars . . ."

Giovanni intoned the last lines of the hymn: *Laudato si, mi' Signore, per sora nostra morte corporale, da la quale nullu homo vivente pò skappare . . .*

The sun was sinking below the horizon. No cars could be seen on the motorway. A donkey walked slowly along a path accompanied by a boy.

I heard someone sobbing beside me. The Stone Woman's eyes were full of tears.

"Don't cry, Concha," someone said, although I don't know who.

The crying didn't stop. Not knowing what to do, the group stood motionless until, finally, our guide thanked the monk and, jumping down, headed off down the hill with his wife.

"Right, let's go and have supper!" he said.

"She lost her husband six months ago," he told me as he passed. Then he went over to her, to Concha, and told her what was on the supper menu that evening.

No, that isn't what happened at all. The visit we made to Assisi didn't end like that. Our guide did organise a reading of "The Canticle of the Sun" and brought a monk called Giovanni to join him, but the Stone Woman wasn't there, and no-one told me that she had been widowed recently or anything of the kind. That was a fantasy created in the head of the second member of the Basque Minority, needless to say, me.

The Stone Woman did not change. She remained exactly the same, like a block of stone. Her reaction to the *Pietà* was an exception. On the day of our visit to Assisi – I found out later – she decided to stay in the hotel, because she thought the town looked "pretty crappy".

BRIANNA DENISON

Of all the nights we spent in Reno, none seemed as silent as the night of 19 January, 2008. The university car park was empty. There were no cars in College Drive either. The Terrace, a bar where, on Saturdays, they played music and held barbecues, was closed and dark.

"I think there's some event going on elsewhere in the city," Ángela said. "All the students must be there."

We had got into the habit of going for a walk after supper, from our house as far as the lake on the campus, but that night we couldn't. The girls refused to go.

"Don't you want to see the swan?" I asked Sara.

"No," she said.

"Why not?"

"It feels like something bad is about to happen," Izaskun said, answering for her sister.

When we read the *Reno Gazette-Journal* on Monday, January 21, those words seemed like a premonition. The news was on the front page: on that same silent Saturday night, Brianna Denison, a nineteen-year-old student at Santa Barbara University in California, who had come back to Reno, her hometown, for the snowboarding festival SWAT 72, had been kidnapped from the home of the friends she was staying with.

The newspaper showed a small map of the scene of the kidnapping. The house was almost next to ours, on the junction of Sierra Street and College Drive. It was only fifty or sixty yards from our door to theirs.

The article gave more details. The pretty petite young woman, only five foot tall and weighing about a hundred pounds, had been kidnapped after attending a concert in the park next to the Truckee river, while she was asleep on a sofa just a few feet from the front door. According to the police, the criminal had acted alone and had simply opened the door and carried her off. The girl's friends, sleeping in the other bedrooms, had heard nothing. Nor it seemed had the friend's dog, which was also in the house, because it didn't even bark. Since the front door was made of glass panes through which you could see into the interior of the house, it was possible that the whole thing had happened by chance, and that the predator saw the girl through the glass door and decided there and then to commit the crime. The police, however, thought it more likely that the criminal had seen his victim beforehand, perhaps at the Hotel-Casino Sands Regency, where she'd had a meal before the concert, and that he had followed her back to the house.

On Tuesday there was more information. The police were linking the kidnapping with the sexual assaults that had taken place near the university in the last few weeks. In both cases, the victims had been girls of slight build, like Brianna. The newspaper repeated the information published when those two assaults had taken place: the first on October 22, 2007 in the Whalen Parking Complex, the second on November 13 in the parking lot of 401 College Drive.

"We're in his territory," I said to Ángela.

"Right in the middle," she said, and we both looked through the window at the house where the kidnap had taken place. It was a really pretty house and had recently been repainted a reddish colour.

We were trapped beneath a taut membrane, which captured and amplified every sound, every movement: the police sirens, the clatter of helicopters overhead, the checkpoints on the exits from the interstate, the interrogations that took place in the street itself and in people's houses. In the normally deserted area around Izaskun and Sara's school, there were now policemen apparently called up from the reserves. And they weren't the only people who were armed. Some fathers went to pick up their children wearing a gun at their waist.

At night, I was aware of a kind of vibration, the effect of everything that had happened during the day, and I found it hard to sleep. The police had told us that the criminal was probably still going about his normal life in the area between North Virginia Street and Rancho San Rafael Park and between the McCarran beltway and the I-80. As Ángela said, College Drive was right in the middle.

When I couldn't sleep, I saw things differently. I would look out into the garden and discover suddenly that the trees growing behind the hut formed a small wood, full of shadows and hiding places; I would look up at Earle's house and realise that the windows facing College Drive corresponded to the rooms reserved for guests, not to the kitchen or the living room, and that, should the predator decide to visit us, Earle would be unlikely to notice anything. Then again, the windows of the girls' bedroom were less than six feet from the ground. More importantly, Izaskun was about the same height and weight as Brianna. She might still only be an adolescent, but could pass for a petite young woman.

Ángela and I were the first people to be interrogated by the police. Had we seen anything odd on the night of January 19 to 20? No, but we had seen something odd that afternoon. A well-dressed man had got out of a limousine and dumped a leather suitcase in one of the trash cans in the street.

"Which trash can was it, exactly?" one of the policemen asked, stepping out onto the porch. I showed him.

The police came back a second time. Thinking it was Ángela, I opened the door in my dressing gown, my face still covered in shaving foam, and I felt so embarrassed that I couldn't understand what they were saying until Izaskun and Sara came and translated for me. They had come to search the house. I let them in and they searched the garden, the raccoon's hut and the cellar.

"Good idea," one of the policemen said when he saw that the small cellar windows, at ground level, were covered with pages taken from newspapers and magazines. This had been Mary Lore's idea. She knew that Izaskun and Sara used to play there and thought that the criminal might be able to see them from the usually deserted passageway that led from the garden into College Drive.

February arrived and with it came cold weather and grey skies, the latter something of a rarity in Nevada. On the 2nd, it snowed. The 3rd was a brilliant day of blue skies. On the 4th it snowed again. Indifferent to these meteorological changes, the *Reno Gazette-Journal* kept us up to date on the police investigation: the bloodstain on the pillow Brianna Denison had used belonged to the girl herself and so could not provide a D.N.A. sample from the criminal. The investigation was taking a different direction now. The police were questioning registered sex offenders who had committed rape or acts of paedophilia in the past. They appealed to the public to help, but not to call the police with mere trivia. Too many calls would simply slow down the investigation.

The vibration affected the whole city now. Female students going home at night took taxis laid on by the university. Posters bearing a photograph of Brianna Denison were put up in supermarkets and tied with blue ribbons to traffic lights and bridges and to the street lamps along by the Truckee river. The police also distributed reproductions of an Identikit picture of the criminal, based on descriptions given by the two students who had been attacked earlier: a simian, Neanderthal face, difficult to imagine as a real face. Can you really recognise someone without knowing what their eyes or voice are like? Every time I looked at the Identikit picture on my way to the library, it seemed to me that without eyes or voice, many bodies would be completely interchangeable.

"Oh, I agree absolutely," Dennis said, when I mentioned this to him. "You could take that picture and create another hundred different faces on the computer."

On the 7th, the temperature rose, and the piles of snow that had accumulated in shady areas melted and filled the streets with puddles. On the 8th it froze again, and the membrane covering the town seemed to lose its ability to vibrate, leaving a dead, lethargic calm. More cold days followed, more icy temperatures. The town seemed to have just one inhabitant: him. He moved about freely, getting on with his normal life, going to work, perhaps even teaching at the university and going back home to sleep. What's more, months earlier, one of the girls he had raped before kidnapping Brianna Denison had said – and the newspaper quoted her words again now – that he was clearly a professional rapist who, as Dennis had told me, shaved his pubic region so that not a single hair or any other organic substance would betray his D.N.A.

The 12th was different. Sara slipped on the steps when we were leaving for school and banged her head, an injury that, at first, seemed rather serious. She kept falling asleep on the way to the McCarran Medical Centre, and we had to shout at her to keep her awake. The anxiety of the next few days – she was kept under observation for forty-eight hours – freed us from the situation we had been living through. Our fear of what might happen to Sara was far greater than our fear of the criminal.

On the 16th, at around five in the morning, I picked up that day's copy of the *Reno Gazette-Journal* from the porch and went into the kitchen to read it. The news was all over the front page. Brianna Denison had been found strangled on a piece of waste ground near the airport.

The whole town was shaken. There was a continual wailing of sirens, but nothing happened. It soon became clear that the only hope was that he would try again – rapists always do – and that the victim would be able to use a pepper spray on him or shoot him. Otherwise, only a tip-off would lead to his arrest.

We couldn't leave Reno. Izaskun and Sara had to stay until the end of the school year, and Ángela still had work to do at the university. As Adam García, the police chief in charge of the case, put it, we must carry on as normal, but without allowing ourselves to succumb to a false sense of security. We must remain vigilant.

REVIEW AND SUMMARY OF WHAT HAPPENED IN THE DAYS FOLLOWING BRIANNA DENISON'S KIDNAPPING

SNOW

It snowed in Reno on the three days after the kidnapping, on January 20, 21 and 22. Every flake that fell was like a word, always the same word, the one we heard everywhere: *Rape! Rape! Rape!* It gave me a headache. One morning, I noticed raccoon tracks on the snow covering the garden porch, and for a few hours, until Ángela calmed me down, I was gripped by the absurd belief that our raccoon had turned rabid. I wondered, too, how we would defend ourselves if the criminal attacked at night, and when I found a ski pole in the cellar, I decided to keep it under the bed, just in case.

When it stopped snowing, there was a void, like the silence when an engine suddenly stops running.

THE HELICOPTER

As soon as the weather improved, the helicopter started patrolling the skies over Reno. You would often hear it during the day and at night as well.

I called in at the Center for Basque Studies and found Mary Lore looking very depressed.

"He'll kill her, I'm sure of it," she said.

When I went to buy a coffee from the stall outside the library, I repeated this remark to Earle and Dennis.

"It's not that he *will* kill her," Earle said. "The girl's already dead."

"We mustn't lose hope, Bob," Dennis said, and his eyes grew moist with tears.

I asked about the security helicopter.

"I think they're looking for the vehicle," Earle said.

"Probably," Dennis said. "In any case, there's loads of information on the Internet. People are giving the police various clues to follow up. We mustn't lose hope."

SPECIAL AGENTS

A note published in the *Reno Gazette-Journal* on January 23 informed readers of the arrival from Chicago of policemen who specialised in investigating sex crimes.

The snow returned. It was snowing in town, in the Sierra Nevada, in the desert. The cold crept in through the cracks in doors and windows.

RENO POLICE BULLETIN

Eight days after the kidnapping, on January 28, 2008, the Reno police published a bulletin, a single, well-produced sheet on high-quality paper. It bore a photograph of Brianna Denison and asked the public to collaborate in the task of tracking down the criminal. It added that Brianna's kidnapper and the man who committed the sexual assault that took place on December 16, 2007 in Terrace Drive were one and the same person, which meant that they had a D.N.A. sample.

"It is important to know that because the D.N.A. that has been collected is valid and conclusive, any person who is brought to police attention can be easily, definitively, and unobtrusively eliminated or identified as a suspect."

The bulletin ended with descriptions of the suspect and the victim.

DESCRIPTION OF THE SUSPECT

"White male, approximately 28 to 40 years old, taller than 5 feet 6 inches but not excessively so; a stomach that was described as not excessively large and firm but not flabby; an "innie" belly button, shaved pubic region, a light covering of hair on his arms; and facial hair about a quarter to a half an inch long below his chin which was soft."

DESCRIPTION OF THE VICTIM. BRIANNA ZUNINO DENISON

"19 years old, 60", 98lbs, long dark brown hair, blue eyes, her nose is pierced on the right side, and she has a scar on her left knee. She was last seen wearing a white tank top with pink angel wings, rhinestones and 'Bindi' on the back and pink sweat pants."

A BABY'S SHOE

The police bulletin added a detail to the description of the criminal's car. One of his previous victims had noticed a baby's shoe underneath the passenger seat.

MESSAGE TO L.

How easy everything is in that story about the glass slipper. "The gentleman made Cinderella sit down and, placing the shoe on her foot, he saw that it fitted perfectly. Her two sisters were astonished, and even more astonished when Cinderella produced the second shoe from a bag and put it on her other foot." Outside the story, though, things are much more complicated. If the police had found the baby's shoe seen in the criminal's car, and then scoured Sparks and Reno, trying it on every baby they found, the result would have been a useless list of a thousand or more addresses. Magic doesn't exist in real life.

QUICK RESPONSE FROM L.

No, magic doesn't exist. I was taking a new, supposedly miracle drug to combat diabetes. But it has no effect on me whatsoever, and the doctors have advised me to stop taking it. Not to worry, though. They assure me that soon other drugs will become available, and that one of them will cure me.

THE FIRST SUSPECTS

According to the *Reno Gazette-Journal*, they had done D.N.A. tests on thirty-four registered sex offenders who lived near the university. Since all these tests proved negative, they would have to widen their search to all of Reno and Sparks. Collections would be made at football and basketball matches to pay for these tests.

213

The newspaper published photographs taken in different parts of the town. These showed posters tied onto street lamps with blue ribbons and bearing a message directed at the criminal: "Bring Bri Back."

DENNIS'S CONTRIBUTION

The five of us, Mary Lore, Earle, Dennis, Ángela and myself, were having lunch in the university diner. Mary Lore was feeling very low. It had been two weeks since Brianna Denison was kidnapped, and the ubiquitous blue ribbons had an increasingly hopeless air about them. The criminal was still at large, and it didn't seem as though it was going to be easy to track him down.

"They'll find him," Earle said. "That shoe will be the clincher, I reckon. The mother of the child is bound to have her suspicions. Men don't usually shave off their pubic hair."

"Perhaps she knows, but doesn't want to report her partner," Mary Lore said.

Earle disagreed.

"Any accomplice to a kidnapping risks spending the rest of her life in jail. I'm sure she'll think it through, and if she wants to go on living with her child, then her only option is to go to the police."

"Maybe she's very submissive and doesn't dare," Ángela said.

Earle made a gesture as if he were cutting his throat.

"She'd better dare, because she's risking her own life."

I told them what I had written to L. After all, Cinderella had a fairy godmother to rely on, but the Reno police had only themselves.

"I've made my contribution," Dennis said.

We waited for him to explain. He hesitated.

"Come on, Dennis. You're among mature adults," Earle said. "Well, three mature adults and one old man."

"It was something I read in *Lolita* that gave me the idea," Dennis said. "The paedophile in the novel hires the services of a prostitute who looks like a child. I thought that perhaps there might be such prostitutes in the brothels of Nevada. And it turns out that they do offer that service. They take on prostitutes who are over eighteen, but who still have the body of a child. To attract paedophiles, I suppose."

214

He paused.

"Brianna is or was very petite. And so was the girl he raped last year. He has a taste for little girls. He's like Humbert Humbert."

Dennis looked at us.

"I mean the character in *Lolita*," he explained.

"I hope he isn't like Humbert Humbert," I said. "Not only was he extremely intelligent, he also had access to divine help. God got him out of every sticky situation he got into."

"I'm sure he's not like him," Earle said.

Dennis continued to expound his theory:

"Well, I just thought that a man with those tastes would probably go to brothels and would choose prostitutes who looked like children. If so, the cameras in the brothels would have filmed him on various occasions. I told the police they should analyse those images and ask the prostitutes if they remembered any client of theirs who had a shaved pubic region, for example. They seemed very interested."

"A very good idea, Dennis," Mary Lore said, and we all agreed.

Earle whispered to me:

"If the police took up his suggestion, they'd be faced by the same situation as they would with the baby's shoe. They'd have a list of hundreds of men."

Dennis asked what he was saying, and Earle patted him on the back.

"I was just saying that prostitutes tend to have very poor memories when they talk to the police."

"It's all so depressing," Mary Lore said, and with those words we brought lunch to a close.

PSALM 37

February 3 was a Sunday. Around nine o'clock in the morning, someone knocked on the door of our house in College Drive, and I thought, because it was early for a Sunday morning – Izaskun and Sara were still in bed – that it must be another visit from the police. When I opened the door, I found two young men. One of them was about thirty, and his companion about twenty. They were both very pale-skinned and very blond. They were wearing dark suits and white shirts, with no tie, and each was carrying a bible.

Ángela asked them what they wanted.

"We want you to allow us to read Psalm 37," the older of the two said. Then, when we agreed, he indicated to his companion that he should open his bible and read. The page was marked with a red ribbon.

The reading lasted for a couple of minutes. When it was over, the older man spoke to us again:

"Read Psalm 37 every day. If a lot of us read it often enough, Violence and Evil will vanish from the world."

They spoke and moved very gravely.

We didn't have a bible in College Drive, so when they left, we looked for the psalm online, having found the young preacher's English rather hard to understand.

> "Fret not thyself because of evildoers, neither be thou envious against the workers of iniquity. For they shall soon be cut down like the grass, and wither as the green herb. Trust in the LORD, and do good; so shalt thou dwell in the land, and verily thou shalt be fed."

FEBRUARY 17. POLICE STATEMENT

Reno Gazette-Journal: "Saturday afternoon, Reno Police announced that the body discovered Friday in a field near a busy industrial area was Brianna 'Bri' Denison, 19, who was kidnapped Jan. 20 from her friend's home near the University of Nevada, Reno."

MESSAGE TO L.
RENO, FEBRUARY 18, 2008

There are lots of blue ribbons in Reno in memory of Brianna Denison. We put some up too.

Yesterday, the murdered girl's aunt spoke for the family:

"We are not giving up until we find that bastard. This shouldn't have happened. Now we are on a manhunt. In my heart of hearts

I know someone knows him. They may not even suspect him, but, people, please, [you] just really need to take a look at your husbands, boyfriends, brothers, nephews, or your neighbor."

In other statements, the family said that the murderer had definitely chosen the wrong person and the wrong state, meaning that the Denisons were an important family, and the death penalty is still in force in Nevada.

Many people will doubtless disapprove of the family's crude desire for revenge, because from an intellectual perspective the suffering-cum-beam in the other person's eye is invisible or seems trivial in comparison with our own suffering-cum-mote. However, bearing in mind that Brianna's mother spoke again and again on local and national television, begging the kidnapper to show mercy, and after almost a month of agony, all the family has been given is a body discarded like a piece of trash, what can one expect? What do you think?

L.'S RESPONSE

King Kong must die.

THE OFFICE NOTICEBOARD IN THE CENTER FOR BASQUE STUDIES

Dennis and Mary Lore were standing by the office noticeboard, reading a cutting from the obituary page of the *Reno Gazette-Journal*. They had decorated it with a blue ribbon, and they both looked tearful.

"Sorry," Mary Lore said when she saw me. "It's just so moving."

Contrary to what I had imagined, the obituary had nothing to do with Brianna Denison. It was in memory of Patricia Ann Marini, an attractive, fifty-something woman looking frankly into the camera with what one sensed would have been green eyes. I read the dates underneath the photograph and discovered that she had died ten years before, on February 2, 1998.

"She wasn't a relative or anything, I put it here because I thought the poem her partner wrote for her was just so beautiful," Mary Lore said.

"Someone should write something similar for Brianna," Dennis said, "but it seems like no-one thinks about her now, just about her murderer."

The poem dedicated to Patricia Ann Marini was signed with the initials K.E.F. and occupied a whole column. It described, in the form of a letter, something that had happened two months before she died. "Christmas 1997. I gave you a mauve Moleskine journal with a red woven silk bookmark. We thought recording our ideas, emotions, moments – capturing our dreams – would be fun to read on Christmas Eve '07 . . ."

That wish foundered because Patricia Ann Marini died afterwards, and the mauve journal had been lost until, on the very date they had talked about, Christmas 2007, it had suddenly, serendipitously, reappeared. K.E.F. found in its pages some pastel drawings by Patricia followed by her signature in dazzling blue ink, along with a promise of love: "Love forever, Christmas 97." K.E.F. wrote that, sometimes, after turning out the light, when the moon's rays cast blue-velvet shadows on the bedroom wall, he would run his finger over her signature. The journal had found a use. "In it now, I write *my* dreams, *my* memories – those silent ships in sail."

"Compare what you've just read with the farewell dedicated to this other Patricia," Dennis said.

Immediately below Patricia Ann Marini's obituary was that of a woman called Patricia Susek. Five lines, a few names, two dates and a note stating that it would be a private funeral.

I said nothing, and Mary Lore interpreted my silence as a criticism.

"I know," she said. "We're all still feeling depressed about Brianna. That's why we keep fixating on obituaries and suchlike."

"What I feel is fear," I said.

"It's not so dangerous now," Dennis said. "It will be a couple of months before the murderer tries anything again. He knows the police are looking for him everywhere."

This was true. There were even police checkpoints in College Drive.

"They always catch the criminal in the end, and they'll catch this one too."

"How would you analyse that poem by K.E.F.?" Dennis suddenly asked.

We had known each other for about six months, and this was the first time he had asked me anything related to my work as a writer. He was an I.T. expert, capable of solving whatever problem the students threw at him. Perhaps he wanted to know if I was equally competent in my own field.

I tried to give him the explanation he wanted. The poem – I said – placed Patricia Ann Marini in a noble setting, relating her to the mauve Moleskine notebook with its red silk bookmark, along with drawings of flowers, velvet shadows and a night lit by the full moon, and that this was a way of embellishing his beloved's final image. And that, after all, was something that had been happening since the world began.

According to Lucan, when Apollo accidentally struck Hyacinth on the head with a discus and killed him, Apollo made a delicate flower spring from the drops of blood spilled, the flower that bears Hyacinth's name. But that need to embellish the dead occurs in real life too and not just in myths. When Lawrence of Arabia was buried, they placed on his shroud the golden dagger he had been given at Mecca. And what about the countless black orchids and wreaths that adorned Eva Perón's coffin?

Instead of gold or flowers, K.E.F.'s poem preferred ordinary objects, personal things, and made of them a kind of Japanese flower arrangement, an *ikebana*, in keeping with Patricia Ann Marini's personality. And that was all. No hopes. K.E.F. did not raise his eyes to heaven like those who, like Lazarus's sisters, believe in resurrection. No invocations. No prayers. No mention of God. In that nothingness, that silence, his wishes and dreams after the death of the woman he loved had become "those silent ships in sail". A line from Gerard Manley Hopkins came into my head: "Our prayer seems lost in desert ways, our hymn in the vast silence dies." K.E.F.'s words were more truthful than many Christian metaphors. After death, nothing. Only, sometimes, a few flowers, a notebook, a poem, and someone who tends the memory of the person who has gone.

Dennis was standing with arms folded, his left hand on his chin.

"You mentioned the moon being full, but how do you know that?"

I didn't understand what he meant at first and had to reread the poem before offering him an explanation:

"K.E.F. says that on some nights, after he has turned out the light, the moon casts velvet shadows on the walls of his bedroom. I think that would only be possible if the moon was full or almost full. Otherwise, it wouldn't be bright enough."

"Yes, you're right. I see what you mean now," Dennis said.

Mary Lore looked thoughtful.

"You should write an article for the *Reno Gazette-Journal*," she said.

"I don't think I could. I only seem to have sombre thoughts at the moment."

"It's a sombre situation, that's for sure," Mary Lore. "If they don't catch the murderer soon, we're all going to go mad."

"*I* certainly will," Dennis said.

WOLF PACK VS. HOUSTON COUGARS

There was going to be a basketball game at the Lawlor Center between the Wolf Pack and the Houston Cougars, and I went to watch it with the Laxalt family and a few other friends. Even though it was only a tournament and didn't count in the university league of the N.C.A.A., the stadium was packed with more than ten thousand spectators.

The dominant colours were the navy blue of the Wolf Pack and the pale blue of the ribbons left in memory of Brianna Denison. A collection was taken before the game began.

"None of the D.N.A. tests so far have led the police to the perpetrator," Monique Laxalt explained. "Brianna's murderer obviously isn't a registered sex offender in Nevada. That means they're going to have to do more D.N.A. tests in the surrounding states, and that costs money."

I suddenly remembered that Ángela, Izaskun and Sara were alone at home, and it was as if all the other spectators had suddenly had the same frightening thought about Reno's King Kong, because everyone fell silent for a moment; then the game started and the shouting began, the Houston Cougars went five points into the lead, and our ears and eyes immediately transported us to another world. Seconds later, the only white player in the Wolf Pack scored a triple, and we all burst into wild applause.

MOMENT

I was having supper in a place on Virginia Street and gazing out through the window at the mountains beyond the desert. The light from the evening sun rested, in turn, on one peak and then another, as if it were the beam from a torch. It lit one peak, tingeing it with pinks and pale oranges, then changed, and the pinks and oranges shifted to the next peak. It occurred to me that a child would have said that the sun was jumping from one mountain to the next, and I wanted to try out that idea on Izaskun and Sara, but by the time they got back from the birthday party being held for one of Mary Lore's daughters, the sun would have settled on a distant peak, apparently for good, as if it lacked the energy to make another leap.

A plane left the airport and rose diagonally up over the town. The sky was edged with a coppery light, and the plane was a bright fragment of mirror in the vastness.

CONVERSATION AT THE FUNERAL HOME
(A MEMORY)

We three brothers were in the waiting room at the funeral home; our father, with a rosary twined about his fingers, was lying in a coffin in a small room next door. A man came over to us carrying a file that resembled a restaurant menu, except that it was full of photographs of bouquets and wreaths and baskets of flowers and their respective prices.

"Thanks," my brother said, "but that won't be necessary."

The man was even dressed like a maître d', in a black suit, and his whole appearance was reminiscent of the ageing romantic leads in films from the 1950s: wavy hair slicked back, elegant eyebrows, blue eyes, perfect teeth. Had my father come back to life and seen him, he would have made a joke, something along the lines of: "I haven't even got to heaven yet and already I'm seeing angels."

"Did you have something else in mind?" he asked.

"I own a florist's shop," my older brother said. "So I'll take care of the flowers."

This wasn't, in fact, true. While he did own various businesses, the main one being a limousine rental firm, he definitely didn't own a florist's shop, but that was his style: keep things short and to the point.

The man left and we were once again alone, waiting for the other visitors to arrive. After a while, my younger brother stood up and went into the room where our father was lying. He returned at once.

"Whose bright idea was the rosary?"

"Nobody's," I said. "It must be the custom."

"What do you mean the 'custom'?"

He swore, oblivious to the crucifix on the wall. I imagined Jesus sternly wagging a finger at him for using such language. I got a fit of the giggles then and covered my face with my hands.

"We have to remove that rosary – now!"

And my younger brother went off to fetch the man in the dark suit.

"Revolution in the funeral parlour!" said my older brother.

"What flowers are you going to take to the church?" I asked.

"Hyacinths."

Our father's name was Jacinto.

"It's logical if you think about it."

My older brother had a particular love of flowers, and even organised his holidays around them. He would visit Saint-Pierre or some other island to spend a week photographing flowers or go on tours of the world's finest botanical gardens. When Ángela published an article about Atanasio Echeverría, a botanical artist who accompanied some of the eighteenth-century expeditions to North and Central America, my brother bought her a print of one of Echeverría's illustrations from Madrid's botanical garden and gave it to her as a present.

My younger brother returned, accompanied by the undertaker.

"I see your point, but we couldn't remove the rosary even if we wanted to. He's been dead for too long. You have doubtless heard of rigor mortis," the man said angelically. We were causing him endless problems, but he seemed nevertheless to like us.

"Well, if there's nothing to be done . . ." my younger brother said.

"Besides," the man-angel added somewhat hesitantly, "the fingers of your father's right hand were not exactly presentable, shall we say, and I thought it best to disguise them a little."

Our father, Jacinto, had lost the tips of the thumb and middle finger of his right hand, the consequence of two minor accidents in his carpenter's workshop.

"The marks of his profession and nothing to be ashamed of," my younger brother said. "On the contrary."

"Continual struggle, permanent revolution," murmured my older brother.

"I respect your point of view, of course, but if you wanted a purely secular affair, you should have gone about the whole business differently and organised the funeral and the service outside the church."

"The whole business . . ." When he left, I started laughing. Then my older brother joined in, and my younger brother. For some reason we found that expression deeply comical, as well as the angel's suddenly stern expression.

"We must calm down," my younger brother said, stopping laughing. "People will be arriving soon."

Indeed, only a few seconds later, our aunt and uncle appeared with their children, the entire Albizu clan. We all embraced, and they went in to see our father. We three brothers and my aunt stood in the doorway.

"How's María?" she asked. Her family always called my mother María rather than Izaskun.

"She's fine, but she didn't want to come today. She'll be there at the funeral, though," my older brother said.

"Do you remember how we always used to have lunch together during the feast of San Juan? Now we never see each other. What changed?"

We said nothing. That was when José Francisco had been alive. Our aunt was addressing the chorus in her beautiful voice, but the chorus could not answer.

A burly, bald-headed man entered the room.

"This was my father's best friend," I told my aunt. "He was the last person to make him laugh."

"I told him about a trick some rather loutish young men played on a poor woodsman," the man said, shaking my hand.

"There's never any shortage of loutish young men," my aunt said, and she went into the room to see my father.

"Ah well, so it goes," I said to my father's friend.

"Yes, we'll all end up here one day, if not today, then tomorrow. But there's one thing you must be quite clear about: your father has gone over to the other side having lived as happily here as the Shah of Persia."

THE SUBJECT OF STEVE FOSSETT RETURNS
FEBRUARY 15, 2008

The remains of Steve Fossett and his plane had still not been found, and a judge in Illinois had declared him officially dead. The news was in all the papers.

"It's a shame we can't ask the vermin who ate him for his whereabouts," Earle said when we talked about it.

The Internet was soon full of weirdos with their questions: "How could an experienced pilot like Fossett die in such a stupid way?" "Why are they in such a hurry to declare him dead?" "What private interests lie behind the official declaration?"

The days passed, and the weirdos' hypotheses became ever weirder. One of them, who signed himself "Oxo", wrote:

"The day he disappeared, Fossett was carrying a million dollars in a suitcase. Why did he need so much money on what was a routine flight? To pay off the aliens perhaps? According to a close friend of his, Fossett was worried about growing old and about the boring future that awaited him and he wanted to buy immortality from the aliens."

"That's true," responded Moon Cat. "But, according to Dr Mattriss, the most common kind of alien in the Nevada deserts are the carnivorous cuneiforms. If Fossett had met them rather than the ones selling immortality, they would have eaten him."

A third weirdo signed himself "American Soldier".

"I agree with some of the opinions given here and not with others. Fossett did have a problem with getting old. He was clearly losing his physical vigor, and he couldn't accept it. Perfectly normal in a man who held more than a hundred world records. It was painful to him to go on living like a little old grandpa and die in his bed. He longed for a heroic death. That's why he headed off from the Hilton Ranch in his Citabria and flew straight to Area 51. And that's no joking matter. Any plane entering Area 51 airspace is immediately shot down by a missile, end of story. That's how Fossett died. The remains of his Citabria would be crushed, turned into scrap and dumped in some warehouse."

I told Earle and Dennis about what I had read when we met at the coffee stall near the library.

"If they had to pay what we're going to pay for these coffees for every comment they made, they might have a little less faith in aliens," Earle said. "That's the trouble with faith. It's free."

Dennis raised one finger, the way students do when they want to ask something in class.

"You're right, Bob, but Fossett is a special case," he said. "Have you ever seen anything like it? Eight Civil Air Patrol planes and three helicopters, more than a thousand flying hours in total. Then there were the National Guard search parties who spent more than three weeks scouring the mountains, not to mention the Internet users who did their bit by scanning thousands of satellite photographs . . . So, yes, obviously, that stuff about aliens is all fake, but there are still a lot of unanswered questions about Fossett's disappearance."

Earle addressed the student serving at the coffee stall.

"Dennis will pay for our coffees, O.K.? I just noticed a little glimmer of faith, and he's not getting away with that for free."

The student couldn't possibly have known what we were talking about, but he burst out laughing.

The stranger was wearing a black cape and a hood that covered his face. He was sitting hunched on a round rock. I thought he must be ill and I looked about me to see if there was anyone who could help him. I realised then that the rock was in the middle of the blue waters of Lake Tahoe. Where was the white boat that did tours of the lake and that could have transported the sick man to shore? Nowhere to be seen.

I looked again at the stranger and saw that he had stood up.

"Are you feeling better, Casey Jones?" I asked.

"What do you mean by calling me 'Casey Jones'?" he exclaimed, taking off his hood, and before me stood Bob Earle.

I stammered a few words of apology, but he appeared to be thinking of something else. I noticed that he looked sad.

"Time passes, and the fundamental themes begin to float to the surface the way buoys do that have become tangled up under the water," he said. "And do you know what is the most important of those themes?"

I shook my head.

"Faust!"

"Faust?"

"Yes, Faust. Goethe's not Marlowe's. Haven't you, at your age, already given it some thought?" he asked, surprised. "I'll be frank with you: I wouldn't hesitate to sell my soul to Mephistopheles if I could have my youth back. I'd do it right now!"

A memory rose up from the depths of my consciousness, like those submerged buoys he mentioned. I saw Earle in a deserted park in Reno, sitting on a wooden bench. Beside him, wearing a short black dress, was Natalie, Mary Lore's niece, the one who had shared our Thanksgiving supper, the captain of the university hockey team.

"May I change metaphors, Bob?" I said. "I'd like to forget about buoys and water and revert to the earth."

"I've nothing against the earth," he said, opening his arms wide as if to embrace the whole world. We were sitting now in an apparently neglected vegetable patch. There were roots and weeds and stones everywhere.

"Bob, don't expect to find gold coins beneath ordinary earth!" I exclaimed with unexpected vehemence, unexpected even to me. "If you dug a hole in this patch, for example, if you dug a thousand holes like the moles do, what do you think you would find? Gold coins? Love? No, Bob. Under the earth you will find only more earth. I mean it, Bob, don't fall in love with Natalie! The story of Faust is just that, a story! *Os vellos non deben de namorarse!*"

"*Os vellos non deben de namorarse?* What kind of language is that?" he asked.

"*Gallego*," I said. "It's the title of a short play by Castelao."

The conversation had taken an absurd turn, even for a dream. I made myself wake up. There I was in the house in College Drive. Seven o'clock in the morning. Izaskun was sleeping snuggled up beneath a duvet. Out in the garden, the first blue jays of the morning were cackling in the trees, and underneath one tree sat the raccoon, gazing up at the birds.

INDIAN COUNTRY GUIDE MAP

The spring vacation was nearly upon us, and we asked Earle where he thought we should go. He didn't hesitate. We should, he said, visit what was known as Indian Territory.

We got out our guide to Nevada so that he could show us the route on one of the maps, but he didn't even bother to open it.

"No, no, we need a really good road map, and the A.A.A. maps are the best. They have one that includes the whole of Indian Territory."

"We'd better buy a copy," Ángela said.

"No, they're not for sale. They're issued free to A.A.A. members."

"But we're not members," I said.

"Yes, but I am. We can go to their office right now if you like. It's only ten minutes away."

I went with him. We drove five or six miles down the I-80 to a complex including offices, shops and restaurants. The parking lot was vast and full of advertising hoardings. A particularly large one showed a model with short blond hair, wearing a blue bra, and with the name of the lingerie manufacturer printed across her belly. I recognised her at once. It was Liliana, "the Russian flower" from the swimming pool. She had a gold chain around her neck; however, the pendant was no longer the Russian Orthodox cross, but the manufacturer's logo.

Earle noticed me looking at her.

"She's certainly pretty," he said.

"Her name's Liliana."

As we were walking over to the A.A.A. office, Earle suddenly grasped my shoulder.

"Be careful, my friend. *Os vellos non deben de namorarse!*" And he said this with a strong American accent of course. "Old men shouldn't fall in love."

"Where did you hear that?" I asked. "Since when have you spoken *gallego*?"

"Don't be so surprised. Years ago, I took a few undergraduate classes in one or two of the Iberian languages."

I wasn't so much surprised by the fact that he knew some *gallego*, as by the truly perplexing coincidence between my dream and reality. By then, however, we were inside the A.A.A. office, and so I said nothing.

One of the tables was piled high with road maps, and, after first showing his membership card, Earle picked up several. One bore the words *Indian Country Guide Map*.

"This is fantastic," he said. "It covers five whole states."

When we got back onto the I-80 – Reno's casinos were on our right, unlit by neon and looking strangely dull – it occurred to me that perhaps living in Reno wasn't that easy for a man approaching seventy, however rich he might be and however fit and healthy.

"*Os vellos non deben de namorarse!*" I said.

"Never a truer word said!" Earle said, laughing.

"Can I say something a little strange?"

"Feel free."

"An idea has been going round and round in my head ever since the Thanksgiving supper."

We were just about to take the exit onto Virginia Street. Three more minutes and we would be at the university.

Earle was listening.

"If you remember, Mannix asked us to talk about our favourite smells. And one of the people sitting at the table chose liniment. The girl who plays hockey for the university team, Mary Lore's niece . . ."

"Natalie," Earle said, looking slightly surprised. "How did you guess?"

"Because of your reaction when she said the word 'liniment'. Mannix pulled a face, but you didn't. On the contrary."

"I can only conclude that you have alien powers. When you go back to Area 51, send greetings to your fellow aliens."

The university car park had a space reserved for emeritus professors. Earle parked there.

"Don't tell anyone, XY120. Not even telepathically," he said when he turned off the engine. Then, with a great rolling of r's, he added in Spanish: "*Es amor prohibido.*" A forbidden love.

MARKING THE MAP

We spread out the Indian Country Guide Map on the office desk. It was a big map, about 3½ feet by 3½ feet. Earle picked up a black pen and began marking out our itinerary, explaining as he went along.

"If you leave Reno by the usual route, you'll reach Carson City. Then you follow Route 95, which takes you through Tonopah, and when you reach Goldfield, you can always turn off and say hello to those aliens in Area 51. You can spend the night here, in Beatty. The second night here, in Las Vegas. Then you keep going until you reach Mesquite, and from there you go on to Utah, then over towards Arizona, until you come to Kayenta . . ."

He mentioned many more names, marking in black the roads and the places where we could stay the night.

MESSAGE TO L.
BEATTY (NEVADA), MARCH 19, 2008

Today we drove over three hundred miles across the desert, from Reno to Las Vegas, and now we're in a small town called Beatty. It's twenty past five in the afternoon, and the temperature is 28 degrees C. According to the motel receptionist, this is nothing to complain about, especially when you consider how hot it gets in summer. Death Valley, which is not that far from here, holds the world record for the hottest air temperature: 60 degrees C.

The motel has two floors, but the first floor is really a casino, with one-armed bandits on either side and three poker tables in the middle. It was packed with people when we arrived, slightly emptier when I went back up to our room.

I'm alone at the moment, and from the window I can see Ángela, Izaskun and Sara. They're in the jacuzzi in the inner courtyard. The jacuzzi is tiny, just big enough for three.

On the journey, when we left Route 50 and joined Route 95, leaving Fallon behind us, we saw rows of small domes. They looked like glass bubbles that had popped up from the ground. I was expecting something odd and unusual, because Earle had told me that this part of Nevada is home to the biggest arsenal in the world, and that all kinds of weapons and bombs – nuclear and plutonium and who knows what else – are stored in artificial underground caves, but having only seen the satellite images Dennis downloaded from the Internet for me, I hadn't imagined anything like those rows and rows of domes. The satellite images had shown giant targets and landing strips traced out on the desert floor.

We drove for miles and miles and still the domes were there. The whole area is fenced off, and there are lots of roadside signs: WARNING: RESTRICTED AREA. WARNING: NO TRESPASSING. WARNING: MILITARY INSTALLATION. PHOTOGRAPHY OF THIS AREA IS PROHIBITED. Very intimidating.

About eighty miles from Beatty, three planes appeared; they looked like flying knives. A second later, they had gone and, in front of us, on the side of the road, as if the planes had deposited it there, was a white yacht. If it had been a real yacht, I would have found the image deeply disturbing – as Francis Bacon said, the mind cannot tolerate absurd images – but it had been converted into a house. A man wearing red shorts and a vest was hanging out his washing on the deck.

We don't know exactly how many miles Beatty is from Area 51, probably about eighty, but since the film "Independence Day", this place has apparently become a magnet for tourists hoping for an encounter with a flying saucer or a little man with a very big head. Most, though, choose to visit Death Valley. That's what we're going to do tomorrow. We're setting off really early, making sure to wear our hats and to apply plenty of sun cream, especially on our ears.

MESSAGE TO L.
LAS VEGAS (NEVADA), MARCH 22, 2008

We're in Las Vegas now, in the Excalibur Hotel. With its red and blue cone-shaped towers, it looks like an imitation of the medieval castles you read about in fairy tales. The casino on the ground floor is huge, and is constantly criss-crossed, as if they were on skates, by uniformed employees offering customers various forms of entertainment. As soon as you escape one, you're tackled by another: "How're you doing, sir? Take a little look at this. You won't find a better show in the whole of Las Vegas."

When we were walking down Las Vegas Boulevard, we were given a handout, a black-and-white photocopy, entitled *Things to Do with Children*. So Las Vegas does think about children too, although, of course, it thinks much more about other things. Ten minutes after receiving that photocopy, and when I was alone – Ángela and the girls had gone to see the gondolas in a hotel called the Venetian – another distributor of leaflets handed me a very different one, *Las Vegas Sundown*: sixteen full-colour pages containing about fifty photographs of girls: Susie, Brandi, Amy, Celeste, Angel and Robin ("college students"), Nissi, Roxy, Candy, Kiki and many others, all half-naked. "Real girls. Directly to your room. Parties for newly-weds. Private parties." And there they are, Tina and Amber – "for those for whom one girl simply isn't enough" – two girls who don't look much older than twelve.

MESSAGE TO L.
SPRINGDALE (UTAH), MARCH 23, 2008

Last night, I went downstairs to the casino in the Hotel Excalibur to have a glass of whiskey, and a man came over to me. He was a rather coarse-looking fellow in his fifties, with muscular arms and a bit of a belly. His breath smelled of drink.

"Don't you recognise me?" he asked.

To judge by his accent, he came from somewhere near the village where I was born, Asteasu. He took off his baseball cap. He had curly hair.

"You're a plumber, aren't you?" I said at last. He had done some work at my parents' house.

He nodded.

"What are you doing here?" I said.

"We're on holiday." And he pointed to a group of men at the other end of the bar.

"We're all plumbers," he said. Then he called the waiter over and raised my glass. "Bring him another one of these."

He explained that they saved up all the money they accumulated from trade discounts and then, once a year, organised "a bit of a jaunt", a Candy, Roxy, Susie kind of jaunt.

I took a sip of my second whiskey.

"What about your family, what do they have to say?"

"You mean my wife?" he asked.

He started to explain, but then stopped and went over to his friends. He returned with a camera.

"We've got hundreds of pictures like this," he said, pressing a button. The photographs started scrolling past on the little screen.

They hadn't been taken in Las Vegas, but in rather more religious places. In most of them, the plumbers were seen posing in front of or inside various colonial churches. I recognised the Basilica of Our Lady of Guadalupe.

"Mexico City," he said.

The plan was a simple one. First, they went to Mexico and spent two days "furiously taking photos". Then they flew to Las Vegas, where they were spending four days "having a high old time". On the seventh day they would be flying back to Madrid via Atlanta.

I couldn't believe my ears.

"Long live Our Lady of Guadalupe, mother of the alibi!" I cried, raising my glass to him. He was not amused.

"I'm a good Catholic, you know," he replied in rather wounded tones. I thought he was going to get seriously annoyed, but it went no further than that. "After all, if the President of the United States can do what he did with Monica, I reckon a plumber can too. That's democracy for you."

"Long live Clinton!" I cried. That second whiskey was clearly having its effect.

The waiter happened to be standing right in front of me, and he smiled broadly.

"I agree, sir. He's certainly the best President for us Latinos."

When I went up to our room, the girls were watching a film, and Ángela was sitting in an armchair, reading. On the wall behind her hung a large picture of Merlin.

"You can learn a lot in Las Vegas," I said.

"Who from? The architects?" she asked, without looking up.

"No, the plumbers."

With the aid of those two whiskies and that silly joke, I slept like a log.

Right now, we're in a small town called Springdale, in Mormon territory. Tomorrow, we're going to visit Zion National Park.

MESSAGE TO L.
TORREY (UTAH), MARCH 26, 2008

The place we've stopped at today is called Capitol Reef National Park. It reminds me of a Zen garden, with gentle sandy paths and rocks worn smooth by the elements.

We walked a lot, going up and down hills, seeing a stone arch here, a rushing stream there; further off, a beautiful clump of trees. Fortunately, it was only when we came back that we noticed the official sign explaining what to do if you met a mountain lion.

Before leaving the park, we were strolling along a narrow path, when we heard the sound of running feet. It was a herd of deer galloping through the trees. Then we happened on a wooden cabin. We looked through the window and saw that there were desks inside. A sign explained that this was a school built by the Mormon pioneers.

I felt like phoning my mother, because it reminded me of the 'school' where she taught, in an old farmhouse in Asteasu, but I thought she probably wouldn't remember and I would only confuse her, so I didn't call.

Tomorrow, we're off to Arizona. There's hardly a soul to be seen, although we have occasionally bumped into a couple in their sixties, who told us they started travelling round the States in their motorhome six months ago and plan to carry on as long as their health holds up.

MESSAGE TO L.
KAYENTA (ARIZONA), MARCH 27, 2008

Today's drive from Torrey to Kayenta was a real test of our nerves. Entirely our own fault. We should have stopped to fill up in the first town, Hanksville, but it was seven o'clock in the morning, the girls were asleep in the back seat, and so we decided to keep driving. We didn't even feel suspicious when we saw two huge gas stations in a one-horse town like Hanksville, and we drove straight past them making jokes about American consumerism. Stupid. The gas stations were there for the simple reason that the two hundred and fifty miles to Kayenta are pure desert, possibly the most deserted desert in the whole of the West.

We left the UT-24 at Hanksville and took the UT-95. At first, we were fine. There were the usual roadside signs: DID YOU CHECK YOUR VEHICLE BEFORE SETTING OFF? HAVE YOU CHECKED YOUR TIRES? PLEASE DO NOT TRAVEL WITHOUT WATER. The girls were still sleeping, and Ángela and I said nothing. Outside, only desert.

Half an hour passed, and the road was still utterly deserted. An hour went by, and still nothing. For the first time, I looked at the petrol gauge.

"What a desolate place!" Ángela said softly.

Another half an hour. I examined the map Earle had given us and noticed that halfway along the route, the Colorado river widened out and, when it reached Glen Canyon, seemed to form a lake. I thought it likely that there would be a service area there, a restaurant-cum-gas-station, like the Crosby Bar at Pyramid Lake. On the map I found a dot that gave me hope: Fry Canyon Store. I again looked at the gauge. The tank was half-full or slightly less.

We drove on for another twenty minutes at sixty-five miles an hour. No-one. Five minutes later, a big truck came towards us from the opposite direction. The driver waved to us, and we waved back.

"I think we'll probably start seeing more traffic now. We're very close to Glen Canyon," I told Ángela.

Another half an hour, and when we reached Glen Canyon, another disappointment. It was more like a deep ditch, and the road simply snaked around it. Ten minutes later, when we drove over the Colorado river, we saw two trucks transporting sand along an orange-coloured esplanade. At least it was a sign of life. Meanwhile, I kept a careful watch on the road ahead. According to the map, we were near Fry Canyon Store. The needle on the gauge was now below half.

"No services." I had spotted the sign from some way off. There was no gas station at the Fry Canyon Store. It was a hut, with no windows.

Ángela and I started exchanging reproaches, raising our voices slightly. Why had we not filled up in Hanksville? Hadn't we seen that the area on the map was a complete blank?

I studied the map again: a surface unmarked by dots or names and traversed only by a thick blue line, the Colorado river, and our road marked by Earle in black.

"When we drove through Hanksville, we weren't worried about the journey at all," I said to Ángela. "Our sole concern was not to wake Izaskun and Sara."

"At least they don't know what's happening, that's one good thing,"

Ángela said softly. It was twenty past ten. The girls had been sleeping for nearly three and a half hours.

I had done some calculations in pencil. According to the map, there was a fairly large town, Mexican Hat, about fifty miles from Glen Canyon.

"We'll get there easily, I think." As soon as I said that 'I think', I realised it was surplus to requirements.

Another half an hour. The only difference was that the desert seemed slightly less harsh and, to use Daniel Sada's image, it was gradually coming to resemble a stage set: the occasional tree, some scrubland.

"I don't understand why there's no traffic," Ángela said. "If Mexican Hat is a town, where are the cars and trucks of the people who live there?"

I had no answer. And yet there were more and more trees on either side of the road, and it wasn't hard to imagine that there must be an inhabited place somewhere near, with houses, a river, a church perhaps – and a gas station.

We had been driving for three hours when we saw the wood, a green fringe on the edge of the sandy desert, and shortly after that, a crossroads. We read the sign very carefully: to the left, following the UT-95, were Blanding and Monticello; to the right, following the UT-261-S, thirty-four miles away, was Mexican Hat.

The road narrowed as we entered the wood and the surface grew more uneven. If the UT-95 was a minor road, then the UT-261-S was a minor minor road.

"If it wasn't for that sign, I would think this road was leading nowhere," Ángela said. It did resemble those 'corridors' through forests made by logging trucks.

About six miles further on, the trees began to thin out.

"It looks like this is where the wood ends," I said.

At that very moment, I saw a traffic sign: 30 m.p.h. The speed limit. Ángela braked, but looked rather sceptical. The road was absolutely straight.

"It must be because of the bad surface," I said. "It's full of cracks."

Another hundred yards further on and another sign: 15 m.p.h. There were fewer trees now, and with the sun shining through the topmost branches, the whole atmosphere seemed somehow less gloomy. Ángela and I looked at each other, not knowing what to say. The road was in a pretty bad state, but not bad enough to require a 15 m.p.h. speed limit.

Suddenly, we saw a handwritten sign: SLOW, PLEASE!!!

We got out of the car to see what lay ahead. Nothing, nothing lay ahead. Only air. We were at an observation point, at the top of one of those rock faces so beloved of climbers. The UT-261-S proper stopped there, and continued two hundred yards below.

We went a few steps closer to examine the near-vertical stretch of road below us. The road that connected the upper part of the UT-261-S with the lower part had been dug out of the rock and was only about nine feet wide. I counted seven bends. Down below, like a dead insect, lay a car with its wheels in the air.

It's often said that in difficult situations, in battles, for example, when you find yourself in danger, someone takes hold of you, as if you were possessed, and you lose your individuality. In my brief experience, that 'someone' who takes hold of us is an automaton. Seeing that we had no alternative but to continue, I took the wheel like an automaton and set off – like an automaton – along the unpaved road.

Halfway down, Izaskun and Sara woke up.

"What's happening? Where are we?"

"Shut up!" we both yelled.

In the end, it wasn't that difficult. Just four minutes and we had reached the bottom.

We got out of the car to look back at the wall of rock. You couldn't even see the road. Sara took some photographs, and Izaskun applauded our Ford Sedan.

The automaton inside me vanished when we set off again, and my head filled with terrifying images: our car meeting another car coming up, with no room for both; a huge boulder in the middle of the road and us stuck there, unable to go forwards or backwards; the car skidding on a curve and plunging off the road . . . Imagining what could have happened, I lost my concentration, and Ángela took the wheel again.

We drove on through the desert on the UT-261-S, but it was much more "stagey" than the earlier parts. Not far ahead, we could see strange-shaped rocks. One of them looked like a figure in a poncho and a Mexican sombrero: Mexican Hat. Twenty minutes later, we reached a gas station.

A Navajo woman served us. Without even asking, she filled the tank right up.

"With what was in the reserve tank and a bit more, we had enough petrol for another thirty miles," Ángela told me.

I'm writing to you from Kayenta, the centre of the Navajo reserve. Ángela and the girls have gone down to the hotel swimming pool. I wanted to buy a beer to celebrate the happy ending to our journey and to cool off, but without even looking at me, the waitress refused point-blank. No alcoholic drinks are served on the Navajo reserve. And so here you find me, in front of my computer, sipping a soft drink.

MESSAGE TO L.
ET IN ARCADIA EGO: DEATH

An image: the Navajo guide is calmly driving the jeep down the sandy slopes, while we're admiring the rock formations. Suddenly, on the other side of a dune, we see a small ravine: at the bottom of the ravine, a pool of crystal-clear water. On the edge of the pool, beneath a leafy willow tree, a dead mole.

MESSAGE TO L.
ET IN ARCADIA EGO: VIOLENCE

We didn't know that, among the Navajo, it's considered rude to give information unless asked, and during the first part of the trip, our guide provided us with hardly any facts at all apart from the various tourist names for the rock formations: Totem, Three Sisters and so on. After a silence, Ángela asked about the education system and if

238

the Navajo could study in their own language. Our guide said only that this was possible in junior school. I spoke then about the protests held by the Hopis to stop their children being taken to white schools, and about the photograph of the Hopi chiefs imprisoned in Alcatraz. Our guide smiled broadly and, with an expressive gesture, described the relationship between the two tribes: "Navajo and Hopi enemies!"

At one point during the trip, we noticed that our guide was looking very tense and kept glancing in the rear-view mirror. Shortly after that, we were overtaken by the Navajo Nation Police. I thought perhaps he was worried because he wasn't supposed to let visitors travel in the passenger seat, where he had placed Sara.

MARCH 30
THE MONSTER

On the return journey, we drove back on Route 95, the same road we had taken on the outward leg of our trip, and we stopped at the gas station in Tonopah. After paying, I returned to the car and noticed that both Ángela and the girls kept peering anxiously at a car parked nearby. When I looked too, I saw the monster: a man with his face completely covered in tattoos. The white and tawny lines formed arabesques and other geometric shapes. He had high, very prominent cheekbones, a mane of reddish hair, pointed ears, and his upper lip was split like a cat's. He resembled a wild animal.

However, it seems he was a friendly monster, because when he said something to the girl at the till, she laughed.

THE CAT MAN

I only had to mention what I had seen at the gas station in Tonopah for Dennis to identify the monster.

"Oh, the Cat Man!" he exclaimed. "He's another world record holder, like Steve Fossett. Apparently, no other human being has made so many changes to his body. Silicone, tattoos, surgery, piercing, he did it all."

An hour later, Dennis sent me various links about the Cat Man. He didn't seem quite so impressive in the photographs, but they were still very shocking. He looked half-cat or half-tiger. According to his biography, he was a Native American, from the Huron tribe.

BACK IN RENO

We were very glad to be back in our house in College Drive after that three-thousand-mile journey. If, as Eric Havelock writes in his book *The Muse Learns to Write*, all life's pleasures are related to rhythm, we were really pleased to return to the rhythm of our Reno routine. The raccoon was in his usual place next to the hut; in the morning, we could hear the blue jays chattering; at the university, Earle, Dennis and Mary Lore were the same as ever; at school, Izaskun and Sara had the same homework to do as before we set off. And yet our happiness was far from complete. The dark side of Reno life continued. Mary Lore reminded me of this when I dropped in at the centre to say hello. Yes, she and Mannix were fine, and so were the girls, but . . .

"They still haven't caught the spider. And it's nearly two months since he killed Brianna. He's probably already preparing to commit another murder. It's just really worrying."

From the way in which she phrased this – "they still haven't caught the spider" – I guessed that she and Dennis had been discussing the matter a lot over the vacation.

On the porch, I found over a week's worth of *Reno Gazette-Journals*, which had been left to pile up during our absence. I glanced through them and again found articles about Brianna Denison. *Et in Arcadia ego*: violence and death.

APRIL 9

AN ARTICLE FROM THE *RENO GAZETTE-JOURNAL*

"A 35-year-old mother of four was jailed on child neglect charges. Officers said her children had been left home alone where they played with knives and tools.

"The woman was arrested on Thursday during her shift at Wal-Mart on suspicion of child neglect.

"Her children, aged 6, 7, 9 and 13, were placed into emergency foster care.

"Officers described the home as in "complete disarray" with rotting food and dirty clothes . . . The children were sleeping on box springs and took knives and razors to bed with them.""

FUNERAL OF A SOLDIER KILLED IN IRAQ

I was lying in bed in our house in College Drive. Once again I was sleeping badly. I would wake in the dark and hear footsteps, a window being smashed, a door handle turning, and I would sit bolt upright in bed, thinking: "Who's there?" But there was no-one, nothing. The house was silent. So was the town. It was the same on that day, April 17, 2008: Ángela was sleeping; Izaskun and Sara were sleeping. All was well. Brianna Denison's murderer had not attacked again. It was said that he might be in Seattle, where, it seems, there had been an identical case of a petite young woman being kidnapped and strangled.

I heard the *Reno Gazette-Journal* land on the porch and went out to pick it up, then took it into the kitchen to read. Before sitting down, I checked to see if the raccoon was waiting in the darkness, among the shadows. There he was in his favourite place, next to the hut. I found his presence soothing. It was a sign of normality.

The protagonist of the main news item was Army Sergeant Timothy Smith, who had been killed when his vehicle struck an improvised explosive device. His body had already been taken to his home town of South Lake Tahoe.

"Fallen soldier returns with honors," the headline said.

A large photograph showed the details. In the background, the snow-covered peaks of the mountains. In the foreground, the coffin, the American flag fluttering in the breeze, a few soldiers standing to attention, and a white aeroplane in the middle of the airstrip. There were two more photographs: one showing an old school friend of his, Lisa Calderón, wiping the tears from her eyes, and one of Timothy

Smith himself. "I'll always remember his bright red hair," Lisa Calderón said. She added: "He just lit up the room when he walked in." And yet the photograph showed a rather sad, withdrawn young man.

Another name to add to the memorial in central Reno dedicated to Nevadans killed in Afghanistan and Iraq. His name would follow that of David J. Drakulich and the other soldiers whose names I had copied into my notebook: Raul Bravo, Anthony J. Schober, Alejandro Varela, Joshua R. Rodgers and Joshua S. Modgling.

There was a note at the end in small print giving details of the funeral service, which would be held at eleven o'clock the next day, Friday, April 18, at the Sierra Community Church in South Lake Tahoe.

I talked to Ángela about the funeral and, twenty-four hours later, after dropping the girls off at school, I set off for South Lake Tahoe, which was an hour away in a normal car, but an hour and a half in our second-hand Ford Sedan.

Car engines take a real hammering going up those mountain roads. The roads are very narrow and appear insignificant in comparison with the rocks and cliffs towering above, and seem even smaller, weaker and more fragile when you look up at the sky and remember that, on many winter days, the road is often buried beneath twelve or fifteen feet of snow. The fir trees are proof of the power of snow: many of the trunks have snapped in two as if they had been under bombardment; those higher up have the rusty look of plants scorched by frost.

In spring, though, the fallen snow seems almost friendly and covers the slopes where the local children, wearing anoraks and warm hats, start learning to ski or snowboard. From a distance, when you see those small colourful dots moving about, they seem odd, out of keeping with the usually dark monotonous mountains; but they immediately become real when you wind down your car window and hear their shrieks of laughter.

As I drove past just such a group of children, it seemed to me that the scene could be made into a haiku, rather like the one by Masaoka Shiki: "In the old still pond, springing into sudden life, a green blade of grass."

With a few judicious changes, the poem could read: "Children in the snow, their laughter restoring life to the sad mountains." That was one possibility. Another would be to connect the sounds the children made with those of the vociferous blue jays. In that case, the poem would read: "Among snow and trees the loud chattering voices of birds and children."

And yet, the road to Lake Tahoe offers other possible subjects to anyone driving along and hoping to write a poem. One of them, probably the main one, begins to reveal itself as soon as you notice the line that cuts across the mountains, halfway up, as if drawn with ruler and pencil, and which is the first transcontinental railway line built in America in the 1860s; a gigantic, monstrous enterprise, the building of which cost thousands of Chinese immigrant lives. It's impossible to look at that line or drive past the tracks without thinking of that poem by Bertolt Brecht: "Who built Thebes of the seven gates?/In the books you will read the names of kings./Did the kings haul up the lumps of rock?/And Babylon, many times demolished,/Who raised it up so many times?"

The official accounts of how the railway was built speak at length about the Union Pacific and the Central Pacific, the companies that financed and organised the work, making special mention of the ceremony held in Promontory, Utah, on 10 May, 1869, when the locomotive coming from the west and the locomotive coming from the east met head on, and when the so-called Golden Spike, the final one, was hammered in. On the other hand, they say nothing of the Chinese immigrant workers who tackled the most difficult section through the mountains, including building the Truckee tunnels. In the photograph taken of the Golden Spike ceremony, you see the two locomotives, a bottle of champagne, and plenty of top hats, Stetsons and caps, but not a single Chinese coolie hat.

In general, nothing is ever said of those who suffer most. Or something is said, but always glossing over the facts, never mentioning the truly horrific part of their story. One of the photographs illustrating the history of the transcontinental railway carries a caption that reads: "Chinese railroad workers perform their duties in the snow."

They could have put this in the form of a haiku: "In the snow-white snow, black against the grey grey sky, see the Chinese work." That would have seemed more palatable, on a par, for example, with what the visitor can see at the History Museum in Carson City: a miniature Chinese village, a sentimental scene in which the children play, the old people tend their caged birds, the women cook and pick flowers, and the men stroll up and down the now completed railroad.

The truth is quite different, though. The ice that freezes the fir trees freezes people too. Chinese-American novelists like Hong Kingston are producing a revised version of the history of the American West, and, according to them, many, many railroad workers lost noses or fingers to frostbite. Harsher still, workers were forbidden to speak to each other, even in English. No-one cared, not even the socialist parties and trade unions, because the Chinese were considered a human subspecies as evidenced by the Exclusion Act of 1867.

Beau comme le premier jour, as lovely as the first day of the world, of creation. That is the thought that comes to mind when, at last, after climbing for more than an hour, the landscape opens out below, and you see Lake Tahoe. The fir trees conceal the roads along its shores: beyond its blue waters stand the snow-capped mountains. It could be considered just a perfect picture postcard, but it's not that either: the space it occupies is immense, and mere cameras cannot do it justice. Initially, you think that what you will remember is its sheer size, but, no, it is that first impression that makes you sigh and say *beau comme le premier jour*. It seems so innocent, so primordial, as if crossing the mountains were like crossing a frontier in time and stepping back into paradise.

This is not exactly an illusion, but it is only a fleeting reality. As soon as you leave behind you the mountains and enter Incline Village, you join the road that skirts the lake, and then you become aware, over and over, of the world's soiling presence. A hoarding warns you of bears and mountain lions. Another tells you that you're not far from the Ponderosa ranch, where the television series "Bonanza" was shot. Then come the mansions built along the lake shore, and later, after a few miles of uninhabited beauty, the small prefab houses with third- or fourth-hand pickups parked outside. Further on, there are the housing developments that spread up the slopes of the mountains and disappear among the fir trees.

This soiling presence becomes still grimier when you read about South Lake Tahoe. A kidnapping took place there in 1963, when Frank Sinatra Jr was snatched from his room in Harrah's Hotel, and wasn't freed until a few days later, when his father paid the ransom money. In 1991, there was a second kidnapping. Eleven-year-old Jaycee Lee Dugard was waiting for the school bus when a man forced her to get into his van. Her adoptive father, who wasn't far from the bus stop, realised what was happening and ran to save her, but the van sped away and disappeared from sight.

On the day of Sergeant Timothy Smith's funeral, 18 April, 2008, there were still a lot of posters bearing the little girl's photograph and a note stating that she had disappeared seventeen years earlier. I knew about the case, because it had been mentioned in connection with Brianna Denison's kidnapping and murder.

It took me a while to find the Sierra Community Church because it was quite small and hidden among trees, and by the time I did find it, the funeral was almost about to begin. At the crossroads, the firemen had formed an arch of honour with the ladders on their fire-trucks. Large numbers of policemen in dress uniform were present. Even more numerous were the Patriot Guard Riders standing next to their Harley-Davidsons, each bike flying the American flag. Outside the main entrance to the church a line of cadets formed a guard of honour.

Along one side of the church stood a long table full of photographs of the deceased, and there the congregation were waiting, some sitting on folding chairs, but most standing. I counted about a hundred people. Apart from the occasional crying baby or the grating cries of the blue jays, not a sound could be heard. The loudspeakers in the porch on that side of the church had been turned off.

A white limousine drove slowly under the arch provided by the firemen. Behind it came another stretch limo, equally long and equally white. The police stood to attention, the Patriot Guard Riders formed a neat line. A very tall man, dark-haired and dark-suited, walked into the middle of the road sobbing and waving his arms about. He seemed utterly distraught. A woman took him by the arm and drew him back into the group.

The coffin was removed from the first limousine. The family emerged from the second limo: parents, brother, sister, wife and son, the son could only have been about two years old. The cadets outside the church gave a military salute, and the cortège entered the church. From inside came the notes of a harmonium. Then a melodious voice: "We are gathered here today to say a final farewell to an American hero, Sergeant Timothy Michael Smith." Various eulogies followed, first, from his school friends who spoke almost incomprehensibly, sobbing hysterically; then his brother and sister, who were both, understandably, deeply moved; after them came a colleague from the same battalion, who had travelled from Iraq in order to attend the ceremony; he spoke very serenely.

The tall, dark-haired, dark-suited man continued to sob and kept going over to one of the loudspeakers as if to drink from that chalice, from the sorrow in those voices. This must have been annoying for the rest of the congregation, but no-one stopped him.

The priest with the melodious voice spoke again, repeating over and over, like a refrain, the three key words of the service: Honour. Duty. Sacrifice. Sometimes, like one melody superimposed upon another, he was accompanied by the harmonium. This was followed by more voices and more eulogies, among them one by a general. However, because of my imperfect English, I found it too tiring to listen to every speech and decided to go and look at the photographs on the table.

In many of them, Timothy Smith was shown standing beside his mother, who was attractive and surprisingly young. Quite a few showed him as a boy in the family pickup, beside the lake, at a Christmas party or dressed as Father Christmas. He only looked genuinely happy in two of them: one in which he was pictured hugging his mother, and in the only photograph of him and his wife. However, the main picture on display showed him on the day he graduated from Military School.

I picked up a couple of memorial leaflets. One contained copies of some of the photographs and a poem entitled "Through the Eyes of a Child": "There comes a time in our lives when we must face the facts and look at ourselves, because there is no going back. We can all learn a lesson from our little ones. When they seem to know nothing, that is when they are beginning to know everything. They have wonderful faces. So when things aren't going so well, take a look at life through the eyes of love, through the eyes of a child."

The second leaflet was the official one and included Timothy Smith's military record, his medals and mentions in despatches, and, on the back, in a larger font, a text entitled "The Soldier's Creed":

I am an American Soldier.

I am a warrior and a member of a team.

I serve the people of the United States, and live the Army Values.

I will always place the mission first.

I will never accept defeat.

I will never quit.

I will never leave a fallen comrade.

I am disciplined, physically and mentally tough, trained and proficient in my warrior tasks and drills.

I always maintain my arms, my equipment and myself.

I am an expert and I am a professional.

I stand ready to deploy, engage, and destroy, the enemies of the United States of America in close combat.

I am a guardian of freedom and the American way of life.

I am an American Soldier.

Every ceremony presupposes a caesura, a break, an interruption to the flow of life. The hours which, generally speaking, seem so similar, the monotonous hours which, point by point, form a geometrical line, dull and unsurprising, undergo a sudden transformation, and then everything is different. An anonymous person becomes the centre of attention, a hero, a superior being, an empty being, an unreal being. Around him the world changes: the clocks move more sedately, more slowly; words and silence meet to create something new. "Honour," says the priest, then pauses. "Duty," he says. Pause. "Sacrifice," he says.

Pause. And then there are the white limousines, the policemen and firemen in dress uniform, the Patriot Guard Riders' gleaming Harley-Davidsons, the boyish cadets with their weapons. Outside time and space. The distraught man with his dark suit and dark hair isn't strong enough to bear the situation and so he sobs. But he is not the only one.

I was thinking how false the poems were. The first was sentimental and set off along a supposedly consolatory route that didn't console at all. "So when things aren't going so well, take a look at life through the eyes of love, through the eyes of a child." But the real child, Timothy Smith's son – Riley according to the same memorial leaflet – would become a constant, living symbol of the tragedy. Besides, how do you look through the eyes of a child when you are no longer a child? Those words could only make sense in the unreal time inhabited by the funeral ceremony.

As for the second text, it spoke proudly of violence and death. "I stand ready to deploy, engage, and destroy, the enemies of the United States of America in close combat," it said, and added: "I am a guardian of freedom and the American way of life. I am an American Soldier." Those words were like the limousines parked outside the church – big, white, elegant – but, like those limousines, they were usually filled with corpses and suffering.

I put the memorial leaflets in my pocket, left the church and made my way to the car park. And there, next to a special bear-proof trash can, was an enormous sign telling you how to behave if you should happen to meet said plantigrade: "Don't panic! Don't approach it! Leave it alone! If the bear hop-charges toward you, clacks its teeth, sticks out its lips, huffs, woofs, or rushes a few steps toward you and slaps or scratches the ground with its paws, you are too close! Back away!"

More advice and explanations followed, but I stopped reading. I had suddenly remembered a poem I had read out on a radio programme after the terrorist attacks on March 11, 2004 in Madrid: "Life is life / And not its results. / It isn't the big house / High up on the mountainside, / Or the cups or medals / (gold or fake) / that fill the shelves. / Life isn't only that. / Life is life / And the most precious thing of all. / To lose a life is to lose everything."

I felt proud of those lines. They seemed to me truer and more realistic than the soldier's creed or the sentimental poetry in those memorial leaflets. Suddenly, though, I felt my legs go weak. Not because I had seen a bear, but because I had just imagined myself reciting that poem at Timothy Smith's funeral service: "Life is life / And the most precious thing of all. / To lose a life is to lose everything."

What would happen when the loudspeakers broadcast those words? They would cause real consternation. Another image came into my mind: the distraught man, tall, dark-haired and dark-suited, who had not stopped crying throughout the ceremony, would hurl himself at me and punch me. Then the policemen in dress uniform would arrest me and lead me away under the stern gaze of the Patriot Guard Riders.

I thought: "They would be quite right too." Regardless of whether my poem was true or not, its only effect would be to increase their grief, while not increasing their knowledge one iota. "Life is life and the most precious thing of all. To lose it is to lose everything." Timothy Smith's family would have said: "We know that. Everyone knows that. It's obvious, so why say it again?" A member of the Patriot Guard Riders would have hammered in the last nail: "You know what I think? A poem that can't be read at a funeral shouldn't be read anywhere." The distraught man, tall, dark-haired and dark-suited, would have come over and said: "Look, my friend, a poem written for a particular occasion may not be worth including in a book, but a poem that has been included in a book should be suitable for all occasions." Then a policeman in dress uniform would arrive and say: "Perhaps you should find a different job."

I felt bad. Not because of what could have happened if I had read the poem out in that small church in South Lake Tahoe, but because I suddenly became aware that I'd already recited the poem over a loudspeaker a hundred thousand times more powerful, on a radio programme with a big audience. Perhaps I had been seduced by a desire to be forceful and emphatic, perhaps the poem was filled, as a tyre is filled with air, by the flippant, foolish arrogance of someone who is convinced he is right.

A round of gunfire wrenched me from my thoughts. It was the salute fired in honour of the fallen soldier. There was no applause, only perhaps a bugle call or a short piece of music. I saw that the funeral procession, headed by the four cadets carrying the coffin, was making its way into the car park, and so I stepped back into the shade of the trees.

The cadets put the coffin back in the white limousine, having to relinquish a little of their stiff military rigour as they did so. From close to, they looked to me even younger than when I first saw them at the door of the church. They would have been at most eighteen or nineteen. Two of them were extremely fair, with very white skin, as Mormons often are; the third had Latino features; the fourth was red-haired like Timothy Smith.

The various family members were standing next to the second limousine, their arms about each other, weeping. All except one, because Riley, the little boy, wasn't crying.

Then came the roar of the Harley-Davidsons, and the Patriot Guard Riders filled the street to form the guard of honour for the two white limousines. Someone gave the command, and the procession set off, flags flying as if it were a military parade, then they drove back under the firemen's arch and disappeared.

In the silence surrounding the church, the prayers and tears and words from the funeral hung in the air like dust motes. A woman started collecting up the photographs and memorial leaflets from the table. Two men took charge of folding the chairs and taking them out to a truck. One of the men was the distraught fellow, dark-suited and dark-haired, who now looked as bent and weighed down as an old man. Two maintenance men in orange hi-vis vests came out from among the trees. When they passed me, the older of the two pointed to the sign warning about bears and asked jokingly: "Seen any yet?"

I left South Lake Tahoe unable to clear my mind of the priest's velvety voice, and I kept hearing over and over those three words: Honour. Duty. Sacrifice. And hearing, too, even more loudly, his pauses and his silences. If he was a man who, as Stephen Spender wrote in *World Within World*, "had made the return journey', a man who had taken a stance after a voyage into the very depths of life, depths that teach you not only the value of birdsong – even the "song" of the blue jays – but also show you the monstrous soul of human predators, kidnappers of children or young women, then he surely must have realised the absurdity of repeating those three words at the funeral of a twenty-five-year-old man, father of a two-year-old boy, a soldier killed in a war like the Iraq war, which many deemed to have been an immoral war. If he did, if he knew the truth and, despite everything, had decided to keep that refrain – Honour. Duty. Sacrifice – then that was a problem I could not resolve.

I stopped for a moment at the top of Incline Village. The sky was blue, as was the lake. Just then, the white tourist boat, the only one, was setting out from the jetty at South Lake Tahoe.

Once I was behind the wheel again, I tried to find some way of repairing what now seemed to me a bad poem. I considered changing "To lose a life is to lose everything" to "Whoever takes that life takes everything", but that didn't work either. A poem wasn't like a dog that comes to whoever whistles for it or gives it a biscuit. That change would have been interpreted by the congregation as a reproach to the insurgents in Iraq who had taken Timothy Smith's life; in a very different context, read in some city in Iraq, it would have been interpreted in exactly the opposite way. It would have been seen as a reproach to Timothy Smith and the other American soldiers, in short, a poem-that-comes-when-whistled-for.

The steep slopes and bends that had overheated the car engine hours before made driving difficult and they were, besides, a metaphor for what was happening to me and that poem: bend to the right, bend to the left, look out, a precipice ahead, a pothole, bend to the right again. I braked, or, rather, I reached a decision: I would delete that poem the moment I got home and turned on my computer.

When I came down from the mountains and rejoined the Reno highway, I remembered a song I'd learned in a village in Castile: "Last night I went to a dance to dance, but never danced; I lost the ribbon from my hair as well, what a waste of a day." It pretty much expressed what I was feeling, and so I came up with my own version: "I crossed the mountains to write a poem, but wrote nothing; indeed, I lost a poem I had written earlier, what a waste of a day."

FUNERAL FOR A BASQUE SHEPHERD

The main park in Reno is called Rancho San Rafael, although the ranch itself is long gone. There's an arboretum, a couple of play-grounds, some ponds and picnic areas and wild areas too, and, on a small hill, there's a sculpture by Néstor Basterretxea dedicated to the Basque shepherds – *Bakardade*, "Solitude". The monument also serves as a memorial with bronze plaques recording the names of hun-dreds of Basque shepherds who lived and died in the American West.

With the arrival of spring, we began visiting the park once or twice a week. It was usually C., Monique Laxalt's friend, who would suggest going for a stroll, saying that she needed Izaskun and Sara's help to get her border collie, Blue, out of the house. We would walk to the park, which was only five minutes away, meet up with Earle, Mary Lore and Mannix, and do the whole circuit, which normally took about an hour. At first, Dennis used to come too, but he stopped doing so when an old college friend came down from Chicago to help him improve the university's I.T. system.

The day after my trip to South Lake Tahoe, I spoke to the others about Sergeant Timothy Smith's funeral service. In addition to Izaskun and Sara, there were four of us: C., Ángela, Earle and me.

"As it happens, there's going to be a funeral here as well," C. said. "For a Basque shepherd." Her tone was deliberately enigmatic.

Earle expressed surprise.

"Here? At the monument?"

"And with no priests either."

"Unheard of!" Earle said.

"Such things *were* unheard of once," Ángela said. "All the shep-herds were devout Catholics."

C. did not respond at once. She had aroused our curiosity and was savouring the moment.

"Those were the dead man's wishes," she said at last.

"Did they kill him?" Earle asked. "The Basque community I mean, for being a bad Catholic."

Blue ran over to us to fetch the stick that Izaskun and Sara had thrown for her, but C. picked it up first and made Blue wait for a moment, until Blue started barking; then she threw the stick as hard as she could. It fell into a bush.

"He wouldn't have been easy to kill," C. said "Apparently he was a giant of a man. Mary Lore told me about him. He worked on the family ranch."

"Killing a man is easy enough, especially in Nevada," Earle said. "Remember what happened to the boxer, Ringo Bonavena, at Mustang Ranch. A single bullet was all it took to despatch him to the next world. And Bonavena was a heavyweight who had won more than fifty fights."

"So he was like our shepherd," C. said

"Why? Was he a boxer too?" I asked.

"No, he wasn't a boxer, but he was a frequent visitor to brothels, and not just to Mustang Ranch either. Mary Lore didn't tell me that bit, of course, she's far too discreet."

The part of the park that extended as far as the mountains was on the other side of McCarran, and we always headed in that direction because Izaskun and Sara wanted to see the owl "who lived in a tree". They had seen him once and, ever since, always insisted on going to visit him, even though he was rarely "at home".

We went through the McCarran underpass and along a path. Izaskun, Sara and Blue ran on ahead and didn't stop until they reached a small wood and a pond formed by a stream, into which Blue immediately plunged, splashing the bushes and grass all around. At that very moment, Izaskun and Sara started shouting. They had found what they were looking for.

The owl became agitated, moving his head from side to side and walking nervously back and forth along the branch. Blue kept barking, and Sara began clapping her hands.

A ranger who had been walking just behind us asked the girls to be quiet. Izaskun and Sara obeyed at once, but the presence of that uniformed woman only made Blue even more excited and she began barking even louder until C. whistled to her and she immediately ran over to join us.

"Sit!" C. said, and Blue sat.

"If you don't leave him in peace, the owl will get angry and leave the park," the ranger told Izaskun and Sara. She was in her fifties and had very short hair. The badge on her sky-blue uniform announced that her name was Dorothy.

"It would be a real shame if the owl were to leave, Dorothy," Earle said, "but rather less of a shame if the geese left. Not all of them of course. A few could stay."

Dorothy responded with unexpected good humour.

"Oh, I agree, sir," she said and laughed loudly.

The meadows and paths of Rancho San Rafael should have been a delight for visitors to the park, but this was not always the case. There were more than a hundred geese living there and their droppings were everywhere. In some areas, it was like walking over white carpets of guano.

"It's not entirely the fault of the geese, Earle. It's your fault too. I think you're the only person who comes here wearing white sneakers," C. said once the ranger had left.

It wasn't only his sneakers that were white. Earle was dressed from head to toe in white. He looked closer to fifty than seventy.

Earle did not respond. He was more interested in the shepherd's funeral.

"His ashes will be scattered near the monument at six o'clock in the evening. Then we'll all go back to Mary Lore and Mannix's place for supper."

"All of us?" Ángela asked.

"There'll be about ten of us, and about the same number at the ceremony too."

In the end, some twenty people turned up for the ceremony, more than C. had expected. The owner of the ranch where the shepherd had worked arrived accompanied by Mary Lore. He was carrying a small urn containing the ashes, and he and Mary Lore took charge of scattering the ashes on the area surrounding the sculpture. The very spot where, just the other day, Blue had been sniffing around for the stick thrown to her by Izaskun, Sara or C. was now the shepherd's grave.

At the beginning of the ceremony, Mary Lore gave the name of the deceased, Policarpo Aguirre, then stood aside to allow the ranch-owner to speak. He began on a somewhat unfortunate note: "*Apur bat ulerkaitza da hainbeste andrakaz ibilitako gizonak inor ez izatea hemen beragatik negar egiteko . . .*" "It's hard to understand why a man who went with so many women should have no-one here today to weep for him."

He was wrong. A young girl of twelve or thirteen was crying bitterly. I looked at the man who was standing with his arms around her. He was tall and completely bald. Now and then he would look at me too. He seemed vaguely familiar, and I tried in vain to remember where I knew him from.

Standing next to Mary Lore was Natalie in a very elegant, pearl-grey dress; beside her stood the intellectual-looking young man who had come to the Thanksgiving supper with her; then there was Earle and the teacher at the School of Journalism who had played Beatles songs. Both men were wearing dark suits and white shirts. The suit looked rather better on Earle. The other people who had come stood in a group before the sculpture. Most looked like farmhands and seemed to be Mexican in origin.

The ranch-owner spoke at greater length in English than he had in Basque. He had been speaking for five minutes and showed no signs of stopping. Izaskun and Sara were getting bored.

"Why didn't C. bring Blue?" Sara asked.

"Nobody takes their dog to a funeral," Izaskun said.

"I can't see Mannix or C. or Dennis," I said to Ángela.

"They're back at the house preparing supper. Mary Lore told me."

The bald man was staring at Ángela now.

"Do you know that man over there, the one next to the tall girl who's crying?" I asked.

Ángela said she didn't.

The ranch-owner finally stopped speaking, and one of the Mexicans spoke instead.

"We ask God with all our heart to take our *compañero* Policarpo to his bosom. They say he often broke the seventh commandment, but we know nothing about that. We only know that he never broke any of the other nine commandments, and that all the time he worked at the ranch he was a good and generous friend."

Now and then, a few people walking in the park came up to the monument, but as soon as they saw that a ceremony was taking place, they turned and went back the way they had come, in the direction of the arboretum, avoiding the ponds. The geese put in an appearance too and kept flying over our heads in twos or threes. They looked prettier in the air, cleaner.

The ceremony ended, and the ranch-owner thanked everyone present. Then I finally got a good look at the man embracing the little girl. He was wearing a dark green velvet jacket, and, however loose and baggy, it could not conceal his misshapen body. He had a hunchback and a bulging chest. His legs seemed too long and out of proportion with the rest of his body. I was almost sure I knew who he was, and any lingering doubts vanished when he came over to me, holding out a pack of Dunhill cigarettes.

"Would you like one?" he asked.

"Adrián! What brings you here?"

When I saw him close to, his eyes took me back forty years, to the day when I first met him in the stables at Loyola. We may lose our hair, our eyes may acquire crow's feet and bags, our eyebrows may grow sparse, but the look in our eyes doesn't change. It might become darker, meeker, clearer, harder, but basically – beneath the disguise – it's the same when you're fifty as it was when you were sixteen.

"The shepherd who died was Nadia's biological father, that's why we've come. I'm her other father. Her cultural father if you like."

As with the look in our eyes, our voice doesn't change very much either. When I heard Adrián's voice, I suddenly saw him as he was when he was a long-haired youth. As for his smile, it seemed more serene than I remembered.

He lit a cigarette and gestured to his daughter.

She had a Slavic air about her and bore a vague resemblance to Liliana, "the Russian flower", who we used to see at the swimming pool.

"Hi, Nadia, how are you?" Ángela said.

Nadia was almost as tall as Ángela and Natalie. Her eyes were red from crying.

"A bit sad, but otherwise O.K., thank you," she said. She had a very soft voice.

After supper, Adrián and I went out into the garden with the gin and tonics Mannix had made for us, and we sat down in the wicker chairs to talk. The other guests were gathered in the conservatory in two groups. To the left, sitting around a rectangular table, were the ranch-owner, Ángela, Earle, Natalie, Natalie's intellectual-looking friend, the teacher from the School of Journalism, and Mannix himself; to the right, sitting at a round table playing cards, were Izaskun, Sara, Nadia, Dennis, Mary Lore and her three daughters. Dennis's friend from Chicago, a man with a black beard, was with them too, and he would smile at me whenever our eyes met. The only person missing from the group of friends was C.

It was a warm night, combed (as the poet says) by the desert breeze. The red, fuchsia and green lights of the casinos seemed more muted than on other days, like boiled sweets. At that moment, Reno was, as Nabokov describes it in *Lolita*, a dreary town.

For a while, we sat like two surveillance policemen observing the people in the conservatory. Everyone seemed very happy. Mannix was doing most of the talking. The ranch-owner also had plenty to say. The teacher from the School of Journalism spoke quite a lot too, but seemed happier talking one-to-one, sometimes with the ranch-owner and sometimes with Natalie. Earle sat in silence, playing with his glass.

Ángela got up and joined Mary Lore, Dennis and the girls. Natalie stood up too and went to talk to Mannix. She wasn't wearing the pearl-grey dress she had worn at the funeral, but a close-fitting red leather suit with a black top and red stilettos.

"Very sexy," Adrián said when he saw her stand up.

C. came to the door, holding Blue by the collar.

"She'd rather be outside. Don't worry, she won't bother you," she said, letting go of the dog. Blue immediately started whining. I called to her, but she didn't want to stay with us.

Mannix came over.

"A few raccoons have made their home in a hole in one of those trees. Blue can smell them, that's why she's so excited," he said.

He looked at Adrián.

"What did you think of the gin and tonic?"

"The best I've drunk in a long time."

"Good, well, in exchange you can give me one of your Dunhills."

We each took a cigarette, and Adrián lit them for us. His lighter was the same mother-of-pearl model I remembered from our schooldays.

Blue was crouched beneath a large tree in the garden, gazing upwards.

"The raccoons are in that hole in the trunk," Mannix said. "Three babies and the mother. Blue would have to jump very high to reach them."

He began walking back to the conservatory. He was holding his cigarette between thumb and forefinger as if it were a very delicate object.

"Come and join us if you like," I said.

"No, I'm going back in. Alexander's trying to solve a problem I have with my computer, and I want to see how he's getting on. I'll leave you two in peace."

Alexander was Dennis's bearded friend.

Blue followed Mannix, and as soon as she got inside, she ran over to the girls, where Sara flung her arms around her.

Adrián was still observing the group sitting at the rectangular table. Suddenly, he grabbed my forearm.

"Look over there, but be discreet. There's a lot of below-table activity."

258

Earle had his leg outstretched trying to touch Natalie's leg, and the teacher from the School of Journalism was doing the same. Seated between them, oblivious to their manoeuvrings, was Natalie's intellectual-looking friend, who was earnestly explaining something to her.

Earle and the teacher from the School of Journalism suddenly withdrew their respective legs. Adrián chuckled, as if to say, "What an absurd world, what absurd people." He'd had the same laugh ever since our schooldays together.

"They were both trying to touch Natalie's leg and ended up touching each other," I said.

This time we both laughed. Adrián lit another cigarette and sat looking at the table where the girls were sitting.

"Being attracted to a pretty young woman is fairly normal, but very different from the feelings you have for your own children. I really love Nadia, and I play her all my records. She likes the Beatles, especially 'Yellow Submarine', although, personally, I still prefer 'In My Life'."

He began singing softly: "There are places I'll remember all my life though some have changed, some for ever not for better . . .'

"A great song," he said. "I understand it now, more than I did at school."

"Same here."

We raised our glasses in a toast. They barely clinked.

"The other day, I visited L. in hospital," Adrián said. "He's in a really bad way."

I had been expecting this news for a long time, but it still affected me deeply.

"I've been writing to him fairly regularly since I've been in Reno."

"Yes, I know. He said he really enjoys getting your emails. Does he ever reply?"

"Sometimes, but only briefly."

"He doesn't have the strength. When I saw him in hospital, he could barely stand."

Blue came out into the garden again. She raced past us and sat under the tree where the raccoons were. We shouted at her when she began barking, and she immediately fell silent.

The darkness had thickened, and the neon lights on the casinos seemed brighter. Adrián made a gesture with his hand. He didn't want to talk any more about L. Nor did I. It was too painful.

"My favourite casino is that emerald green one," I said, pointing to the Silver Legacy.

"If you like we could spend a night gambling."

I couldn't do that. Brianna's murderer was still on the loose, and I didn't want to leave Ángela and the girls alone in the house. The police warned us on an almost weekly basis not to lower our guard.

"Why don't we have breakfast together tomorrow? It's late now, time to go to bed."

As if in agreement, the group at the rectangular table were getting up as well. C. came out into the garden.

"Come on, Blue, we're leaving. Say goodnight to the raccoons!"

"Which hotel are you staying at?" I asked Adrián.

"Ascuaga's Nugget. The ranch-owner is staying there too. He was the stepbrother of Nadia's biological father."

"I have an idea, Adrián. Tomorrow morning, I'll pick Nadia up from the hotel and drop her off at College Drive so that she can spend the day with Izaskun and Sara. Then you and I can go for a stroll by the Truckee river. You haven't told me anything about Nadia yet."

At that very moment, the three girls came over to join us. Izaskun and Sara were both tall, but Nadia was almost six inches taller.

"Can Nadia come over to the house tomorrow?" Izaskun asked. "It's Sunday, and we're free all day."

"It's already arranged," I said.

"How are you doing?" Adrián asked Nadia.

"I'm fine," she said in her soft voice.

THE STORY OF ADRIÁN AND NADIA
(ACCORDING TO THE VERSION HEARD ON THE BANKS OF THE TRUCKEE RIVER)

Adrián was the son of the owner of the biggest sawmill in Guipúzcoa, and the gnarled, misshapen tree that stood next to the pool in the Obaba river constituted the Centre of the young Adrián's territory.

There were other important places in his life too: the Colegio La Salle in San Sebastián, the School of Engineering in Bilbao and the hospital in Barcelona where he had been operated on several times during his adolescence, but his memory avoided them as skilfully as a prudent hand avoids the nails sticking out of a plank of wood. As for places nearer to home – the bars and restaurants in the village or the cinema that was only a mile or so from his house – he only visited them early in the morning or late in the evening, when he was less likely to meet anyone. He liked his neighbours and enjoyed chatting to them over a beer or a coffee, but he preferred to be alone. Often, in a restaurant or at the cinema, he would feel a sudden urge to go back to his Centre and, on the slightest excuse, he would get up and leave.

He had felt bound to that gnarled, misshapen tree ever since he was a child or, to be precise, ever since the day he went swimming in the pool in the river and one of his school friends pointed to the tree and said:

"Look, Adrián, that tree could be your brother!"

He must have been about five then, and, at the time, being compared to that tree had seemed to him a compliment, a recognition of his singularity, and he continued to think so until, ten years later, conscious now of his hunchback and his misshapen body and what this meant in terms of his social acceptability, he decided to distance himself from that "brother", from the sawmill and from the pool, and become an eccentric adolescent who wanted not only to live like Oscar Wilde, but to be buried like him, "in a green velvet suit". That phase passed, though, and six years on, a minor, even banal incident again changed the direction of his life. One day, he was heading towards the School of Engineering in Bilbao, when he found a fallen swallow lying on the ground next to the pond in a park. The bird had seemed to him like a kind of avian dandy, dressed for its funeral like Oscar Wilde, in a silk jacket, half-blue, half-white. When he went to pick it up, however, the bird suddenly fluttered. It wasn't dead, after all, but simply unable to take off because its wings were so long that they touched the ground. Very gingerly he picked it up and launched it into the air over the pond. The swallow, the avian dandy, flew over the water and disappeared.

This, Adrián felt, was a sign. Not the answer to an enigma or the solution to some mathematical problem, but – or so he chose to interpret it – an order, a command, sent to him via that messenger by some superior power. He had to change. The jackets and hats he wore were unconventional, as were the Dunhill cigarettes he smoked and the music he listened to – the Doors and Kraftwerk – but those choreographic details aside, his life followed the same libretto as any other student. And that was wrong. He was different. He was misshapen and hunchbacked. And he had fallen to the ground like that swallow. He knew his fellow engineering students called him "Quasimodo", a slightly more literary equivalent of the nickname he'd been given at Colegio La Salle. It was absurd trying to live among normal people. Normal people had the souls of chickens and it was painful to have to listen to their clucking.

He looked around him. Not far off, hundreds of swallows were lined up on the telegraph wires. They were leaving. So was he. Yes, he was leaving too. He wouldn't stay in Bilbao for the fourth year of his degree. He would go back to the village, to the sawmill, to that tree, his Centre.

L., who had been his best friend since they were at school together at Colegio La Salle, understood and supported his decision, perhaps because he, too, had been the butt of jokes on account of his physical appearance, in his case because he was rather short, but he was the exception. Most of the people he knew tried to dissuade him, especially Beatriz, the daughter of the accountant at the sawmill.

"I heard that you'd decided to leave engineering school and devote yourself to the sawmill. I hope that's not true," she said when the Christmas holidays arrived and she came to see him. They had grown up together in the house that their respective fathers had built in the grounds of the sawmill, and she spoke to Adrián with an almost sisterly familiarity.

"No, it's true. I've been home for over a month, and I won't be going back to Bilbao."

"You're obviously suffering some kind of regression. I can't believe it. I mean, going back to childhood has its charms, but it's simply not possible. Work's no joking matter, you know."

Adrián looked out of the window at where the beech and the oak logs were drying. He didn't want to discuss the matter with Beatriz.

"Do you remember that gnarled, misshapen tree near the pool?" he said at last.

"Of course I do. How could I forget?"

The tree and the pool were about three hundred yards upstream from the sawmill, but he didn't recall ever having seen Beatriz there. She and the other village girls played elsewhere, usually up near the church.

"I'm going to learn my father's trade. Then I'll build a kind of workshop next to the tree where I can make unusual things, toys and bits of furniture."

"So it's true," Beatriz said with a sigh. "When I was little, I used to dream that we would study together and then get married. Now I feel as if I've overtaken you and I don't like that."

They were the same age and had gone to the same school until Adrián's long stays in hospital had separated them. Beatriz was now a doctor and about to marry a fellow medical student.

"Don't go all melodramatic on me, Beatriz. It's great that you're doing so well," he said. He wanted to change the subject.

"I just don't understand your decision," she went on. "Your father told me you were still getting good marks. Besides, you're not strong enough to work with wood."

"As I said, I'm going to be making unusual things, not loading trucks."

"Well, I wouldn't build a workshop over there if I were you. It's very damp and that wouldn't be good for you."

Adrián had a sense that, from then on, Beatriz would maintain that doctorly tone, and he urgently wanted to end the conversation.

"You don't understand. That's where I want to be. We cripples should stick together."

He regretted his words as soon as they were out of his mouth. He found all this talk about his health upsetting.

"That's not funny, Adrián. No self-pity, please. It's so unattractive."

When they were children and they got angry with each other and started hurling insults, she would call him "pigeon breast". It seemed to him that her present attitude was equally aggressive.

"Leave me alone, Beatriz. You're becoming a real pest."

"I'm sorry, Adrián," she said and kissed him on the cheek.

Adrián was an only child and had been crippled since birth. His legs were very long and his torso short and bulbous, and there was something almost equine about his long neck and head. It was said in the village that, because their main house was still being built, Adrián's mother had spent the nine months of her pregnancy in an apartment immediately above the sawmill and that the almost continual vibration from the machinery below had damaged the foetus. He preferred the version given by the doctors in Barcelona, who blamed his deformity on the illness that finally took his mother to her grave. It was not a matter of neglect. It was simply the blind malice of nature, which doesn't count its children in ones and twos, but in thousands, millions, and knows nothing of suffering.

The second version wasn't exactly definitive either – the doctors in Barcelona spoke only of probabilities – but he would fiercely defend this hypothesis during the Christmas festivities or at fiesta time, when his father, prompted by memories and possibly by too much wine, would begin weeping and laying all the blame on himself.

"How could I have let her spend the whole nine months there? How could I not have realised?"

"You always say the same thing, Dad, but you're wrong. The vibration from the machinery had nothing to do with it," Adrián would insist, and everyone else sitting round the table, Beatriz's father and the three or four longest-serving workers would all nod vigorously in agreement. "Besides, what does it matter? I've told you countless times that I don't care about my deformity. Have I ever complained?"

The guests would nod again, and his father would end up wiping away his tears. It was the same every year.

*

Adrián's positive frame of mind was not a pretence. As a child, he had enjoyed a privileged position in the village, because he was a member of an important local family – the owners of the sawmill. His school friends thought of him as rich, but also, and above all, as lord and master of the best playground in the whole area, and they would accept him as leader in exchange for being able to leap over the piles of sawdust and play with the axes used to lop off the smaller branches from the trees brought in from the woods. The sawmill remained a valuable playground later too, because the castles of planks and piles of logs proved to be excellent places for smoking a furtive cigarette or for any early romantic dalliances; even some of the village dances were held there, behind one of those walls of wood, with the band standing on a caterpillar truck used for transporting the logs along the forest tracks. And as Beatriz explained when he returned from his first operation in Barcelona, even having to spend long periods in hospital gave him a certain prestige.

His mother had died when he was nine. Just days before, she had summoned him to her side and told him yet again, and for the last time, that he enjoyed a privileged position in the village, in life and in the world.

"Adrián, always remember how lucky you are, remember all your good qualities, which can never be destroyed by whatever bad things may happen to you. People who make fun of you because of your physical deformity are mere nothings beside you. You are much richer and far more intelligent than they are. Besides, you have a beautiful face and very noble eyes."

When he did not respond, she made a comparison that was easier for him to understand, because it referred to one of the games they played at the sawmill.

"For example, can any of you shift Tártaro? No, you can't. Well, it will be just the same with you and your good qualities."

Tártaro was the name of one of his father's workers, a giant weighing almost twenty-three stone and measuring over six foot tall. Tártaro used to sit on the rear of a cart, so that the back end touched the ground, while they, Adrián and four or five other boys would hang from the shafts that were then pointing skywards and try vainly to pull them down.

The example given by his mother on her deathbed remained fixed in his mind, and he would remember it whenever he found himself in a difficult situation, when he fell ill or when someone, whether intentionally or not, made fun of his appearance.

"I won't let that throw my scales off balance," he would think. "Tártaro will not be moved." It became a formula, a kind of magic spell.

Later, the bad things weighed much more heavily in the scales than he had at first thought, when he was still not entirely aware of the consequences of his condition; but he managed to stand firm throughout, at Colegio La Salle, in hospital in Barcelona, and during his first years at engineering school. The memory of his mother sustained him and helped him carry on. It wasn't all triumphs, though. He received some very hard blows, and then not even that counterweight could keep his scales steady, not at least initially. For example, he had recently been told that he wouldn't be able to have children. A doctor in Bilbao had said:

"You have a problem with your reproductive system. And I'm sorry to say that, for now, there's no solution, either pharmacological or surgical."

That was when he made the decision to abandon his studies and go back to the village and to the sawmill, to his Centre. It was a response to that painful news. He could withstand people's insults or mockery, he could place in the scales the Good that outweighed the Bad and move on; but what he couldn't bear was the Bad continually being thrown at him by Nature. He didn't act immediately. He didn't want to go scurrying back to his Centre like a sad Quasimodo figure. He would return eventually, but as someone intending to conquer new and hopefully more pleasant territory; he would go back in order to live and to triumph. He would do so when he felt mentally prepared, when the scales were more evenly balanced.

It took him a year, more than a year. Then, on the day he found the fallen swallow in the park, when he received that message, he felt ready. It was time to go home.

*

266

When he started working at the sawmill and took over some of his father's responsibilities, the young Adrián's life changed completely. One day, he would be setting off with the loggers to the Pyrenees and spend whole weeks overseeing their work in the forest; another day, he would go with his father and the accountant to buy a piece of new machinery; on yet another day, he would be directing the building of a hut in the Centre of his territory, beside the pool and that gnarled, misshapen tree, and he began to study how to make furniture and toys.

It was a new era for him. Life seemed to consume time more and more quickly, as if it were fire, and time were a heap of tinder-dry wood; as if the calendar advanced by leaps and bounds and jumped suddenly from June to September or from November to March. Events rushed forwards at full tilt: he learned that Beatriz was expecting a baby, then that she'd had the baby and it was a girl, and, shortly afterwards, that the baby was three months old and he was invited to the christening.

The celebratory meal was held in a restaurant in the village, and he took with him, in his jacket pocket, a doll he had made.

"Oh, how lovely!" said Beatriz when he gave it to her. "Did you make it yourself?"

"The wooden part, yes, but I haven't yet learned how to sew."

"Well, it's really pretty. Thank you."

Beatriz seemed different, as if another woman had emerged from her body, smaller and paler than the previous one, but much happier. She was a beneficent presence, and all the guests responded to her influence, laughing and talking, pleased to be there. Even Adrián's father seemed cheerful, which he never usually was at such celebrations. When coffee was being served, he said to Adrián, winking at Beatriz's father as he did so:

"We've been working together for a while now, son, and so far we've had no secrets from each other, but it would seem that things are changing. A little bird tells me that you've been storing wood down at the hut by the pool without your foolish father even noticing."

His father was smoking a very slender cigar and pretending to take a great interest in the smoke rising up from it.

"This little bird of yours, is he about six foot tall and weighs in at about twenty-three stone?" Adrián asked, poker-faced.

"Yes, Tártaro. And quite right too. Otherwise, I would still be entirely in the dark."

"I'll have to have a word with that little bird, and tell him that neighbours should be more discreet."

The giant who used to play with him years before was still working at the sawmill and lived in a cabin in the wood, about a hundred yards from the gnarled tree. He chose not to live in the village and, as he himself admitted to Adrián when they happened to meet one day, instead of paying rent to a landlady, he preferred to spend his money on women. And this wasn't just idle talk on his part: he was famous for his nocturnal adventures. Adrián found it hard to believe that the two Tártaros, the one from his childhood and the one who was now his neighbour, could be the same person.

"I understand you've been buying cherry and walnut wood," his father said.

It was true. He had spent some time examining and buying those two kinds of wood and currently had ten logs soaking in the dam. He had read in a book that walnut becomes purple in water and cherry wood turns maroon.

"I'm thinking of building a small workshop once I've finished the hut," Adrián said after a pause. "I enjoy making furniture and toys, like the doll I made for Beatriz. But only in my spare time. It's just a bit of fun."

His father again winked at Beatriz's father.

"Your mother wouldn't be pleased to hear that you were spending money on 'a bit of fun'. And the worst thing is you're buying poor-quality walnut wood. Next time, take Tártaro with you. He'll teach you how to tell good from bad."

The meal ended in the same high good humour. Then, at his father's suggestion, all the guests were invited back to the sawmill to continue celebrating there.

Adrián arrived after all the others, because Beatriz had left the doll at the restaurant and he had to go and fetch it. This circumstance – as banal as him finding that swallow in the park – would prove decisive in balancing the inner scales on which he now and then weighed up Good and Bad.

When he reached the house, he pushed open the door and went towards the living room, where all the guests were gathered; first, though, he turned and peered into his bedroom to see what it was lying on his bed. There she was, partially wrapped in a white towel, the newly christened baby. She was moving her little feet very slowly, and her eyes, still blue then, were gazing up at the ceiling.

Then he understood. The beneficent presence at the meal, and which he and all the other guests had felt, had been the baby not Beatriz, and now his bedroom seemed calmer and more luminous than ever. He sat down cautiously on the edge of the bed, and his thoughts, which he did not try to force or direct, gradually took on the rhythm of the baby's gently kicking feet. He thought:

"This is how life is propagated, this is how pain and misfortune vanish, this is how death is vanquished, with the continuous intertwining of the generations, with the bodies that emerge from other bodies. That would be my way out too, to take part in the game and make a leap towards health, to cancel out the backward leap that took place before, either with me or my mother; but that happiness will be denied to me too, because I'm impotent and cannot have children."

When he emerged from these thoughts, he met the baby's blue gaze. She was looking at him as if to say: "Here I am, a little marvel, and I wasn't born of you." He felt his inner scales totter, as if he were again staggering from the blow he had received from that doctor in Bilbao.

"Thanks for keeping an eye on her. I couldn't find her clothes," he heard someone say. It was Beatriz, who had just come into the room. "Bath time, sweetie!" she said, dangling the child above her head.

"Sorry to have commandeered your bed, Adrián, but don't worry, we'll get out of your way now so that you can lie down," Beatriz's father said from the door.

"I wasn't intending to lie down," Adrián said.

"Did you find the doll, Adrián?" Beatriz asked before leaving the room with the baby. "You did? Well, give it to me now so that I can put it in my bag. I wouldn't want to forget it again."

Adrián took the doll out of his pocket and handed it to her.

The christening party was followed by a few weeks of slow time, and Adrián began to feel uneasy. He wished the hours and days would continue to be consumed like dry wood, that the calendar would keep advancing in leaps and bounds, that life would pass rapidly from action to action, with no thoughts, no memories, and without the image of that baby lying on his bed. It proved impossible. On occasions, as he had when he was younger, he would visit the restaurants in the village or go to the cinema, but time continued to pass painfully slowly, and he sank lower and lower.

Fortunately, his father sought his help in salvaging an old project.

"You see this?" he said. Before him stood a butcher's block on which the wood was very cracked and shrunken. "It's made of oak, but that's still not hard enough. A meat cleaver can reduce it to pulp within a couple of years."

"It certainly looks in a bad way," Adrián said, touching the wooden block. "What did you have in mind?"

He knew he could trust his father to come up with a good idea. Although in many ways a very ordinary man, his father knew all there was to know about wood.

"Butchers are fed up with having to replace their blocks every few years. If we could make a really good, solid block, our business would really take off. We could sell it in Spain and in France too. Why don't you see what you can come up with? There's no rush."

Adrián spent the summer and the autumn researching, studying and travelling to France and other European countries to look at different types of butcher's block, and his enthusiasm for the task filled up all the empty corners of his life, even in his dreams; in the winter, the first models and trials took him completely out of himself, carrying him into new territory where the talk was all of mistakes and adjustments; with the spring, though, came success – an extraordinary block made up of thousands of compressed wood particles – and then it was all celebrations and preparations, the buying of new machinery, meetings and publicity campaigns. Shortly afterwards, when summer was about to return, Adrián felt as if he were in the middle of a bonfire in which time was vanishing like smoke and feeling that he, too, had half-vanished; he had forgotten not only the baby lying on his bed, but everything; he had even forgotten about his Centre and his plan to build a workshop in which to create his own things. He decided to stop. He summoned Tártaro and suggested they spend their Sundays buying the trees he needed – mainly fine walnut trees – to make furniture and toys.

"I've been expecting you to ask me that," Tártaro said. "Your father had already mentioned it."

"Will you help?" Adrián asked.

Tártaro nodded.

"I don't usually leave the cabin on Sunday mornings, because I tend to sleep in to recover from my Saturday night exertions. But from now on, I will. I respect your father enormously and, frankly, if he asked me to lie on my back with my legs in the air, I'd do it."

He spoke almost like a child.

The secret of finding a good walnut tree was easy enough to learn. You just had to use a brace and bit to drill a hole in the base of the tree and see how long it took before a dark, almost black shaving appeared, because that was the unmistakable sign of quality. However, even though Adrián didn't really need Tártaro, he nevertheless preferred to take him along with him on his excursions and buying expeditions. Tártaro was really impressive when seen from close to: his strong, muscular back as he strode along a mountain path or the veins in his neck when he picked up a log or a stone, or the ease with which he handled an axe, as if it were light as a feather. He may have been six foot tall and weigh twenty-three stone, but he wasn't just a human beast of burden. His movements were quick and precise.

Tártaro liked to talk too, mostly about sex. He recounted exploits which, to Adrián, seemed logical enough and perfectly in keeping with the size of Tártaro's hands and the thickness of the veins in his neck, but he nevertheless found them astonishing. Would they astonish those who led more normal lives than he did, married people, people who had a lover or visited brothels? He was sure they would.

"Do you think of nothing else but women?" Adrián would say to him, as a way of detaching himself from what he was hearing.

Tártaro's response was always the same.

"What can I do? If I didn't have so much spunk in me, I'd stay at the sawmill and happily work forty days on the trot, but the spunk drives me crazy."

One Sunday, at the beginning of July, Adrián noticed that Tártaro was unusually silent. He didn't regale him with a single anecdote and spoke not a word on a journey which, because the walnut trees were in a more mountainous area, took them more than an hour. It was the same when they were testing the trees for the quality of the wood.

"How much spunk have you got, Adrián? A lot or a little?" Tártaro suddenly asked him when they were driving back.

"A little," Adrián said somewhat reluctantly.

"Well, be grateful to God for that. You will never be as unfortunate as me. You will never live in a cabin in the woods and you'll never get shot at the way they shot at me. They almost killed me."

Adrián didn't know what Tártaro was talking about, but he did remember seeing him once using crutches.

"The problem now is different, but just as serious," the giant went on. "I've asked your father to give me leave from the sawmill for a while. He's agreed and told me not to worry. Your father's a good man."

"So you're leaving," Adrián said, surprised. "I didn't know."

Tártaro's answer surprised him even more.

"I have some cousins who live in Nevada. They have a ranch with more than three thousand sheep. If all goes well, I'll be having lunch with them next Sunday."

The workshop Adrián had built in his Centre included a small living area – lounge, bedroom and kitchen – and he would sometimes sleep there if he happened to work late on a particular piece of furniture. If it was a very hot night, he would leave the workshop and go and lie beneath the gnarled, misshapen tree, and stay there for hours, keeping very still, listening to his own breathing and to all the other sounds: the water slipping through the cracks in the dam, the rustling leaves, the singing of the toads and the night birds in the wood. Of all those sounds, though, only one really penetrated his mind: the singing of the toads. "Oh!" said the toads. "Oh! Oh!" and it seemed to Adrián that something must have impressed them so deeply that they could not stop exclaiming "Oh! Oh!" over and over, and the stars seemed to be keeping time too, blinking on and off to the rhythm of the toads' "Oh! Oh!" The sound penetrated still deeper inside him, and Adrián could then clearly see the scales balancing Good and Bad. He could see that the positive side of the scales was full, fuller than ever thanks to the success of his butcher's block, but that wasn't enough. Nothing could console him for the misfortune that Beatriz's daughter had so clearly revealed to him. It was very hard to be excluded from the march of life, from the march of those intertwining generations. How he would love to take the logs he was keeping in the pool and make furniture from them that he could then offer to a woman like Beatriz! And then choose the finest wood to make a cradle! "Oh! Oh!" sang the toads. "Oh! Oh!" Adrián would get up at that point and go to his bed in the workshop.

It was a particularly hot night. Adrián suddenly heard a different noise. On the path that led to Tártaro's cabin, a dry twig snapped.

"Are you back already?" he asked, sitting up. He could see nothing.

More sounds of snapping twigs, which took on the rhythm now of someone's footsteps. Soon Adrián could make out a shadowy figure.

"Where is he?" the shadow asked. It was a woman and she spoke with a foreign accent.

"Do you mean Tártaro?" he asked. He knew what the answer would be, but he needed time to adjust to the situation.

"Where is he?" the woman asked again.

"He's gone to Nevada," answered Adrián.

The woman let out a scream, an incomprehensible word. Doubtless a curse.

"Look, we can't see anything here, why don't we go inside. We'll be more comfortable there," he said.

They went into the workshop and sat down in the lounge.

She was a rather plain young woman and heavily pregnant. She told Adrián that she was Russian and worked in a bar near the motorway.

"Tártaro was my lover. A very stubborn man. He refused to take any precautions and so in the end the inevitable happened," she explained, sitting down and lighting a cigarette. She seemed tired, but not particularly upset. "Anyway, I didn't come here for sentimental reasons. I'm in this country illegally and I need money for the baby."

"Why didn't you have an abortion?" Adrián asked.

"Precisely because I'm here illegally, and I thought that if I had the baby, Poli would marry me and then I'd be eligible for Spanish nationality."

He was amused by the name "Poli".

"His name's Policarpo, but everyone calls him Poli," she said, as if guessing his thoughts. "By the way, my name's Nadia," she added, holding out her hand.

"I'm Adrián."

They shook hands. The woman stubbed out her cigarette in a saucer on the coffee table and asked for a glass of water.

"River or bottled?"

"Bottled."

"I'm going to make myself a gin and tonic. Would you like one?"

The woman hesitated and glanced at her wristwatch.

"It's a bit late. I start work at half past eleven," she said. "I work at the bar now that I'm pregnant. I'm eight months gone."

She made as if to shoo away a fly.

"Oh, what the hell, I'll have one too," she said.

She had a strong accent, but spoke very fluently.

The fluorescent light in the kitchen transformed the ingredients of the gin and tonic as he took them from the fridge: the little bottles of Schweppes sparkled; the ice cubes glittered like glass; the green of the gin bottle took on an emerald tone; the yellow of the lemons gleamed like wax.

He cooled the glasses first by swishing the ice cubes round inside them; then he poured in the gin followed by the tonic water. Suddenly, as he was squeezing the slices of lemon on the edge of each glass, he had an idea, a plan.

He handed the woman her drink, then sat down in front of her. They both took a sip.

"That's the best gin and tonic I've had in a long time," she said. "The ones they serve at the club practically drill a hole in your stomach."

"What are you going to do with the baby, Nadia? Do you want it?" Adrián asked.

She lit her second cigarette.

"Even if I did, I couldn't keep it," she said. "Besides, I'm planning to go to the States. Apparently, they treat Russians well over there."

The smoke from her cigarette dissolved before it reached the ceiling. Outside was utter darkness. A moonless night.

"Listen, you and I are going to make a deal," Adrián said. "We won't leave here until we've come to an agreement."

Once those words had rushed out of his mouth, he felt an enormous sense of relief. He had taken the first step.

After that night, time seemed to stop. The days, hours and minutes were no longer made of tinder-dry wood, but of stone, which neither burned nor was consumed. Adrián neglected his work at the sawmill and spent his days going back and forth; he couldn't sleep and felt increasingly weary; nevertheless, he went ahead with the plan he had drawn up after his conversation with Nadia. One day, he visited his lawyer; on another, he wrote a document in which he acknowledged that he was the father of the child she was about to give birth to; on yet another, he visited the Russian embassy and picked up the papers he needed to arrange a proxy marriage with a woman 'resident in Russia'. He accompanied Nadia to the clinic where she was going to give birth and paid all the costs up front. He was trying to do with his plan what he had done with the butcher's block, gathering together a thousand fragments and compressing them into a solid block, except that he was dealing with people now and his calculations could not be as exact. He would occasionally shut himself up in his workshop and try to work on a piece of furniture or perfect a new expression for the face of one of his dolls, but he would soon abandon the task and go and lie beneath the gnarled, misshapen tree and wait for night to come. And night would come, but the toads would not sing. Autumn was approaching and it was getting colder.

One September morning, when he was beginning to think his plan was a mere chimera, he saw his father coming down the path to the workshop. In his right hand, he was carrying a piece of paper, which flapped about as limply as if it were a handkerchief.

"Someone's left a baby outside our door, and according to this document, it's yours," his father said once the two of them were face to face.

Adrián saw that there were two signatures on the document. Nadia had kept her word.

"So it's a girl," he said, laughing. "Excellent. Now Beatriz's daughter will have a ready-made friend."

They walked back together towards the sawmill, when he was suddenly assailed by doubt.

"Is she healthy?" he asked.

"Absolutely, and she's big too," answered his father.

When they reached the sawmill, Adrián ran up the steps into the house. The newborn baby was lying on his bed just where Beatriz's daughter had lain that other day; she was wrapped in a blanket decorated with little flowers and other folksy Slavic motifs. A souvenir left by Nadia for her daughter.

The little girl had reddish, wrinkled skin and was fast asleep.

"Hello. How are *you*?" Adrián asked, taking her hand. The baby gripped it hard. "Good! I can see you're going to grow up to be a big strong girl!"

His father was standing at the bedroom door.

"More than that," he said. "In future, she'll be able to haul whole tree trunks along, like Tártaro."

He was beginning to understand what had happened.

WILD HORSES

Earle and Dennis had an appointment with someone at the office of the silver mine, and I was waiting for them in Earle's Chevrolet Avalanche. The sky was blue, the desert an ochre yellow that took on a reddish tinge on the round hills beyond; the wind was blowing over the bushes, combing them clean.

I found the sky, the desert and the warmth inside the car very comforting. They were combing my mind clean too, dissolving what remained of the unease I'd felt an hour before when I spotted a rattlesnake as we were walking among the rocks decorated with petroglyphs – the drawings made by the Indians thousands of years ago.

As happened with Sara when she slipped on the steps at College Drive and hit her head, I was struggling to keep awake. Gradually, the image of that snake just three feet away from my shoe evaporated from my memory. I closed my eyes.

Then I opened them. Standing right next to the nose of the car were two wild horses looking at me. They were very still. One of them had a white star on its head like the horse at Loyola that Cornélie used to ride. Where would Cornélie be now? I hadn't heard from her for possibly thirty years. An image came into my mind: the head of a horse peering over a stable door, and a figure nearby smoking a cigarette: Hump or Adrián.

The other horse was black, like the one in my village that got electrocuted, although that had been a much bigger breed, a Percheron. His bones would still be lying in the empty plot of land behind the house where I was born, although it was no longer an empty plot, but a parking lot.

There were more wild horses about three hundred yards away. One of them started galloping, like in the Marilyn Monroe / Clark Gable film, but not because it was being pursued by a hunter. Horses were only hunted on the reserves of the Paiute and other Indian tribes.

The Indian tribes: Paiute, Comanche, Sioux, Cheyenne, Kiowa, Apache, Arapaho, Navajo, Oglala, Iroquois, Dakota . . . I was reading about their history in Dee Brown's *Bury My Heart at Wounded Knee*, which was even sadder than Sarah Winnemucca's account. It made one want to weep for Crazy Horse, Sitting Bull, Cochise, Geronimo and all the other Indians who lost the war against the white men and were driven from lands they had inhabited for eight thousand years – because that's how old some of the petroglyphs are.

In a passage devoted to Crazy Horse, Dee Brown explains that for Crazy Horse, the world we inhabit was merely the shadow of another world, of the real world, and that he could only get into that real world through dreams, and in his dreams he saw his horse dancing wildly, crazily, which was why he called himself Crazy Horse, and it was in his dreams, too, that he acquired his skills as a warrior, because it was there, in the real world, that he discovered new ways of fighting the white man.

I, too, wanted to enter the real world and, for a moment, I did. The two wild horses in front of the car started whirling round and round as if they were on a carousel, and with them whirled Cornélie's horse, Franquito's black horse and all the other horses that were part of my past. It seemed to me – although, as I said, only momentarily – that this was an image of my life, and I thought how easy it would be to place human creatures alongside those horses, or indeed replace them entirely with, for example, the woman who used to read *Reader's Digest*, the man in hospital who felt caged in like a monkey, José Francisco, Didi, Adrián, L., myself, Ángela, Izaskun, Sara . . . Once around, twice, three times, four times, and so on until the carousel stopped. But where was the centre? Where was the axis around which everything was turning?

The two wild horses remained quite still, looking at me. I opened the window and, as José Francisco's mother, my aunt, used to do, I addressed them as if they were a chorus:

"Tell me, horses, what axis are we turning around? What is it that gives order and unity to our lives?"

"Shh," Dennis said. He and Earle were standing next to the car.

Hours before, when we drove into the desert and Earle suggested we drive over to look at a herd of grazing horses, Dennis had been firmly opposed to the idea. They were wild animals. We should respect them. They were a living symbol of the American West.

Now he was speaking to me in the same way.

"You'll have to do as he says," Earle said. "Horses are sacred here, like cows in India."

Earle was happy. He had been equally happy while we were studying the petroglyphs, and later too, after seeing the rattlesnake, as we drove to the silver mine. Sometimes, he wouldn't just smile, he would laugh out loud.

"So you talk to horses, do you?" he said as he got into the car. "I thought that only happened in films."

"I was saying goodbye. I don't think I'll ever come back here," I said.

When Earle started the engine, the two horses drew back a little, but stayed where they were.

"We know the moment to say goodbye is getting close," he said, "and that's why we're going to Virginia City. Dennis and I want to buy you a present. A souvenir of Nevada. A dried rattlesnake skin."

This time it was Dennis who laughed.

We set off very cautiously, so as not to startle the wild horses. It would take us an hour to get to Virginia City. There were no roads in that part of the desert.

"To be honest," I said, "I find even the dried variety alarming."

What they really had in mind was a pair of leather boots. Dennis confessed as much as we were passing the area where we had seen the petroglyphs.

"We'll buy you some special ones if you want, like the boots Ringo Bonavena wore," Earle said.

Earle seemed so happy that I immediately thought of Natalie. *Os vellos non deben de namorarse* – old men shouldn't fall in love – but maybe Castelao had been wrong.

"Do you know the story about what happened to Bonavena in Nevada?" Earle asked.

"I know he was killed here. You told us that the other day."

"He bought a pair of boots from the very shop we're going to now. The boots had a sort of compartment in which you could hide a small pistol."

I found this astonishing.

"I don't know that story," Dennis said.

"What ignoramuses!" Earle cried, who really was very happy indeed. *Le rire était dans le cœur*, laughter was in his heart.

RINGO BONAVENA AND THE ANGELS
A FANTASY (BOB EARLE'S VERSION)

Ringo Bonavena bought himself a pair of cowboy boots in Virginia City and wore them day and night. During the day at Mustang Ranch, he went up and down the brothel's carpeted stairs in them and only took them off when necessary; at night, in the streets of Reno, going from casino to casino, he would show them off to the other poker players. Afterwards, he would return to Mustang Ranch, to sleep in the caravan he had parked there. He would place his boots on a shelf, lie down in bed and dream of angels, for it is a well-known fact that boxers have very innocent dreams.

Bonavena wasn't in Reno by chance, with, as his sole aim, going up and down the stairs at Mustang Ranch, but because the owner of the brothel, Joe Conforte, had bought his contract and was his new owner. He didn't pay him very well, sixty thousand dollars a fight, but then, at thirty-three, Bonavena wasn't exactly at his peak. Well, perhaps he was when it came to going up and down stairs, but not as regards boxing. In February 1976, in a fight that took place in Reno itself, he twice knocked down his rival, Billy Joiner, but failed to knock him out.

That night, while he was sleeping, one of the angels, his guardian angel, said to him:

"Go back to Argentina, to your mother. You have fought enough."

Traditionally, angels have always been right, as was the one who spoke to him then. Bonavena had fought sixty-eight fights since the day he turned professional in Luna Park, Buenos Aires, and he had won fifty-eight – forty-four with a knockout. Added to this list of achievements was the splendid memory of his fights with Muhammad Ali and Joe Frazier. In other words, he had money and fame. Why not go back to his mother? Boxers usually love their mothers, and he was no exception.

"Not yet," Bonavena whispered to his guardian angel, not quite waking up. "I love Annie, and it would break my heart to have to leave her."

His guardian angel accepted this reason unquestioningly. May God's will be done. However, a devil, the security guard at Mustang Ranch, was not of the same opinion. His name was Ross Brymer. He went to Joe Conforte's office and said:

"That Argentinian wants to screw Annie for free."

Traduttore, traditori. Bonavena's delicate words did not deserve such a crude translation.

As a businessman, Joe Conforte valued peace above all else, because peace, along with his talent for innovation, was what made Mustang Ranch the best brothel in the world. Ross Brymer, though, was a tenacious man, and he spoke to his boss sternly, as if he were his son:

"It makes me sad to see what's happening, Joe. You were one of the country's pioneers, and there isn't a brothel in the world worthy of the name that doesn't model itself on Mustang Ranch. Listen to me, Joe. This Argentinian bull is insatiable. Not content with having Annie, now he wants Mamy. Your wife, Joe! If you don't do something, the same people who call you 'the father of legal prostitution in the United States' will start calling you 'Cuckold Joe' or, even worse, 'Chicken Joe'."

The word "chicken" was a loaded one. Many in the United States would remember Bonavena sneeringly calling Muhammad Ali "chicken".

"Throw him out, Joe," Ross Brymer said. "Get him off Mustang Ranch land. I hate seeing his caravan parked in our drive."

It's hard to know what went through Joe Conforte's mind when he heard those words, because his genuine feelings were usually about as easy to find as a needle in a haystack, hidden beneath a thousand insubstantial trivialities; but he was probably thinking about Mamy and Annie. There was a nearly forty-year age difference between the two women. Could Bonavena cope with such a wide chronological range?

The telephone rang and interrupted his thoughts. It was Mamy calling him from Harrah's.

"Joe, I'm going to Los Angeles with Ringo. I want to show him the sights."

Joe Conforte made a joke before hanging up.

"Fine, sweetheart, but don't show him anything else."

Joe Conforte found himself in a dilemma. If he gave in to Ross Brymer and expelled Bonavena from Mustang Ranch, Mamy would be most displeased, and Mamy was irreplaceable, the most efficient brothel manager in the whole country. On the other hand, he didn't want to displease Ross Brymer either. He was the "main man" of Mustang Ranch, good with his fists, good with a gun, brave, loyal and even capable of picking up a guitar and entertaining the clients. In a way, he was irreplaceable too.

"Ross, I know things have got a bit out of hand since Ringo arrived," he said at last. "Up until recently you've been the main man here, and now you've had to take a step back. In a way, that's inevitable, Ross. After all, Ringo has faced Muhammad Ali and Joe Frazier in the ring, and he deserves some respect for that alone. On the other hand, I agree. Ringo would be much more comfortable in a room at Harrah's than living in that caravan. And he'd be even better off in Argentina. It's always good to be with your mama."

Ross Brymer touched his hat. He had heard all he needed to hear. He was about to open the door of the office to leave, when Joe Conforte spoke again:

"Another thing, Ross. Annie tells me Ringo has a small pistol, but she doesn't know where he keeps it. She's searched his clothes, but it's not there."

Ross Brymer pulled a face.

"It isn't his small pistol I'm worried about, it's his big one."

He wasn't always so coarse and, according to some of the brothel's regular clients, he was as good as Doc Watson when it came to singing country-and-Western songs; however, the new situation at Mustang Ranch was driving him to distraction.

Angels, especially guardian angels, listen to everything and understand everything, and Ringo's guardian angel tried to tell him about that conversation between Conforte and Brymer, but couldn't. Ringo was swanning around Los Angeles with Mamy and, despite its name, that city was not a good place for angels. In a word: the angel failed to talk to him.

On their return from Los Angeles, Ringo left Mamy in Joe Conforte's arms and went to the other end of the chronological range. Annie, however, had changed. She was nervous and asked a lot of questions: "When did you fall in love for the first time?" "'How old were you when you first made love?" "Is Buenos Aires a pretty town?" "Do you ever phone your mother?" "Have you ever been to France?" "Where do you usually keep your little pistol?" The first five questions were the haystack, the sixth, the needle.

"It's inside my right boot," Ringo said.

"You're kidding," Annie responded, laughing.

Ringo showed her the boot, which had an inside pocket in which the pistol fitted snugly.

On one of those nights, the caravan caught fire and burned to the ground.

"No matter, I'll buy another one," Ringo said.

His guardian angel was still concerned. The message from that fire was clear: "Get out of here! Leave Mustang Ranch! This is your final warning!"

The guardian angels also have their own backup system. They are guardians who have guardians, counsellors who themselves receive counselling, and they form an endless series, A1, A2, A3, A4, A5, A6, A7 . . . Ringo's guardian angel – say, A212 – consulted colleagues about the best way to handle this serious situation. The angel's closest friend in that infinite series, A162.400, immediately said:

"There's nothing you can do. Ringo's a boxer, he knows no fear. He called Muhammad Ali 'chicken', remember. For him, being chicken is the worst thing in the world. So be in no doubt, he'll go back to Mustang Ranch and continue playing around with Annie and with Mamy, and even more brazenly than before."

That night, A212 went to Ringo's room at Harrah's, where he had been sleeping since his caravan burned down.

"Ringo, buy a proper pistol and carry it in your belt or in a holster under your arm. That miniature pistol in your boot is no use at all."

Ringo listened.

"Tomorrow, I'll buy one in the gun shop next to the hotel," he promised the angel before going back to sleep.

In the morning, A212 again consulted A162.400, who was sceptical:

"Ringo was asleep when you spoke to him and it may have seemed a good idea at the time to go about armed like Billy the Kid, but he won't remember when he wakes up."

A162.400 was right. Ringo rose late and spent the day playing poker. Then, that night, he went to Mustang Ranch in one of the casino's limousines. When he got there, he tipped the driver a hundred dollars and set off to look for Mamy and Annie.

Brymer shot him from the main door of the brothel. He told the judge he hadn't intended to kill anyone, and that the grille protecting the door had deflected the bullet into Ringo's heart. He couldn't claim self-defence, because why would he need to defend himself against a person whose only weapon was a small pistol hidden in his boot? The judge sentenced him to a few months in prison, denying him the reprieve requested by the Mustang Ranch's lawyer.

Ringo's body was returned to Argentina to lie in state at the Luna Park sports arena in Buenos Aires, where more than a hundred thousand people filed past to pay their last respects. His guardian angel was impressed by the crowds and commented to his colleague A162.400:

"It reminds me of that other man they crucified two thousand years ago. That was a special death too."

"They're hardly comparable," A162.400 said.

"Maybe not, but it was still a shame."

MAY 7

THE COST OF LOOKING FOR STEVE FOSSETT

The *Reno Gazette-Journal* carried an article about Steve Fossett prompted by comments made by Jim Gibbons, the governor of

Nevada, to the *Las Vegas Review-Journal*. It seems that the governor intended sending a bill for $687,000 to the millionaire adventurer's widow for costs incurred by the Nevada National Guard and the Civil Air Patrol in their search for her husband.

These comments caused great controversy. "We do not charge the rich or the poor," said Frank Siracusa, director of Nevada's Division of Emergency Management. "You get lost, and we look for you. It is a service your taxpayer dollars pay for."

The article explained that the hotel magnate Hilton, the owner of the ranch from which Fossett had set off on his final journey, had made a voluntary contribution of $200,000 to cover some of the search costs. On the Internet, most people agreed with Frank Siracusa. One of the few in agreement with Jim Gibbons, however, was very aggressive: "Why should we pay to look for some adrenaline junkie?"

According to the article, the problem was money. The state of Nevada had budget problems because of the cuts.

TELEPHONE CALL

I called my older brother on his mobile phone because it was my mother's day to go to the hospital, but he didn't answer, she did. I heard her voice and the sound of a truck honking. They were in the car.

"Who is it?"

Her voice sounded unusually soft and mellifluous, as if she were speaking to a child.

"It's me," I said.

"Where are you calling from?" she said, after a silence.

"I'm in my office at the university. Are you in the car?"

"Yes, I am. You've no idea the number of trucks on this road."

"Can I speak to my brother? Just for a moment."

"Transportes Patinter!"

"Can I speak—"

"Transportes Azpiroz! Transportes Mitxelena! Autocares . . . !"

She paused, and my brother took the telephone.

"She's getting all worked up about these trucks. Call back later."

"Bengoetxea! Autocares Bengoetxea!" my mother shouted. "We've just overtaken them! We're going really fast!"

"O.K., I'll call back later."

"Yes, whenever you like. Bye."

MAY 12
SEVEN TELEPHONE CALLS

My two brothers called me, so did a doctor, as well as Adrián and another three friends from our schooldays. All gave me the same message: "L. died today."

DREAM FOLLOWING THE DEATH OF L.

I dreamed I was in a huge rubbish dump, surrounded by mounds and even mountains of detritus and rubble. There were thousands of bags filled with trash. One area was blue and, from a distance, resembled a lake. However, when I went closer, I saw that it, too, was filled with bags of trash, except that these were newer and made of shiny plastic and arranged more neatly. A man was going around opening and examining them, although without actually rummaging around in the contents. I didn't speak to him because, in the dream, he was always about fifty yards away from me. I took the opportunity, however, to examine the contents of the bags as well.

"They're full of metaphors!" I thought with some surprise. This was an absurd idea, but I could see the bags and their contents, and it all seemed very real to me.

The metaphors were not as substantial as potato peelings or milk cartons, nor did they have any definite form, and yet, despite their ineffable nature, I could easily associate them with natural things and creatures. In several of the bags I opened, I found what looked like ants; in another, horses; and in still others, trees. There were some, too, that resembled books, houses or even walls.

I knew that a small bag could not possibly contain things that were

286

ten or a hundred or a thousand times larger, but I didn't care. All I cared about were the metaphors.

I studied those that were like ants and those that were like horses and those that were like trees, books, houses or walls, and I soon realised that, regardless of size or shape, they were all speaking about life after death. Then I heard a voice saying:

"Now when Jesus came, he found that Lazarus had already been in the tomb four days."

I turned and saw that it was the old man who I had been unable to approach before. He had taken a book out of one of the rubbish bags and was holding it open before his eyes.

"Allow me to continue with the story of Lazarus," he said and then read out loud: "Jesus said, 'Take away the stone.' Martha, the sister of the dead man, said to him, 'Lord, by this time there will be an odour, for he has been dead four days.' Jesus said to her, 'Did I not tell you that if you believed you would see the glory of God?' So they took away the stone. And Jesus lifted up his eyes and said, 'Father, I thank you that you have heard me.' When he had said these things, he cried out with a loud voice, 'Lazarus, come out.' The man who had died came out, his hands and feet bound with linen strips, and his face wrapped with a cloth. Jesus said to them, 'Unbind him, and let him go.'"

The old man walked over to the blue bags, and I myself – I, the author of the dream, the creator of the images that kept recurring as if on a kind of closed circuit – could see that they were not bags exactly, but containers resembling yoghurt pots.

"Greek yoghurt," the old man said. "Quite a different class of metaphor."

He removed the lid of one of the containers and took out, not the creamy white substance I was expecting, but a wall.

Then, in another instant transformation, the wall became a book.

"I'm going to read the passage that describes the funeral of Patroclus," the old man said.

I noticed that he looked very much like a teacher I had at school, who had been the first person to talk to me about classical literature and to urge me to read the *Iliad*.

The old man looked down at the book and began to read: "At length Achilles sinks in the soft arms of sleep, when lo, the shade, before his closing eyes, of sad Patroclus rose, or seem'd to rise; in the same robe he living wore, he came; in stature, voice, and pleasing look, the same. The form familiar hover'd o'er his head, 'And sleeps Achilles? (thus the phantom said:) Sleeps my Achilles, his Patroclus dead? Ah, suffer that my bones may rest with thine! Together have we lived; together bred, one house received us, and one table fed; that golden urn, thy goddess-mother gave, may mix our ashes in one common grave.'"

The old man was walking briskly now, skirting round the yoghurt pots and occasionally turning to me to tell me what each one contained.

"Here we keep the Koranic metaphors," he said.

Immediately, a young man emerged from among the containers and began walking alongside the old man. He wore a turban and could have been a page boy. Without stopping, but gesturing theatrically, he began to recite:

"According to the Koran: 'In Paradise there will be rivers of water incorruptible; rivers of milk of which the taste never changes; rivers of wine, a joy to those who drink; and rivers of honey pure and clear. In it there are for them all kinds of fruits; and Grace from their Lord.'"

The containers became houses, and the three of us – the old man, the page boy and I – walked along a very straight path towards an arch. We went through the arch and emerged onto an esplanade whose vast size and reddish colour reminded me of the Arizona desert. There were thousands of trucks, many of them stationary, but all with their engines running; others were constantly on the move, approaching, driving away, passing. On top of a strange-looking rock, above the esplanade, was a hoarding the size of a hundred cinema screens, on which was written: AREA FOR THE LOADING AND UNLOADING OF METAPHORS.

I went over to a man wearing fluorescent yellow overalls and who was going from truck to truck with a clipboard and a pen, and I asked him, just to be sure, what the trucks were carrying.

"You're obviously not from around here," he said, without even looking at me and all the while noting down the information given him by the driver of that particular truck. Then he added: "All the trucks parked here are transporting metaphors to the beyond. And to be honest, we've barely been able to cope lately. Apparently, an awful lot of people are dying."

The man went over to the cab of a second truck and again noted down the information given. He seemed almost hyperactive. He spoke very quickly and was always on the move.

"Do you see that fleet of white trucks over there?" he said, pointing to a line of trucks painted in a colour, which, in real life, is usually reserved for spaceships. "They're all carrying metaphors to do with reincarnation. Apparently, there's more and more demand for them. Do you know what reincarnation is?"

He kept moving, going from truck to truck, cab to cab. I found it hard to keep up. I was beginning to get tired.

"Well, reincarnation is the theory that the soul leaps from one body to another, and thus never ceases to live. The other day, a truck driver was telling me the story of an American boy. Apparently, he had proof that he'd been a sailor in an earlier life and had died on the *Titanic*."

He paused to light a cigarette, then went on:

"He also told me a story about General George Smith Patton. Apparently, an admirer said to him: 'General George Smith Patton, you should have fought with Napoleon.' And General George Smith Patton replied: 'But I did. I fought beside him at Waterloo.' Do you understand? He meant that General George Smith Patton had, in a previous life, been one of Napoleon's soldiers."

The man sat down on a stone bench. He took a long drag on his cigarette, exhaled the smoke, then exclaimed:

"You know, I really like that name: George Smith Patton!"

"You don't say," I said.

"From what I've read, he was a great general. They say he should have been given the Nobel War Prize," he said.

I looked around, wondering where the old man had gone, the

one who had read me those passages from the Bible and from the *Iliad*, and where the page boy had gone too, because they had both vanished.

I suddenly found myself, as if by magic, and quite unaware that I had risen up, on a high peak from which I could see part of the esplanade, the Area for the Loading and Unloading of Metaphors. This confirmed my first impression: what lay before me resembled the reddish desert with the strangely shaped rocks that I had driven through with Ángela, Izaskun and Sara. Except that it wasn't a vast, empty space, but a vast space filled with trucks approaching, moving away, passing and sending up clouds of dust. How many trucks were there? How many tons of metaphors? One hundred thousand trucks? Two million tons of metaphors? I remembered that famous line: "I had not thought death had undone so many."

The man in the yellow overalls was still smoking.

"If I ever marry and have a family," he said, "I'd like one of my sons to be the reincarnation of George Smith Patton."

Hoping to change the subject, I pointed to one of the loading bays. There were hundreds of pallets piled high with books ready to be transported. I looked more closely and saw that although there were many books, they were all the same.

"What book is it?" I asked.

I was hoping it would be an anthology that included one of my favourite John Donne poems: "Death be not proud, though some have called thee mighty and dreadful, for thou art not so . . ."

"John Donne? The name doesn't ring a bell, I'm afraid," the man in the yellow overalls said. He was still smoking what seemed to be an interminable cigarette. "He must be in the old part of the dump, or perhaps in sector M7 for minority metaphors. Some people think it's wrong that they should be kept in such an inaccessible place, but that's the way it is. Stories like the one about General George Smith Patton are far more popular, and so, of course, they're at the head of the queue."

I felt in need of air and a desire to move and walk over to the desert, towards the horizon where the red earth and blue sky met, beyond all those trucks, beyond the Area for the Loading and Unloading of Metaphors. But I couldn't.

"You asked me about the book on the pallets. Well, it's called *Life After Death*. That's where the story about the general comes from . . ."

"Oh, I see!" I said and leapt into the air. At last, I had recovered the power of movement.

"It certainly seems to sell well," he went on. "Last month alone, it sold twenty thousand million copies. There's another best-seller being loaded onto the trucks called *The Fourth Dimension*. Apparently, on the sixth day of the sixth month of 2006, a crystalline door opened up in the christic, metafactual consciousness, an intergalactic pathway along which the Great Energy began to flow . . ."

"Your cigarette seems to be never-ending," I said, interrupting him.

"Yes, apparently it's eternal," he said, exhaling another cloud of smoke.

Apparently, apparently . . . Unable to bear any more repetition, I woke up.

What had begun as a dream – one of those confused digressions, part-image, part-thought, that surface when you're only half-asleep – suddenly became a febrile vision, a nightmare.

I tried to find an explanation for those images.

"It's that journey from Torrey to Kayenta," I told myself. "The dream recreated the landscape we passed through, and then there was the news of L.'s death, because I spent hours trying to come up with metaphors so that I could write something to celebrate his life."

While I was thinking, I had the impression that I was back in the Best Western Hotel in Kayenta. I looked out of the window and noticed that my computer was still on one of the tables in the foyer, along with a can of soft drink. I must have been dreaming, because my computer and the can of drink could not possibly still be there. It was equally impossible that I was in Kayenta, because we had come back to our house in College Drive over a month ago. Knowing this did not help though. The effort of thinking logically became too much and I again fell asleep.

The one-storey hotel in Kayenta had sixty rooms and was built in the shape of a U. Inside the U was a swimming pool surrounded by parasols and loungers all in turquoise blue, the Navajos' favourite colour. For a moment, as if I had risen up into the air like a bird, I could see everything from above: the hotel, the swimming pool, the parasols, the loungers, and, about three or four hundred yards away, at the bottom of a hill, there was a green wood, the only one to be found near Kayenta.

I could hear my two daughters shrieking with laughter and imagined them splashing about in the pool, glad to be able to have somewhere to swim in a place as hot as Kayenta. I was glad too that all was well. We hadn't had an accident and, more importantly, we hadn't plunged off the edge of the terrifying road we'd had to drive down to reach Mexican Hat.

The girls' shrieks grew still more jubilant. In General Patton mode, Izaskun shouted: "Attack," and Sara burst out laughing. Ángela shouted something too, but only once, then I heard a splash.

"I can't save you. That would be against the rules," someone said.

That's L.'s voice, I thought.

I had a feeling he and I had arranged to meet at the hotel, and that I had forgotten. Anyway, L. was obviously there already and I had to leave my room and go and find him.

I looked at my watch. It wasn't eight or nine o'clock in the morning as I had thought, but a quarter to six in the evening.

Izaskun asked L. if he lived in Kayenta.

"No," he said. "I live in the south of Arizona, in Tempe, near Phoenix."

My daughter asked him what he did.

"I teach physics at the Arizona State University," he said. "I specialise in optics."

"Why is your nose so flat?" Sara asked suddenly.

"What's that got to do with you?" Ángela said.

L. laughed.

"I was in a fight, or, rather, in twenty-three fights. For a time, I was a professional boxer. I called myself Lawrence."

I knew the story well. It was during our time at Colegio La Salle. A fancy-dress party was held in Loyola, at the house behind the stables, and most of us got dressed up in wigs, garish shirts and dark glasses with mirror lenses, like our favourite singers of the time. At the end, something unusual happened: all the lights went out, and into the room came a figure dressed entirely in white and with his face half-covered. He looked every inch a Bedouin, and the white fabric – I found out later that it was impregnated with phosphorus – glowed and formed a kind of aura about him. We – Katia, Maribel, Cornélie, Luis, López, Vergara and everyone else who had been dancing – were mesmerised by this phosphorescent figure. Then Adrián appeared. He waited for the noise to die down before introducing the man in white: "Ladies and gentlemen, today is a special day. Lawrence of Arabia has agreed to honour us with his presence. Please pay homage to the hero of the desert." Cornélie and the other girls joined in the game and began curtseying and bowing. However, the boys, once they had got over their initial surprise, became aggressive, and López, one of the cross-country team, tore away the cloth concealing the stranger's face. We all saw that it was L., a boy with an English mother, who was Adrián's best friend at La Salle. "You really can't stand the girls to look at anyone else, can you?" Adrián said. López was dressed like Johnny Hallyday, with a curly blond wig, and by his side was a girl who resembled Sylvie Vartan. López pointed to her and said to L.: "You should have dressed like her, in a mini-skirt." Someone turned on the lights. The record player started up again, with, oddly enough, a song by Sylvie Vartan. Adrián and L. left.

The following day, in the recreation area, López became even more insultingly insinuating. He minced over to L., calling him offensive names, saying, hello, sweetie, how's your little arsehole. L. hurled himself at him, and we all assumed that López would beat him to a pulp, because he was nearly four inches taller and, being a cross-country runner, physically very fit. Instead, exactly the opposite happened; López didn't land a single punch on L., who dodged every blow with just the slightest movement of his waist. L. then punched López hard, four times, twice in the stomach and twice in the face, one-two, one-two, and López fell flat on his back. He staggered groggily to his feet. The boys who had gathered round to watch the fight started applauding.

L.'s name boomed out over the tannoy, with an order to go at once to the Prefect's office. And it was the Prefect himself speaking. He repeated the order several times.

Adrián and I, and a few other students, protested: why summon L. when it had all been López's fault? L. didn't deserve to be punished, because it was perfectly legitimate to respond to such grave insults with your fists. At that moment, we were sure he would be punished and would, at the very least, lose points for bad behaviour.

Ten minutes later, we saw L. heading for the door of the college carrying his files and books. "He's been expelled!" Adrián cried. We ran over to him.

L. greeted us with a broad smile. He wasn't going to be punished for the fight. On the contrary.

"The Prefect asked me where I learned to box," he said. "I told him my uncle was a boxer in England, and that he coaches me in the holidays."

This was news to Adrián and to me. All we knew was that his mother was English.

"The Prefect gave me permission to leave school early," L. went on. "He wants me to go and see Paco Bueno and ask if I can train at his gym. He says Bueno has the best technique of any boxer in Spain and would be a good teacher for me."

With that, he said goodbye and headed off downhill towards the bus stop.

At that moment, it all seemed like a joke, and yet L.'s visit to Paco Bueno proved to be a turning point. L. fought on the amateur circuit in Spain and, later, because he had British nationality, as a professional in the United Kingdom and in Europe. When he retired, the sports journalists said he had been just four inches short of being a champion. L. was only five foot three.

*

The wind got up a little, and the parasols around the swimming pool in Kayenta began to flutter. Izaskun, who had just taken part in a science project at Mount Rose School, asked L. about a subject that had been preoccupying her for the last few weeks: the origin of the human species. It seemed that there were many people in America who rejected the theory that we had evolved from monkeys. Izaskun's teacher did not share this unscientific view and neither did she. What did he think?

The wind prevented me from hearing L.'s answer. What I did hear, though, because the wind suddenly dropped again, was my eldest daughter's next question: Had he enjoyed the film "2001: A Space Odyssey"? She hadn't quite understood the first part. In fact, she hadn't really understood any of it, and the only part she had enjoyed had been the death of HAL 9000 while he sang "Daisy Bell".

"I can sing that song. I learned it at school," Sara said.

Not wanting to be ousted from the limelight, Izaskun continued talking. She was genuinely annoyed not to have understood what the director of "2001: A Space Odyssey" had been trying to say in the first part of the film, because it had to do with human evolution.

Sara started singing: "There is a flower within my heart, Daisy, Daisy. Planted one day . . ."

"That isn't the bit the dying computer sings," Izaskun said, interrupting. Then she hurriedly explained what it was that was worrying her.

In the film, you saw a few men who looked like monkeys, and one of them picked up a big bone from a skeleton in order to throw it at another man-monkey; then, suddenly, the bone whirled up and away and became a spaceship.

"With no evolution!" she exclaimed.

"There is a flower within my heart, Daisy, Daisy . . ." Sara continued to sing, although without much conviction now.

"I think the scene is very true to the facts," L. said. "Compared with the time that elapsed between the monkey-monkeys and the moment when the semi-monkeys learned to use stones, sticks or bones as weapons, the next period of time, between that and spaceships, is a mere instant."

"My birthday's on 2nd July," Sara said.

"But we have to be entirely true to the facts," Izaskun said, ignoring her sister. "We would have to know what the difference is between the monkey-monkeys and the semi-monkeys."

This seemed to me the moment to interrupt the meeting and say hello to L. I walked over to the turquoise-blue parasol where they were sitting. The sun was turning the Arizona sky yellow.

We embraced and stood face to face, looking at each other. I hardly recognised him. He was very thin and was wearing glasses with coffee-coloured lenses that concealed the blue of his eyes. He was also holding a cigarette. L. had always gone around with the smokers at school, but had never been a smoker himself.

It was getting dark in the Arizona desert, and I found myself walking with L. towards the little wood a few hundred yards from the hotel. When we got there, I saw that the wood was actually in a canyon and that the trees were taller than I'd thought. Among the trees, in an area of pebbles and moss, was a spring, a pool of crystal-clear water.

"It's like a garden," L. said.

He was right, because as well as the moss and the trees, there were flowers too, white flowers and yellow flowers.

We went down a path towards that part of the canyon and saw, lying next to the spring, a dead mole. There was no sign of violence, but rather an impression of peace: a small animal who had succumbed to sleep when he went down to the water to drink. The breeze was gently stirring the leaves of the trees, apparently with the sole aim of helping the mole to sleep more soundly. L. took a puff on his cigarette and gently prodded the mole with the tip of his shoe. The mole did not move.

"He's sleeping very deeply," he said. "Let's sit and watch over him."

We sat down on a fallen tree trunk, a few feet from the mole, and watched him.

"He won't come back to life again," I said. "I expect there's a book in the literary tradition of moles that tells of a mole called Lazarus, who died one day and then returned to life. And probably right now, in this very canyon, his family and friends will be listening to that story and others that are continually being distributed by the Area for the Loading and Unloading of Metaphors. However, metaphors can do little in the face of death. You might as well try and catch the moon in your hands."

"Another metaphor!" said L., his eyes fixed on the mole.

He was still smoking, and, for a moment, I thought it odd that his cigarette had scarcely burned down at all. I remembered the eternal cigarette of the man in the yellow overalls in the Area for the Loading and Unloading of Metaphors.

"That's how I see it anyway," I went on somewhat uncertainly. "If there's no resurrection, all that matters is memory, especially our memory of someone's final days: how the person who was once part of our life died, if it snowed on the day he died or if the sky was blue, if the funeral was worthy of him, if his grave lies somewhere beautiful . . . In that sense, the mole is lucky. He's lying here among trees and flowers, next to a spring. What's more the walls of the canyon shelter him from the noises of the world. The only sound here is the rustling of leaves."

L.'s cigarette was still not burning down. It seemed eternal.

Somehow he sensed my unease.

"You don't get it, do you?" he asked, standing up.

I didn't know what to say.

"You do realise that I'm dead, don't you?"

"Yes," I said, but the answer surprised even me.

L. began to sing, imitating the computer in "2001: A Space Odyssey": "There is a flower within my heart, Daisy, Daisy! Planted one day . . ."

I began to weep helplessly.

"Stop it, L.!" I shouted.

When I woke up in our bedroom, I felt disoriented, as if the dream had altered time and space. At first, I thought I was still in the hotel in Kayenta; then, that I was in the house where I was born in Asteasu, in the first bedroom I could call my own; then, in the house that Ángela and I rented in Brissac, Mas de la Croix. I finally regained control of my mind and, like someone recovering from a dizzy spell, everything around me – the bed next to mine, the child sleeping in it, the window, the walls, the drawing pinned to one wall – gradually steadied and became clear again. I was in College Drive. The child was Izaskun, over whom I had kept watch at night ever since Brianna Denison was killed.

I got up and went out onto the back porch. Everything was in its proper place: the garden, Earle's house at the far end of the garden, the raccoon's yellow eyes next to the hut.

Ángela found me there.

"What are you doing up at this hour?"

"I had an absurd dream and came out here to get some air."

At that moment, I didn't feel able to give her all the details, and only mentioned the biography I had attributed to L. in the dream.

"In my dream, he was a physicist, specialising in optics at the University of Arizona. How ridiculous. L., a specialist in optics, when he was the only student at school who had chosen to study literature, and was the first boxer in history with a doctorate in seventeenth-century English poetry!"

"It's just so sad about L. He was such a special person," Ángela said, and we both went back into the house.

LAST SUPPER IN RENO

Dennis's house was on the other side of McCarran, in Kane Court Street; it was a very modern building, composed of three rectangular modules. We parked outside the first of these – where there were two garages – and walked over to the large wooden verandah on the ground floor of the second module. It was sheltered from the sun by a dark blue awning. The table was already set for supper, with a white tablecloth and a vase of yellow paper flowers. The music coming from the speakers made the atmosphere on the verandah seem all the sweeter.

"It's Schubert's "Rosamunde" Quartet," Dennis said in answer to my question.

Earle put his arm around Dennis's shoulders.

"Didn't you know?" he said. "Dennis is a man of many parts. Classical music is the second most important of his interests, the first being insects. Have you been to his office recently? He now has *two* black widows and a praying mantis."

Dennis brought us our beers. He seemed oddly flattered by Earle's comments.

"It's a really lovely house, Dennis, and the location is just amazing," I said.

From the verandah you could see the Reno–Sparks plain, an area large enough to accommodate ten towns. In the distance, the desert mountains formed a kind of wall.

"It's prettiest at night," Dennis said.

It was still only seven o'clock in the evening, and the lights of the casinos and the houses had not yet come on. In another hour, the empty spaces of the plain would vanish into the dark, and the smaller area of visible landscape would be enlivened by car headlights.

Dennis showed us the passageway leading to the third module.

"The kitchen's at the back. You could start bringing the food and drink out onto the verandah, if you like. Meanwhile, I'll go upstairs to the living room and set up a movie for the girls."

Izaskun and Sara had already told us that the television screen on the upper floor was ten times bigger than that of a normal television, and that there was a huge rug in front of it covered with multicoloured cushions. Even more amazing – to them – was the fact that the room had a fridge full of cold drinks and a microwave for making popcorn.

We, the guests, went up and down the passageway, carrying food and drink out onto the verandah. There weren't many of us that day, just the usual people – Mannix, Mary Lore, Earle, Ángela and me, plus Alexander, Dennis's bearded friend from Chicago, as well as a friend of his whom we didn't know, a very smartly dressed man in his fifties, wearing expensive cowboy gear: leather boots, jeans, pale blue shirt, black silk waistcoat, dark hat.

The girls – Izaskun and Sara plus Mary Lore and Mannix's three daughters – carried two trays of sandwiches upstairs, accompanied by

Ángela and Dennis. The rest of us sat down at the table on the verandah. The temperature was perfect, about twenty degrees centigrade.

It was clear from the start that Mannix did not take to the stranger. He tended not to like affected people, far less what he called "urban cowboys".

"It's usually considered rude to keep your hat on at the supper table," he said to the stranger as soon as we sat down.

"I thought it was up to the owner of the house to set the rules," the cowboy said in response.

We all tried to take this comment as a joke, but, as any reader of Kerouac would say, we all picked up on the bad vibes.

"Now, let's not quarrel," Mary Lore said.

"No, let's eat!" added Earle.

The table was well provided with food and drink: rice salad, potato salad, tabouleh, chilled yoghurt soup, chicken served in funny red cardboard containers, hamburgers and electric griddles to cook them on, Californian cheese – including one with a Basque name, *Ona* – Californian wines and cold beers.

The cowboy took off his hat, but then didn't know what to do with it. In the end, finding nowhere else, he put it down on a chair.

"Oh, wear it, if you like . . ."

Mary Lore hesitated. She didn't know his name.

"Patrick," the cowboy said.

"Wear your hat, if you want to, Patrick."

Mary Lore held out her hand to shake his. Mannix did the same.

With his hat off, Patrick looked younger, about forty. He had a scar on his forehead, a red mark that extended onto his scalp.

Earle and I also shook his hand.

Dennis's friend, Alexander, came over to me. He was the polar opposite of the cowboy as far as clothes were concerned. He was dressed rather shabbily, in a baggy sweater more suitable for winter than summer, and his curly beard was in need of a trim. He was holding a can of Pepsi.

"Hi, I'm Alexander. We didn't really get a chance to talk the other day," he said.

300

"No, but Mannix told me that you've come down from Chicago to help Dennis sort out the university's computer system."

When I shook his hand, I noticed that it was very cold from contact with his can of Pepsi.

"How's your Dunhill-smoking friend in the green velvet jacket?" he asked.

"You're very observant," I said.

"No, not really, but your friend did seem rather unusual, and I don't just mean because of his physical appearance."

"He left immediately afterwards. His daughter had to get back to school," I told him. Then, pointing at the cowboy, I added: "Your friend seems rather unusual too."

Alexander looked away and said:

"Yes, Patrick works at the airport, for the security department. Security people don't tend to be the nicest people in the world, but he's a good guy."

When dictionaries define the word "vibration", they mention brief, repetitive movements and the tremor that comes either from the air or from certain objects. On the verandah, on our side of the table, I felt something similar, as if there were a magnetic field operating underneath the dark blue awning. It wasn't at all pleasant.

Dennis and Ángela appeared on the verandah, smiling broadly. They had come from the floor above, from a very different magnetic field. They had left the girls alone with the giant screen and the sandwiches, which meant that we could now begin our supper.

There were no empty spaces at the table, apart from Dennis's chair, because he was now walking around, helping us to the salads.

"They held a vote to choose today's movie," Ángela told Mary Lore. "Guess which movie won?"

Mary Lore didn't know.

"'Ratatouille'!"

"Not again!"

"It got four votes out of five. Only Izaskun voted against. She was quite firm about it too."

"Well, it is a movie for kids, and she's not such a kid any more."

"No, she's growing up fast," Mannix said. "The same thing happened to me. Yesterday, I was a little boy and now look at me. Suddenly, I'm a two-hundred-and-forty-pound hulk."

"You can all talk blithely about the passing of time because you're still young," Earle said. "I daren't even think about it."

We raised our glasses to this thought, everyone except the cowboy. He carried on eating his rice salad as if he were entirely alone. At the other end of the table, Alexander was wiping a drop of yoghurt from his beard.

As it was getting dark, Dennis wound back the awning. I saw Izaskun standing at the upstairs window and gestured to her, asking if she wanted to come and sit with us. She shook her head.

Dennis placed two metal boxes containing fluorescent blue lights on the balustrade. These were intended to attract the insects and incinerate them.

"You're being very cruel to those insects, Dennis," Earle said. "There they are thinking you're their friend and flocking to your verandah, and you go and incinerate them!"

Again, there were two exceptions at the table. Neither the cowboy nor Alexander smiled.

Earle whispered in my ear:

"Tell me, XY120, where did Dennis find these two guys? I'd say they came from Area 51. I wonder if Dennis is an alien too, or are you all aliens?"

Without Natalie there, Earle was his usual self.

"I don't think Dennis is," I said.

Izaskun had finished her sandwich, but was still at the window, observing us. What was happening at the table was obviously far more interesting than *Ratatouille*.

"What is it you do, Patrick?" Mannix asked.

He and Mary Lore were standing up, cooking the hamburgers on the griddles.

"I work at the airport, in security. It's not a particularly nice job, but a necessary one," answered the cowboy. This, more or less, was what Alexander had told me.

The conversation turned to the subject of security, but went no further than the usual banal clichés. The air was filled with the smell of hamburgers cooking.

I was struggling to remember. I knew that cowboy; I'd seen him before, but I couldn't remember when or where.

Izaskun was now in the passageway that led to the kitchen, keeping close to the wall, as if she didn't want to be seen. She beckoned me over. When I gestured to her, inviting her to join us at the table, she only beckoned to me more urgently, as if issuing an order. I gave in. When I reached her, I closed the sliding door behind me.

"Don't you remember that guy?" she whispered. "He was in Tacos when the police arrested the fat man with the round head. You wanted to wash your hands and kept trying to get into the bathroom, but it was always occupied."

"Are you sure?"

"Of course I am. He was there in Tacos and he was wearing the same cowboy outfit too."

She reminded me of other details from that night, and I had to admit she was right. It seemed an extraordinary coincidence to meet him at Dennis's house, but there was no doubt about it. The guy at Tacos and the man having supper with us were one and the same.

"You go back upstairs, Izaskun," I told her.

"I'm going to keep watching," she said.

"It's probably more interesting than watching 'Ratatouille' again," I said jokingly.

"You bet," she said, and she *wasn't* joking.

When I returned to the verandah, Mannix and Mary Lore were serving up the hamburgers; Ángela and Earle were discussing Bruce Laxalt's poems and the irreversible state of his health; Alexander and Dennis were studying a small computer, with Alexander explaining a new app that had come onto the market. As soon as I sat down, a mobile phone rang, and the cowboy got up and went over to one corner of the verandah to answer it. When I saw him there, any lingering doubts vanished. He was definitely the man we'd seen at Tacos.

The Schubert quartet that Dennis had put on at the beginning of the supper came to an end, and the ensuing empty silence seemed to endow the town with a larger presence: in the darkness, the white lights of the houses, and the fuchsias, reds and greens of the casinos seemed more intense. A yellow sliver of moon hung above the desert mountains.

The cowboy's telephone conversation was brief. He put the telephone away in his waistcoat pocket and spoke to Dennis.

"There's been an incident at the airport, and I have to leave. I won't be long, though. I'll be back before you've finished your dessert."

"If you like, I'll save you a hamburger," Dennis suggested.

"No, thanks, dessert will be fine."

"I'll show you out," Dennis said.

Alexander stood up.

"I'll go with him, Dennis. Meanwhile, why don't you put on some more music?"

I spotted a figure in the darkness. It was leaning on the window overlooking the verandah. Izaskun was still watching.

Dessert was apple tart and vanilla ice cream. Dennis and Ángela took five servings upstairs to the girls. Then we served up eight more plates and took them out onto the verandah.

"I don't know where Izaskun has got to. She wasn't upstairs," Ángela said when we sat down again.

"And Patrick's not back either," added Mannix.

In the sky above Reno, I could see the lights of a plane making its slow descent. On the ground, at the airport, there didn't seem to be anything much going on. It was the same in the streets of Reno. Most were dark and empty. Including Virginia Street. The only traffic to be seen was on the I-80 and on Route 395: the long-snouted trucks heading for Las Vegas, Chicago, Salt Lake City or Houston passing those going to Sacramento or San Francisco.

Then something changed on the I-80. A helicopter flew over the trucks and landed on the roof of a building. I didn't need to see anything more to know that it was the air ambulance for St Mary's Hospital. This was my ninth month in Reno. In another week, one of the planes taking off from the airport would be ours.

I was worried. Patrick had still not come back. Izaskun was not up-stairs, nor could I see her at the window. My mind began making wild connections, and the palms of my hands were sweating. However, I had reached entirely the wrong conclusion. The cowboy wasn't with my daughter. He was coming back down the passageway onto the verandah.

Rather chattier than he had been before, the cowboy explained the problem that had arisen at the airport. A passenger hadn't turned up for his flight even though he had already checked in his luggage, and the plane couldn't leave until they had unloaded the luggage and returned it to its owner.

"We found him drunk in his room at Harrah's. He couldn't remember a thing, not even that he was supposed to catch a plane. We told the guy, this isn't Las Vegas, you know. You don't fool around like that in Reno."

He was eating his apple pie very quickly, mixing each spoonful with some of the half-melted ice cream.

Then Izaskun appeared on the verandah. She seemed very tense. Even Earle was surprised when he saw the look on her face.

"That man's lying," she said.

The cowboy continued eating his dessert as if he hadn't heard her, eagerly spooning up what remained of the ice cream. On the other side of the table, Alexander sprang to his feet. Mannix, Mary Lore, Ángela, Earle, Dennis and I stayed where we were, waiting.

"He did leave the house, but immediately came back in again through the garage," Izaskun said. "I saw it all from the window on the other side."

Alexander took a step towards Izaskun.

"No, you're getting things all confused, sweetheart," he said, his voice suddenly hoarse. "He left his car keys in the kitchen and came back to get them."

Izaskun was not to be cowed.

"He looked in one of the bedrooms, then in one of the bathrooms. He's been in the house all the time," she told us.

Suddenly, we all had something to say, but the cowboy got in before us.

He stood up, wiped his mouth on his napkin, then took a badge out of his waistcoat pocket. His movements were very precise. He was a cold-blooded fellow, but doubtless a good policeman.

"Allow me to explain," he said, in a more formal, distant tone of voice. "As you know, last month someone kidnapped and murdered Brianna Denison, and the case remains open. That's why I'm here. According to information we've received, Dennis Horace Wilson could be the person we're looking for."

On the other side of the table, Alexander was stroking his beard. I had no doubt that he was our Judas, the one who had betrayed Dennis.

"I came here to collect some hair samples," the policeman said, putting on his hat. "In a few days' time, we'll know if Dennis's D.N.A. matches that of Brianna's killer."

"But why all the pretence?" Earle asked. "Couldn't you just have asked straight out? I'm sure Dennis would have been glad to help, and I'm even more sure that he has nothing whatsoever to do with the murder. That's ridiculous! Dennis wouldn't hurt a soul!"

Mannix and Mary Lore agreed. They felt as angry about this as Earle did.

"Alexander wanted it to be done as discreetly as possible and to carry out the test without worrying Dennis," the policeman said. "But that was clearly a bad idea. It's always best to follow official procedures."

I heard the Judas voice of Alexander in my head. Why were Earle, Mannix and Mary Lore so sure? Was it normal for someone to keep black widow spiders in a jar? And he was, after all, often surrounded by young girls and took photographs too, of Izaskun and Sara for example. Then again, as far as we knew, he had no partner, which was odd for a man in his thirties.

Dennis was sitting with his head in his hands, sobbing. I silenced the Judas voice in my head.

"It will only be a matter of a few days. Meanwhile, don't leave town," the policeman told him.

As he left the verandah, he looked at Izaskun. She was standing there, her arms folded, looking very composed.

"Good job!" the policeman said as he passed her.

"I always tell the truth," she responded.

The policeman headed off down the passageway and vanished from sight, with Alexander at his heels.

TELEPHONE CALL FROM SAN FRANCISCO

"Dennis is a lot better," Earle said, "and having Jeff around has been a great help. Apparently, Jeff has to choose a font for some city council publication or other, and he's finding it very hard to make a final choice. The house is full of bits of papers all bearing the words, 'The quick brown fox jumps over the lazy dog.' I've read it so often now and in so many different fonts that seeing a fox jumping over a dog would seem like the most natural thing in the world. But, as I say, it's good for Dennis. Jeff's obsessions help him to forget about his."

"I'm really glad things are working out," I said.

The police had taken less than a week to announce that there was no match between Dennis's D.N.A. and that found on Brianna Denison's body. Alexander's complaint, based on the photographs of young girls he'd found on Dennis's computer and which were mainly of Izaskun, Sara and Mary Lore and Mannix's three daughters, was declared null and void, but things did not immediately go back to normal. The accusation had left Dennis mentally shaken, and he began to behave very strangely. Earle had found him in his office playing with a spider, letting it run and up and down his bare arm. Earle had immediately got rid of the spider and taken Dennis straight to a psychiatrist.

At the other end of the telephone, I heard Earle sigh.

"He's not as depressed as he was, but the question now is: are we all going to be driven mad by this wretched fox jumping over the lazy dog?"

"Don't you go out for walks at all?"

"Yes, but that's even worse. Jeff keeps asking us to identify the font on every poster and sign we come across."

"Well, good luck with that," I said.

"When are you leaving?"

"The day after tomorrow."

"O.K., have a good trip, and, if all goes to plan, we'll see you and your mountains in the fall."

"Let's hope Dennis can come too."

"I think he will. Anyway, see you soon."

"Yes, see you soon."

FAREWELL TO RENO

On the afternoon of June 19, we paid one last visit to Rancho San Rafael Park, because Sara wanted to say goodbye to the owl. Alas, he wasn't sitting in his usual tree, and so we drove straight back to the house to pack our bags, while Sara went down to the hut to say good-bye to the raccoon.

"*He*'s not there either!" she said. "He's probably gone into hiding because he's sad to see us go."

"Don't be so silly!" Izaskun said.

Mannix arrived at four o'clock the following morning in Earle's Chevrolet Avalanche, just after our daily *Reno Gazette-Journal* had been delivered. He picked it up and brought it into the house.

"Here, take this with you as a souvenir," he said, handing it to me.

"I will," I said.

"We could have gone in my car, I suppose, but the Avalanche is big enough for all your suitcases plus an entire army," Mannix said, taking two of our cases. "Well, perhaps not the American Army," he added, laughing at his own joke.

He drove slowly down Virginia Street, as if wanting to allow us time to take one last look at the web of bright white lights and the red, green and fuchsia lights of the casinos.

"When you come back to Reno, I'll cook you antelope supreme," he said as we drove onto the I-80. "It's pretty straightforward. You leave the fillets to marinate overnight in water, vinegar, garlic and salt. The next day, you pat them dry, dust them with flour and black pepper, then put them on a griddle with a lid and cook over a low flame for half an hour. To finish, you cover them in chicken stock and cook for a further fifteen minutes, then serve with rice. They're really delicious."

The airport was only a couple of miles from College Drive. We reached it before Mannix could finish telling us about a few possible variations on the recipe.

"The raccoon wasn't there," Sara told him while he helped us carry our suitcases to the moving walkway.

"He probably doesn't like goodbyes. That's normal. I don't like them either," Mannix said.

We all gave him a hug and made our way to the check-in desk.

Once we were on the plane, I opened the *Reno Gazette-Journal*. "High-tech device lets public follow Pony Express riders," one of the headlines said. The article described how technological advances had put paid to the Pony Express in 1861, but that one of the latest advances, GPS, was helping to recreate the journey. The contents of the famed leather mail pouch carried by the riders were now rather different. Instead of letters, it contained the GPS that would guide riders safely on their way across eight states.

The plane set off down the runway.

"Here we go," Ángela said.

We rose gently into the air. Day was breaking, and dawn was filling the sky with light.

THE END

FINAL PIECE
IZASKUN IS IN EIBAR

A poet once put love and tripe cooked Oporto style side by side in the same poem, but it would be difficult to do that with death. How would you bring death and tripe together like that?

We three brothers had to eat tripe after our mother's funeral, and we felt ashamed every time we wiped our lips and saw the greasy, reddish stain on the napkin; we felt coarse, rough, brutal. We couldn't just leave the restaurant and abandon our friends and relatives and everyone who had attended the ceremony, yet we longed to be somewhere else, surrounded by flowers, as the coffin had been in the church. As my eldest brother said at the beginning of the service: flowers are one of the few things that seem bearable to someone who has just lost his mother.

The cook came over to offer his condolences, but, a moment later, he was talking about tripe, explaining how long it took to prepare, which is why it so rarely appeared on restaurant menus. In his case, he always took personal charge of chopping it up, marinating it in water and vinegar for twenty-four hours, before cooking it with leeks and carrots and a ham bone. To finish it off, he put the mixture in a frying pan, added tomatoes and chorizo and sautéed the whole thing over a low flame for another half an hour.

"It's really delicious," I said, unable to think about anything but the church and the funeral service, and certainly not about tripe.

*

About eighty people filled the two rows of wooden pews. Before us stood a priest wearing a purple chasuble, and two parishioners who took turns to speak into the microphone. I found it hard to listen to them and to follow the thread of what they were saying or reading and I remained in that abstracted state until the priest, looking directly at the pew where we brothers were sitting, spoke our mother's name: Izaskun. He repeated it several times, and said that she had been a good woman. He resorted to the usual metaphors, saying that Izaskun would live for all eternity at Our Lord's side in Heaven, and we should not be sad because death was not death, but life.

The priest finished speaking, and the singing of the choir filled the dark church. Above them rose the voice of Andrés Garay, the best soloist in the village. My eldest brother whispered in my ear:

"They're singing this part in Latin, as it would have been sung when our mother was a girl."

He had made all the arrangements for the funeral service. It would never have occurred to either me or my other brother to invite the choir to be there, still less to tell them what to sing.

"*Requiem aeternam dona eis, Domine, et lux perpetua luceat eis*," sang the choir. "Eternal rest grant unto them, O Lord, and let perpetual light shine upon them." The organ quietly accompanied each word.

Like the flowers, the music helped and consoled. It went very well with death. "*Requiem aeternam dona eis, Domine, et lux perpetua luceat eis*." The melody was different this time, and the organ played more loudly: the prayer was coming to an end. I looked at the flowers on the coffin. There were lilies, marguerites, carnations, gladioli and a few pinkish flowers that my eldest brother told us were called gypsophila. In their silence, the flowers seemed, like everyone else, to be concentrating on the music. The only person to remain immune to the solemn atmosphere was a fretful baby sitting on the lap of an elderly lady.

*

The priest stepped down from the altar and sprinkled the coffin with holy water. Shortly afterwards, the service was over.

"What are you going to do with the flowers?" he asked us. "Are you leaving them here or taking them to the cemetery?"

My eldest brother had already thought of this and replied unhesitatingly.

"We'll leave them here."

The priest gestured to the two parishioners who had accompanied him during the Mass, and they placed the flowers on the altar steps:

the lilies in the middle, the carnations and gypsophila to the left, the marguerites and the gladioli to the right. My eldest brother stood looking at them, and I thought perhaps he was going to change his mind; however, since we needed him to help carry the coffin out of the church, he ended up leaving the flowers there on the altar.

The village cemetery is on the top of a hill. In the old days, when the Mass was still celebrated in Latin, the family members would carry the coffin on their shoulders to the grave, silently followed by all the members of the congregation. The procession would pass first through a very gloomy place, a dank, moss-covered alleyway that ran alongside the church; then it would go past farmhouses and down a stony, pot-holed track, and it always felt – at least to me when I was eight or nine years old – as though the coffin was leading us down into a ravine; but the next stretch rose gently and had views of the surrounding maize fields and mountains, more and more mountains, all intensely green. Finally, when we reached the cemetery gates, we could see the most distant peaks, some of them over the border in France; for example, Les Trois Couronnes, which looked very blue from there.

Walking the route to the cemetery was like going from the narrow into the broad, from darkness into light, as if doing so fulfilled the desire expressed in the prayer: "Eternal rest grant unto them, O Lord, and let perpetual light shine upon them." *Requiem aeternam dona eis, Domine, et lux perpetua luceat eis.*

Times had changed. A road now connected the church and the cemetery.

We placed my mother's coffin in the hearse and went off to fetch our own cars, as did the relatives and friends coming with us to the burial. My eldest brother, however, preferred to go on foot.

"You'd better come with me," I said. "You'll be late."

I thought that perhaps he didn't want to take his car because, although the road was an improvement on the old one, it was still very dusty and stony, and he had just bought a new Mercedes-Benz S 500. A luxury brand.

"No, I'd rather go on foot," he said. From the boot of his car he took a wicker basket, which, from what I could see, contained a bouquet of black flowers wrapped in cellophane. Then, without any further explanation, he headed off.

The flowers went well with death, like the prayers in Latin and the path through the maize fields with views of the mountains; the cars, on the other hand, were more like the tripe. They seemed out of place, they jarred. More than twenty cars set off almost at the same time and began manoeuvring round each other to get behind the hearse. The noise of the engines really grated on me, and I regretted not having followed my brother's example.

In the cemetery chapel there was a kind of stone pedestal on which they placed the coffin, and the priest again spoke about my mother, this time adding more details. He mentioned the places where she – "our Izaskun" – had lived, the villages of Albiztur, Eibar and Asteasu; he mentioned my father, "a good man who left us four years ago"; he mentioned us – "three sons who, thanks to the sacrifices made by her and by her husband, were all able to go to university"; finally, he mentioned that she had been a schoolteacher and that many of the people at the funeral had been taught to read and write by her. What followed, though, was more banal, a repetition of those metaphors about death and eternal life.

The coffin had to be carried to the grave, as we had when we carried it from the church. I looked for my eldest brother among the thirty or forty people gathered in the chapel, but he wasn't there. A friend offered to help.

"You'd be best carrying it by the handles rather than on your shoulders," the priest said. We followed his advice and began walking rather clumsily, finding it hard to keep in step. The coffin seemed to weigh more than it had in the church.

There was a slight slope up to the family vault, where my father and my aunt and uncle lay.

My eldest brother had never been a particularly sociable person. Ever since he was a child, or perhaps since adolescence, he had always had a rather brusque manner. Nevertheless, he had decided to walk up to the cemetery not because he wanted to be alone, but in order to fill the wicker basket, and when he reached the cemetery, we saw that it was full of grass and sprigs of blackthorn. On top of these lay the black flowers wrapped in cellophane.

My brother was wearing a dark velvet suit, a white linen shirt, very pointed red shoes, and a gold ring in his left earlobe. Add to that the wicker basket, and he cut a somewhat eccentric figure.

The priest stood looking at him, and my brother indicated that he intended to decorate the grave with the contents of the basket. However, he would have to wait. The two young gravediggers had got behind in their work and were only now, somewhat belatedly, removing the gravestone. In the silence of the cemetery, you could hear the clank of crowbars and steel tubes. A few tiny birds were flitting about among the graves.

Removing the stone was no easy task, and the gravediggers were performing a kind of dance, jumping from one side to the other, from the ground onto the grave and from the grave onto the ground, continually shifting the position of the wooden wedges and the steel tubes. After a few minutes, the priest began reading a prayer, but the cows grazing in the nearby field began mooing so loudly that he had to wait for them to stop before he could go on. He glanced at the wicker basket, where a sprig of blackthorn heavy with sloes protruded from beneath the bouquet of black flowers.

From the part of the cemetery where we were standing, you could see one of the tallest mountains in Guipúzcoa, El Hernio – or, as a popular poem calls it, *mendi arkaizti tontor aundiya*, the tall, rugged mountain. It looked taller than it actually was, because it rose very steeply to its height of 3,527 feet and resembled a wall. How long would it take one of those tiny birds flitting among the graves to reach the top? I calculated that, if it flew straight there, it would take about half an hour. I did the same calculation for the cows. How long would it take them to reach the top? Given that they walked more slowly than most people, I thought it would take about four hours.

There were more of us holding the coffin now, because some friends had joined us. Meanwhile, the gravediggers continued their labours, raising the gravestone an inch at a time and constantly changing the position of the crowbars and the steel tubes. How much would it weigh? The only way I could calculate that was by comparing it with the stones that oxen were made to pull in contests at country fairs, and which usually bore a number indicating their weight. I remembered seeing one that weighed 7,500 pounds. The gravestone was longer and considerably thinner, but it could easily weigh maybe 4,500 pounds.

The gravediggers kept working: one inch, two inches, three inches . . . It was taking a long time.

The lower slopes of 'the tall, rugged mountain', El Hernio, were much gentler. As children, we thought the mountain looked like a woman lying down. How many times had we been there with our mother? Thirty times? Forty? And how often would she have climbed it with her parents from the village where she was born, Albiztur? Another forty or fifty times at least. It was her favourite mountain, and the site of one of her favourite stories.

*

One day, our mother used to tell us, two women from Albiztur were walking to Santiago and got as far as Zelatun, at the foot of El Hernio, but three paths lay before them. They weren't sure which of the three would lead to Santiago.

"Let's wait until someone comes," one of them said, and they sat down on the grass.

A day passed, and no-one came. Another day, and still no-one. On the third day, a crow approached them. He wasn't the informant they were expecting, but since no-one else had appeared, they decided to ask him:

"Crow, which is the way to Santiago, this way, that way or the other way?"

In a harsh voice, the crow replied:

"Kra! Kra!"

"What did he say?" one of the two women asked. Her friend answered:

"He said 'kra', which means 'the other way'."

They thanked the crow and set off along that other path. The further they went, the more convinced they were that this was the path to Santiago. The woman who hadn't understood the crow said to her friend:

"It's just as well you speak Spanish. Otherwise, we'd be in a right pickle!"

My mother told this story two or three times a year, and it always made her laugh.

*

The vault was open now, revealing a chamber about ten or twelve feet deep. After putting the coffin down on a slightly raised piece of ground, my younger brother and I climbed onto the edge of one of the side walls, and a cousin and a friend of the family climbed onto the other side. The walls, which were about three feet high, were over a foot thick, so there was no danger of us falling.

The gravediggers passed two ropes covered in cloth underneath the coffin and handed us the four ends. One of the men then went down into the chamber with the help of a third rope and, once there, began giving us instructions. We had to lower the coffin very gradually, keeping it as level and as stable as possible.

"Slowly! Slowly!"

Supporting the coffin with his two hands, he guided it into one of the niches. Once it was in, he scrambled up the rope like a cat. My younger brother, my cousin and I jumped to the ground.

More clanking of crowbars and steel tubes. When, after some time had passed, the gravestone was back in place, my eldest brother began sorting out the contents of the wicker basket. First, the black flowers wrapped in cellophane and the sprig of blackthorn; then a bunch of maize flowers and an armful of freshly cut green grass, neither of which I had noticed before.

"A present from Larre," my brother said, pointing at the grass. Larre was a farmhouse he would have passed on his way to the cemetery.

Someone once asked the Basque stone-lifting champion Urtain what his favourite smell was, and he said it was freshly cut grass. I became aware of the smell as soon as I remembered his response. Or perhaps it was the other way round, perhaps I smelled the grass and then remembered.

My brother was absorbed in decorating the gravestone. He put the grass down as a base, then arranged the maize flowers on top; at the foot of the cross he placed the sprig of blackthorn laden with sloes; lastly, separating each one out from the bouquet, he scattered the black flowers over the gravestone.

The resulting composition resembled the floral carpets with which we used to decorate the streets of our village for the feast of Corpus Christi. My mother always wanted to make sure our house had one of the most striking displays. We used to go with her to the woods in search of materials, then help her make a suitably artistic arrangement.

My younger brother whispered:

"He's brought black orchids! That isn't what our mother would have wanted. We're not supporters of Eva Perón!"

Many years before, on the twentieth anniversary of Eva Perón's death, an illustrated magazine had chosen as its cover a photograph of Evita's hearse adorned, indeed almost covered, with black orchids.

"What a marvellous funeral!" our mother cried, showing us the photograph. "But when I die," she went on, "I don't want any black orchids. I was born in Albiztur, in a house surrounded by maize fields, and a few maize flowers will suit me fine. And if it's the right time of year, a little grass too."

My two brothers had come up with completely contrasting interpretations of that story. My eldest brother saw in her words a hidden desire and a disguised request for us to carry it out; my younger brother's reading of it was more literal. In different circumstances, this disagreement would have ended in a bitter argument, but, as with the tripe, certain ways of speaking did not go well with death.

My eldest brother was still leaning on the gravestone with his back to the rest of us. He picked up a fallen sloe from the ground and put it in his mouth.

Like the carpet of flowers with which he had adorned the tomb, this was another reference, a memory of an old anecdote. One summer day, when we brothers were still very young, our mother had taken us to a very stony place near the house where she was born. It was full of blackthorn bushes, and she encouraged us to taste the fruit.

"Go on, try those little cherries, and see how sweet they are!"

The sloes were extremely sour, and we spat them out as soon as we put them in our mouths, protesting and grimacing. She found this hilarious.

When she fell ill – by then, she was eighty – the woman who looked after her arrived in the house one day bearing a sprig of blackthorn heavy with fruit, just like the one my brother·had brought to the cemetery. My mother picked a fruit and, smiling sweetly, offered it to the woman:

"Here you are, Paquita. Try this little cherry."

"I'm not Paquita, Izaskun. I'm Rosa Mari, the woman who comes every day to help you."

My mother pretended not to understand:

"Rosa Mari? How can you be Rosa Mari? There's no-one of that name here. If you're not Paquita, then you must be Miren."

The woman decided to play along.

"No, I'm not Paquita or Miren. I'm Jesusa."

"Jesusa? Well, you look more like Paquita or Miren," my mother said, again offering her a sloe. "Go on, eat it. These cherries are so sweet."

The woman called my eldest brother that night and told him what had happened.

"She confused me with one of her sisters. And she spoke in a strange voice, like a child."

My eldest brother stayed with my mother for a few days, but there was no repetition of the conversation. Her memory was failing, and she became very exhausting to talk to because she would keep repeating things over and over, but she always called us by our right names.

*

There were five siblings living in Aitze, which was the name of their house in Albiztur. A boy, Bartolito, and four girls: Miren, Paquita, Jesusa and my mother, who was the oldest, and who they always called María rather than Izaskun.

There's a photograph taken outside the house in 1928 of the five siblings and their parents, our grandparents. They look like Gipsies

318

who have just emerged from their caravan, very poor and swarthy-looking, their skin burned by the sun; the children are all wearing rustic smocks, their hair is uncombed, and the overall impression is one of grime. And they look alarmed, as if they've never seen a camera before.

The person who took the photograph doubtless wanted to capture an image of anthropological interest. It was probably the owner of the electricity substation where my grandfather, Ramón, worked or else a colleague of his. That would explain why the photograph was preserved.

My mother's mother, Grandma Leona, hated the photograph. She was ashamed of that image of the family, and said they had been caught unprepared and that, one day, she would throw it on the fire. However, when her husband Ramón was electrocuted at the substation, she had no alternative but to keep it, since it was the only image she had of him.

*

We three brothers were alone in the cemetery. We had told our friends to go on ahead and organise supper at the restaurant in the village square.

"We'll order a few tapas and then *callos*, tripe, for everyone. Apparently, they make the best *callos* in Guipúzcoa," one of our friends said. I would have liked to tell him to order something else, but he was already leaving, and I didn't want to have to shout.

One of the little cemetery birds alighted on the cross on our mother's grave. It had a blue-and-white head, a dark line passing through each eye, and a yellow breast. Suddenly, it fluttered its wings and flew down onto the grass covering the gravestone. A moment later, it was flying off with a worm in its beak.

Were birds like flowers? Did they go well with death? Seeing that bird with the blue-and-white head, I felt that they did, but our experience with other birds had been less positive. When we realised that our mother's mind was going, we bought her a canary, because the doctor had told us that a simple chore like giving the bird some millet or cleaning out its cage would help maintain her brain function. The day after we had given it to her, she called us all to announce that the canary was lying on its back on the floor of the cage with its legs in the air.

It was getting dark, but there was still light in the sky. The apple trees on the hills around were all in blossom. El Hernio resembled a soft, moss-covered wall and was split in two by a bank of mist. The three of us were leaning on the grave opposite our family grave and gazing out at the landscape.

My older brother and I were talking about how spartan our grandparents' house had been. My younger brother had said nothing since his remark about the black orchids.

Gaurkoa badugu, biharkoa seguru. Today we have food and for tomorrow too. This was a saying Grandma Leona used to come out with whenever anyone arrived at the house bringing a chicken or some meat. She was joking, of course, but having enough food was a real concern. There was very little around the house where she lived. Most of the maize fields our mother mentioned belonged to the neighbours. There weren't many animals either: two cows, a breeding bull, and a couple of dozen hens. Our grandfather earned a wage looking after the electricity substation, but the wage was so small that, in the summer, he would make a little extra money by performing as a *dantzari* – a Basque folk dancer – at fiestas in other nearby villages.

Some members of the family left. Miren married an engineer who worked on a fishing boat and she went to live with him in a village on the coast; Jesusa got a job as a kitchen hand in a restaurant in San Sebastián. Bartolito and Paquita stayed near Albiztur, Bartolito in Aizte, as a casual labourer in a quarry there, and Paquita in the nearby inn, where, in time, she would set up a restaurant. Before that, though, and only shortly after the "Gipsy" photograph was taken, our mother's life took a most unexpected turn.

Don Eugenio Urroz Erro came to visit the family. He was the parish priest in Albiztur and by then, towards the end of the 1920s, he had already published several books, among them one devoted to the image of the Virgin of Izaskun.

"I've been appointed archpriest in Eibar. Presumably because they couldn't find anyone better," he told Ramón and Leona when they sat down under the vine trellis shading the entrance to the house. He was a modest man, and few people in the village knew that he had studied in Rome and had a law degree.

"I would like Izaskun to come with me to Eibar," he said. Our mother had been christened María Izaskun on his recommendation, and at the time, he was the only one who called her by that second name.

Ramón had nothing to do with matters affecting the children, and so it was Leona who answered.

"Yes, take her with you," she said.

Don Eugenio was surprised to receive such a prompt reply.

"Before you decide, let me explain what I have in mind."

"I'm sure whatever it is will be good," Leona said.

Years later, she would confess that, the night before the priest's visit, she'd had a dream in which her daughter had appeared to her wearing a very elegant dress, and that was why she had been so confident about accepting his proposal.

"Yes, but I would prefer you to hear me out," Urroz Erro said. He had a lawyer's mind and hated to leave things vague.

He explained that his elderly mother, who was now bedridden, required a great deal of care, and the maid who was going with him to Eibar could not be with her twenty-four hours a day. She needed an assistant.

"I thought of Izaskun, because I know her and know how bright she is, but there's something else," he went on. "She needs to continue her education, and I'm offering to pay for her studies in exchange for her work. There's a very good college in Eibar run by French nuns and I'm going to enrol her there."

Leona responded quickly.

"So far, no-one in our family has had a real education. She'll be the first. Thank you, Don Eugenio," she said. Ramón nodded his agreement.

Two weeks later, our mother travelled by car to Eibar. She was not yet eleven.

*

One of the cows grazing in the field near the cemetery began mooing again, and was soon joined by the rest of the herd. Further off, on the farms in the area, the dogs were barking loudly. None of those animals really went well with death. They couldn't sing like the birds or like Andrés Garay. They were rather coarse, disagreeable creatures.

We left the cemetery. My younger brother and I went to the car park; my older brother walked back down to the church to collect his Mercedes.

"And now, to top it all, we've got to eat tripe!" he shouted, not for our benefit, but his own.

The maize fields, the village and the church were all growing dark now. Some of the windows in the farmhouses were lit. In the distance, Les Trois Couronnes was just a dark smudge. In the opposite direction, El Hernio, "the tall, rugged mountain", seemed suddenly much bigger, as if it had grown while we were burying our mother. I asked my brother if he remembered the story about the two women walking to Santiago who'd had to ask directions of a crow, and he did of course, vividly.

"She was always repeating the same stories," he said.

It was true, but she only told us stories about Albiztur when we were children. Later, her main point of reference became Eibar. The years that she spent in Guipúzcoa's biggest industrial town proved to be a unique experience, probably the most important of her life.

*

"Eibar was a very difficult place for Don Eugenio Urroz Erro and for all practising Christians," my mother used to tell us. "The socialists and the republicans had a lot of power, and very few people went to Mass. More than half the funerals held were secular, and because there were so many atheists in the town, the Church tended to send Eibar the very best preachers, the most admired of all being a priest called Madinabeitia. He was in charge of the Good Friday sermon on the Seven Last Words. That day, the church would always be filled to bursting. Everyone went to hear him: Catholics, socialists, republicans and communists.

"Madinabeitia would arrive in Eibar at the beginning of Holy Week and stay in our house. I remember that the first year he came, I was looking after Don Eugenio's mother when I heard voices. I went into the living room and realised that Madinabeitia was rehearsing his Seven Last Words sermon, and so loudly that he could have been heard out in the street. I sat down in an armchair to listen to him."

Thirty or forty years later, my mother could still imitate Madinabeitia's vehement delivery: "I am thirsty!" "It is finished! *Consummatum est* . . ."

"I wanted to go back to my patient, because I had to change her position in bed frequently so that she wouldn't get bed sores, but I just couldn't make myself get up and leave the room. I was so moved by Madinabeitia's voice that I was almost in tears, especially when he began to call out pleadingly: "Father, Father, why have You forsaken me?" I don't know how long I sat there. When I did eventually get up to resume my work, I noticed Don Eugenio. He was sitting in another armchair, listening. He hadn't even realised I was there. He was a wonderful man, but not a good public speaker, and he admired Madinabeitia enormously."

*

"A lot of people used to come to Don Eugenio's house," my mother would tell us. "Not just preachers and religious people. Once, a hypnotist came. He was a very thin man and a heavy smoker. One day, Don Eugenio gave a lunch to which he invited local councillors and other town worthies, among them the hypnotist. They were all sitting in the living room, smoking, and the other guests started making fun of the hypnotist, saying that hypnosis was mere flimflam, and that they were surprised at a serious man like him presenting himself to the world as an expert on the matter. I heard all this because, on that particular day, I'd been asked to help out in the dining room, which was right next to the living room.

"Initially, the thin man said nothing, but he went out onto the balcony. I thought he had decided to leave the other guests so as to put an end to the joshing. However, that wasn't his intention at all. Pointing down into the street, he said to one of the councillors who had come out onto the balcony to join him: 'When that girl carrying the cakes passes underneath the balcony, call out to her and say whatever comes into your head. I just need her to look up here.' I ran over to the kitchen window to watch. There was the girl with her tray of cakes. They came from Soloaga's, the best patisserie in Eibar.

"The girl reached our house, and the councillor did as the thin man had told him. The girl immediately stopped and came in through the street door. Shortly afterwards, the doorbell rang. I ran to open it, but the thin man, the councillor and other guests all beat me to it. The girl held out her tray and said: 'I thought you might like some of these cakes.' The thin man gave her some money and said: 'Thank you, but not just now. So sorry to have bothered you.' The assembled guests looked astonished. "How did you do that?' they asked. 'Through hypnotism,' answered the thin man. He said nothing more, neither then nor during lunch. Don Eugenio greatly enjoyed the incident and said something in Latin along the lines of 'The victor never explains.'"

*

"In general, the students at the school I went to all came from rich families," my mother used to tell us. "For example, one girl in my class was an Orbea, of Bicicletas Orbea, and another was a Beistegui, of Bicicletas B.H. One afternoon, Don Eugenio gave me permission to visit a classmate who lived on the outskirts of Eibar, and when I arrived, I saw five or six boys playing football in a part of the garden planted with palm trees. My friend, whose name was Agustina, whispered to me: 'They play for Bilbao Athletic.' They were wearing ordinary clothes, but since they really did play very well, I had no reason not to believe my friend. One of them, a rather thin boy with curly hair, took off his shoes and left them at the foot of one of the palm trees, then went back to the other boys and continued playing. 'That's Chirri II,' Agustina told me, and with that, she grabbed my arm and dragged me over to them. She was a very bold girl – not even the nuns at Aldatze could tame her – and so I guessed at once what she was intending to do. She wanted to steal Chirri II's shoes. I tried to pull away, but Agustina kept a firm grip on me. Before I knew it, she had picked up the shoes and stuffed them under her shirt, and since we were arm in arm, no-one noticed. She was laughing, but I was frightened.

324

"I saw the footballers again later on in the house, and there was Chirri II in his socks talking to the owner of the house. He seemed quite untroubled, as if he had forgotten about his shoes, but I hadn't. I couldn't help thinking about them because they were right there, underneath the sofa I was sitting on. Besides, I was alone now, Agustina having gone over to talk to the player she thought was the most handsome, Muguerza. Time passed, a quarter of an hour perhaps, and there I sat, not knowing what to do, but getting more and more worried because it was growing dark, and Don Eugenio didn't like me coming home late. Suddenly, Chirri II sauntered over to me and said: '*Bilbora yoan bia'dot, ta ezin naz zapata barik ibilli. Entrenadoriek kastigue ipiniko deust.*' 'I have to go back to Bilbao and can't go without my shoes. The trainer will punish me.' He spoke in the Biscayan dialect. I felt horribly embarrassed. I took the shoes out from under the sofa and gave them to him. He laughed and talked non-stop while he was putting them on. '*Ze ikisi bia'dozu, ba?*' 'What are you going to study?' he asked. Chemistry, I said, because that was my best subject for which I always got either an A or an A+. He told me he was an engineer and regaled me with all kinds of information about the Engineering School in Bilbao. I was so nervous, though, and found his dialect so hard to understand, that I didn't really take much of it in. He was a really nice lad."

*

We heard these Eibar stories over and over, and they made a huge impression on my younger brother, perhaps because he *was* the youngest and therefore more sensitive to what he heard at home. Once, when he was still at school, he was asked to draw a town, and he filled the sheet of paper with palaces, palm trees and other marvels. The teacher exclaimed: "What kind of town is this? It looks like paradise!" "It isn't paradise, it's Eibar," my brother said. Years later, when he visited Eibar for the first time, he was puzzled to see the real thing, so densely populated and so industrial, and he realised that his mental image of the place had come from our mother's stories. She described the things that had happened there in her youth, and they seemed to be set in an ideal geography. And yet my brother actually preferred the real Eibar to the ideal one, for, by then, he was already a voracious reader of Marx and Lenin.

Our mother told us rather more political stories too, but with the same pleasure as she told us about Chirri II or the hypnotist. For example, she would laugh about the situation in Eibar when the Republic was proclaimed. She said that on the night of April 13, the civil guards were still assiduously arresting anyone who shouted "*¡Viva la República!*" – "Long Live the Republic!" – then, the following morning, they were equally assiduously arresting anyone shouting "*¡Viva el Rey!*" – "Long live the King!" From the war, she recalled only the more picturesque details: the sound made by the rifles, *pa-kun, pa-kun*; the pharmacist's double reaction when he returned from the air-raid shelter after a bombardment to find his house reduced to rubble, and how he jumped for joy because he was alive and then, hours later, wept bitterly for all that he had lost; the times she had to stay at the school when the bombardments intensified, and how, when the siren sounded, the mother superior would scold the girls for not getting down into the cellar quickly enough, and then, when the planes could be heard moving off, would scold them again for the pillow fights and other noisy games they got up to down there.

"The main instigator was always Agustina," my mother would say. "She was an excellent mimic. Somehow she'd managed to get hold of a nun's habit, and when we had to go down to the cellar during air raids, she would put it on and imitate the various nuns. Oh, she did make us laugh! If she'd been caught, though, she would have been punished twice over: first, for making fun of the nuns; and second, for lighting candles, which was totally forbidden during bombing raids."

There was something rather childlike about our mother, a kind of innate joy, but this disappeared or was extinguished on the day they arrested my younger brother and took him to prison.

*

In 1972, on the night before Good Friday, a group of civil guards broke down the door of the apartment where we were living and burst in, wielding machine guns. When I woke up and opened my eyes, two of them were in my room. A third man followed. He was older than the others and had a sergeant's stripes on his sleeve.

"Get out of bed!" he bawled. "Now!"

They were more like soldiers than civil guards, because of their uniforms and, in particular, because of the caps they wore.

I started to get dressed, but the sergeant bawled at me again:

"There's no time to get dressed. I want you out of this room now!"

On my bedside table were some photocopied sheets about the history of the Basque Country that my younger brother had made for me. I was convinced he was the one they were looking for.

My mother and father were in the kitchen; she was wearing a pink nightdress and he was wearing a pair of green pyjamas. I looked at my father. His pyjamas were clinging so tightly to his body that you could almost make out his private parts. The very young civil guard who was with them gestured to me with his machine gun, indicating that I should join them.

The apartment was very large; in fact, it was two apartments separated by a swing door. From the other side came the sound of raised voices. Suddenly, there was the noise of blows and a scream. Turning deathly pale, my father rushed over to the kitchen door.

"What's going on?"

The young civil guard lifted his machine gun to stop my father, who instinctively pushed the barrel aside. The gun fell to the floor and several bullets scattered over the tiles. At first, I thought they were coins.

Two more civil guards appeared, dragging my older brother with them and propelling him into the kitchen. He was in his underpants, and his nose was bleeding.

"Don't you look at me like that, you poofter!" one of the guards shouted, threatening him with the butt of his gun.

My older brother had long, curly fair hair and was wearing a hippy-style bead necklace. His underpants were in the same flower-power style. Apparently, as I found out years later, when the guards burst into his room, yelling that they had come to search the place, he pulled down his underpants and showed them his bum, saying:

"Well, you'd better search up here first!"

The price for this impertinence was a bloody nose.

Sitting on a bench in the kitchen, our mother looked like a sculpture.

"It's alright, it's alright," she said, but only I heard her. The kitchen had filled with loud voices, the loudest of which was the sergeant's.

"What's that gun doing on the floor?"

The young civil guard now looked as pale as my father. He crouched down, picked up the gun and tried to explain.

"And pick those bullets up too!" the sergeant yelled, and left the kitchen. He went through the swing door so violently that the two halves continued to creak for some seconds afterwards.

He returned accompanied by four of his men, who brought with them my younger brother. They formed a line: first, my brother, his wrists handcuffed behind his back; then, three civil guards carrying machine guns; after them, another guard carrying a cardboard box full of papers; and, finally, the sergeant himself. The younger man guarding the kitchen joined them and they all left the apartment.

My mother ran out into the corridor and pushed her way past them.

"Don't worry, I'll be back soon," my brother said. His voice sounded different, somehow hoarser.

We rushed to the window and looked down at the street. The guards were surrounding my brother as if to protect him from some danger. An illusion. When we called to him and he tried to respond, one of the guards pushed his head down hard and bundled him violently into a jeep.

My older brother started swearing and hurling insults.

"Stop that nonsense!" my father said. He was about to say more, but he began coughing and couldn't go on.

We all went and sat in the living room. An hour later, when the clock struck five, my older brother announced he was going to San Sebastián.

"I know the lawyer who deals with these cases. I'll talk to him about what's happened."

My father and I went back to bed and tried to make my mother do the same. She refused and stayed curled up on the sofa.

The following morning, I was woken by the radio, which was on at full volume. It sounded like someone giving a lecture, but it was a sermon on the Seven Last Words. It was Good Friday.

"My God, my God, why have You forsaken me?"

The preacher on the radio relied on repetition for effect.

"Why have You forsaken me? Why?"

My mother was still curled up on the sofa. I thought she was asleep.

"He's not a patch on Madinabeitia," she said.

The preacher assured us that Jesus's cry had been not a cry of despair, but an attempt at prayer. He was trying to recite Psalm 22: "My God, my God, why have You forsaken me? Why are You so far from saving me, from the words of my groaning? O my God, I cry by day, but You do not answer, and by night, but I find no rest." According to the preacher, Jesus was not cast down, but full of hope.

"Not a patch on Madinabeitia," my mother said again. She seemed about to go back to sleep, and so I didn't respond. Peace reigned in the living room. Not a sound could be heard. A dim light filtered in through the window. Outside, it was a grey day.

Then my mother groaned.

"Where will they have taken him?"

I told her that we would know this when my older brother got back from San Sebastián.

"Your father has gone out to buy bread," she said. "But will there be any bread today, on a Good Friday? I can't remember if it's today or tomorrow when the baker's is closed."

There was a knock at the door. I thought it would be my father coming back from the baker's, but I found myself face to face with Andrés Garay. He didn't want to come in.

"Your brother hasn't been taken to Madrid," he said softly. "He's in San Sebastián, in the Ondarreta barracks. We've told everyone we can."

This was all new to me. I associated him only with the church choir. I didn't know he was involved in politics.

We heard someone opening the street door. Then a cough. It was my father. Andrés Garay fled up the stairs to the next landing. I went down to meet my father and offered him my arm, but he declined my offer of help.

When we went into the apartment, my mother was in the kitchen, pounding the wall with her fist.

"Stop that now, or we'll all go mad!" bellowed my father, throwing the loaves he'd brought with him down on the table.

*

We always return to our everyday life; we have nowhere else to go. Sometimes something extraordinary happens, some misfortune, and it seems as if everything has stopped and will never start again. However, the current of daily life keeps flowing, even when it seems to have turned to stone, and the grieving, suffering person still has to get up and have a shower in the morning, have breakfast, do the shopping, go to work, listen to what people are saying about last night's television programmes or the latest football match, or argue with a bank clerk about some mispayment. Gradually, all these activities erase the extraordinary, the misfortune, from his or her head, for just an hour at first, then, later on, for a week or a month. In the end, all that remains in the consciousness is a shadow, a dull ache.

That is what happened in our case. We returned to everyday life. My younger brother did too. He was sentenced to eight years in prison, but was released after less than three years thanks to the amnesty that followed General Franco's death. A few years later, he was absolutely fine, working for a book distributor and apparently contented with his life. During that time, my older brother had made big strides: by the time he was thirty-five, he was already the owner of a company renting out buses and taxis and employing five drivers. As for me, I was teaching languages in a school.

The day we celebrated my father's seventieth birthday, we went over the family history, and the years my younger brother had spent in prison occupied only a couple of minutes, while my older brother's business career took much longer. He had just acquired a white limousine for weddings, and that was the main topic of conversation over lunch.

My mother joked: "It seems strange that someone who rents out wedding limousines doesn't get married himself. When are you going to hire that limousine for your own wedding?"

She hadn't realised that my older brother was gay.

"What do I need a wife for, when I have the prettiest of women here at home?" he said. He knew how to flatter our mother.

We leave behind whatever happens to us, but our way of living changes. To use a metaphor common in religious texts, grass – life – begins to sprout and grow in different cracks in the wall. After his time in prison, the differences between my two brothers became more marked, and they tended to avoid meeting. When they had to meet – on my father's seventieth birthday for example – the tension between them was tangible, and they would sometimes engage in bitter arguments about the current political situation. For my part, I was tired of always being the conciliatory intermediary and made little effort to participate in family life. In this new situation, my father cut himself off and spent time at the local pool or gym, or went walking in the countryside. Our mother changed too.

"You've lost your sparkle," my younger brother would say to her.

It was true, and one of the consequences of this was the loss of the childlike joy that had led her to tell us her stories. She continued telling them, especially the ones about her childhood, the one about El Hernio and others, but only at family get-togethers, when she'd had a drop of champagne. As for Eibar, that vanished completely from her conversation.

Gradually, her stories were replaced by complaints: "I've got terrible back ache today." "It's such a lot of work looking after your father." "Sometimes I don't even feel like getting out of bed." "It's not much fun getting old." A few years later, her mind began to go. We knew this the day she confused Rosa Mari with one of her sisters.

We took her to a specialist in geriatrics, who put her on some medication that restored her to reality – "The very worst place to be," according to my younger brother. Then the complaints started again: "It's not much fun getting old," she would say over and over.

A few months later, one Sunday afternoon, I went to see her and found her sitting in the living room, talking to the village priest. She was frowning.

"You have to understand, Don Eugenio. You don't seem to realise how many hours I spend with your mother in her room," she said in a high, thin voice. She thought she was in Eibar. She was confusing the village priest with Don Eugenio.

"Apparently, the other day, I told her off for playing hopscotch," the priest said, winking at me.

"No, not for playing hopscotch," she shrilled, shaking her head. "For drawing chalk lines on the bedroom floor! But how am I supposed to play hopscotch without making lines!"

"Yes, but it's a wooden floor and the chalk makes a real mess," the priest said, getting up, relieved to be able to hand over to me.

"I can't always be studying," insisted my mother. "I need to have fun and go out. That's what Agustina's always saying, that I should go dancing with her and go and see Bilbao Athletic playing."

"I hope you enjoy Agustina's company," the priest said.

"You know very well that Agustina's my best friend," my mother retorted. "The other day she gave me her sunglasses. She says her eyes are her best feature and she doesn't want to hide them."

"I see," the priest said, moving towards the door.

My mother continued arguing with the supposed Don Eugenio even when the priest had left. I tried to give her some supper, but she seemed so exhausted that I decided to put her to bed. Once in bed, she suddenly burst into tears.

"What's wrong?" I asked.

She gave me an explanation, which I didn't understand. I couldn't tell whether she was talking to me or to someone from the past. I asked her what she could see.

"María Ángela," she said.

"And where are you?"

"In the cemetery in Eibar."

I thought she was referring to one of her school friends. I fell back on metaphors, as priests do, and began talking to her about heaven. María Ángela will be fine, contemplating God.

My mother turned to me, perplexed:

"I'm talking about the street, about Calle María Ángela," she said. "It's been bombed by the Italians. You can see it from the cemetery."

Years later, in a catalogue of photographs by Indalecio Ojanguren, I came upon a photograph showing Calle María Ángela after the air raids during the Civil War. The street itself is almost untouched, but the houses on either side have been reduced to rubble. The tower of Casa Zuloaga is still standing, but is badly damaged by fire and its roof has caved in. The church of San Andrés and the Augustinian convent are damaged too, with great cracks in the walls.

"But that isn't why I'm crying," my mother said.

"Why are you crying then?"

"Didn't you know? Don Eugenio is dead."

Even sixty years later, this news still affected me.

"What happened?"

"Those horrible planes bombed the train taking him to Bilbao. Apparently, Don Eugenio had a heart attack and died instantly. He must have been so afraid. He was always terrified of the air raids. The first time they bombed Eibar, he took me with him to the shelter. We were the first to arrive."

She fell silent for a while.

"What am I going to do?" she said. "I don't think I'll be able to study chemistry now. I'll have to go back to Albiztur."

She took a white handkerchief from one of the drawers in her bed-side table and dried her tears.

When she fell asleep, I called my brothers. They weren't there, but I left the same message for both of them: "Izaskun is in Eibar."

She died two weeks later, without ever mentally leaving the town where she had spent her youth and where she had been happier than anywhere else. She talked a lot, but made little sense. There was just one day when she did manage to make herself understood. She con-fused her carer, Rosa Mari, with one of her school friends and thought she was coming back to Eibar in the train after sitting her exams in Vitoria. She was feeling happy because she thought it had all gone very well, especially the exam in chemistry, and then she started describing something 'really funny' that had happened during the oral exam in philosophy. A student from another school, who clearly hadn't done his revision and kept giving the wrong answers, had so infuriated the examiner that, at one point, the latter leapt up, waving his arms in the air and shouting: "Will someone please bring me some hay for this donkey!" My mother laughed when she told the story.

"That's how I'm going to remember her," Rosa Mari told us when she came to offer her condolences after the funeral. "Laughing."

*

We were in the restaurant eating *callos*, and some of the friends with us were discussing the best way to cook tripe. One said that he cooked it as they had in the nineteenth century, adding a glass of white wine to the sauce, another one followed a Karlos Arguiñano recipe and mixed it with other sorts of offal and coated it in batter, but left out the bay leaf.

One of the women at the table was extremely thin, but spoke with great enthusiasm. My older brother whispered to me that she talked like that not because she liked tripe, but so that no-one would suspect she was anorexic.

"It seems that in your case your enthusiasm is more theoretical than practical," my brother said to her, pointing to her almost untouched plate.

"It's too greasy, that's why I haven't eaten very much," she said. "The chorizo definitely adds flavour, but you need to cook it on its own first to get rid of the grease."

"Have you seen who's over there?" said my brother, ignoring the woman's explanation and pointing at an old man standing by a nearby table.

At first, I didn't recognise him. Then I recalled what he had looked like thirty or forty years ago. At the time, he had criticised our mother for teaching in Spanish rather than Basque in the village school, a criticism that had wounded her deeply. Seeing the man in the restaurant, and thinking that he had probably attended the funeral, enraged my brother.

The situation was beginning to change. Our mother's death had taken us out of the current of daily life, installing us in a separate place, a dream place. For a time, from the moment of her death to her burial, all our thoughts had been focused on her; but as my brother's reaction showed, we were now waking up and returning to reality.

*

The Mercedes was parked in front of the restaurant, and two young men who were looking at it started asking us questions when we came out into the street. My older brother refused to answer, and they didn't insist.

"You could have parked somewhere else," my younger brother said to him. "Why did you have to park it here in full view of everyone? What are you trying to prove?"

My older brother did not respond, and my younger brother returned to the charge.

"Everyone's really very impressed with your new car, not to mention the black orchids. I'd like to know just how much each of those flowers cost."

"Your problem is that you don't know how to enjoy life," my older brother said.

"Look, don't argue now. Wait until tomorrow," I said and went off to find my own car.

We left our childhood village behind us. We left the separate place in which our mother's death had deposited us. We went back to being our usual selves.

NEWS

(*POST SCRIPTUM*)

RENO GAZETTE-JOURNAL, NOVEMBER 26, 2008

"Reno Police arrest James Biela for Denison's murder.

"The Reno police have arrested James Biela for the murder of Brianna Denison. According to the police, Biela's girlfriend, who cares for their four-year-old son, found two items of women's underwear in his pickup truck. She told a friend, and that friend rang Secret Witness on November 1.

"According to the affidavit, Biela declined to give a D.N.A. sample, saying that he had nothing to do with the murder of Brianna Denison, and that his girlfriend could provide an alibi for him.

"Biela's girlfriend called the police saying that she could not account for his whereabouts in the early hours of December 16 and January 20, and she gave them permission to take a D.N.A. sample from her son.

"The D.N.A. matched that found at the Denison murder scene and at the scene of the sexual assault on 16 December. This was confirmed by Chief of Police Michael Poehlman. The D.N.A. also matches that found at the scene of two other attempted kidnappings that occurred in the environs of the Reno University campus.

"According to the police, James Biela worked as a pipe fitter on the new university buildings from spring to fall 2007."

SFGATE, OCTOBER 31, 2008

Experts sure they have Steve Fossett's remains

"The 3 Oct., 2008 picture provided by the Madera County Sheriff's Department shows wreckage from the fuselage of Steve Fossett's plane near Mammoth Lakes, Calif. Searchers have found what appear to be two large human bones near the crash site of Fossett's plane in California's Sierra Nevada, along with the adventurer's tennis shoes and driver's license. The investigators have carried out laboratory tests and say they are now sure they have found the remains of Steve Fossett."

MESSAGE FROM A MOTHER ON THE SCHOOL WEBSITE, MAY 2, 2009

"Hello, my friends, I wanted to tell you what happened to Mary and a friend of hers yesterday afternoon.

"4.10 p.m. Mary and her friend were walking from Waldens to the Whire Caughlin House.

"At one point, a white Ford Mustang with a blue flash down the side drew up beside them.

"The driver wound down the window and told them to get in the car. Both girls refused.

"They turned round and walked back towards Waldens. The driver then told them that he needed their help to find a doll.

"The girls again refused and carried on walking. Then the driver got out of the car.

"The man had half his face covered with a scarf and was wearing sunglasses and a Reno University baseball cap. He said: 'Get in the car so we can fuck.' At this point, the girls ran towards Waldens. The man did a U-turn and followed them as far as the lights at McCarran and Mayberry.

"The girls ran to the house of a family member near Waldens.

"The guy then drove off towards Roy Gomm Elementary School.

"That night, I went to the police with my husband. The guy did everything he could to persuade the girls into his car.

"It's just terrifying. We feel so lucky to have our little girl with us.

"Please send this message to all the mothers in the neighborhood and explain to your kids what happened."

"Brianna Denison's killer, James Biela, gets death

"The murderer of Brianna Denison, James Biela, 28, has been sentenced to death. After nine hours of deliberation, the verdict was unanimous: James Biela will die by lethal injection."

BERNARDO ATXAGA was born in Gipuzkoa in Spain in 1951 and lives in the Basque Country, writing in Basque and Spanish. He is a prize-winning novelist and poet, whose books, including *Obabakoak* (1992), *The Accordionist's Son* (2007) and most recently *Seven Houses in France* (2011), have won critical acclaim in Spain and abroad. His works have been translated into thirty-two languages.

MARGARET JULL COSTA is the award-winning translator of José Saramago, Javier Marías, Bernardo Atxaga, Eça de Queiroz and Fernando Pessoa.

A New Library from MacLehose Press

This book is part of a new international library for literature in translation. MacLehose Press has become known for its wide-ranging list of bestselling European crime writers, eclectic non-fiction and winners of the Nobel and *Independent* Foreign Fiction prizes, and for the many awards given to our translators. In their own countries, our writers are celebrated as the very best.

With this library we mean to make the books you would not want to overlook harder to overlook. The landscape for literary fiction in translation is expanding; we will go on looking beyond our shores and making it possible for readers to share in the most exciting and most renowned international writers.

Join us on our journey to **READ THE WORLD**.

PUBLISHED IN 2017

1. *The President's Gardens* by Muhsin Al-Ramli

TRANSLATED FROM THE ARABIC BY LUKE LEAFGREN

2. *Belladonna* by Daša Drndić

TRANSLATED FROM THE CROATIAN BY CELIA HAWKESWORTH

3. *The Awkward Squad* by Sophie Hénaff

TRANSLATED FROM THE FRENCH BY SAM GORDON

4. *Vernon Subutex 1* by Virginie Despentes

TRANSLATED FROM THE FRENCH BY FRANK WYNNE

5. *Nevada Days* by Bernardo Atxaga

TRANSLATED FROM THE SPANISH BY MARGARET JULL COSTA

6. *After the War* by Hervé Le Corre

TRANSLATED FROM THE FRENCH BY SAM TAYLOR

7. *After the Winter* by Guadalupe Nettel

TRANSLATED FROM THE SPANISH BY ROSALIND HARVEY

8. *The House with the Stained-Glass Window* by Żanna Słoniowska

TRANSLATED FROM THE POLISH BY ANTONIA LLOYD-JONES

www.maclehosepress.com